Small Aircraft Operations Manual

STEPHEN M. LIND, JD, ATP

PAGE PUBLISHING, INC.
New York, NY

First originally published by Page Publishing, Inc. 2019

ISBN 978-1-68456-234-3 (Paperback)
ISBN 978-1-68456-235-0 (Digital)

Printed in the United States of America

Contents

Foreword

As the first student of Steve Lind, I have had the most time to benefit from the foundations found herein. I had my first flying lesson with Steve on March 12, 1994. From that day on, my life changed. Steve was my flight instructor, but he also became a true *mentor*. Not only did I learn to fly, and fly the "right way," but I also became a pilot, an airman, and a man. I learned skills that we rarely see in life. An awareness both in the sky and in our normal lives. Upon reviewing this book, I find myself sitting across his kitchen table, reliving countless stories, examples, techniques, knowledge, and life lessons that I still utilize today.

Foundations are the key, and Steve clearly illustrates what it takes to truly understand what it means to a pilot. Sometimes it's necessary to be blunt; many CFIs (certificated flight instructors) are themselves fresh out of flight school with a few hundred hours, who learned from an instructor with a few hundred hours, etc., etc. It should be evident where I'm going with this. I consider myself to be very lucky to have had my foundations from someone who understands what it means to be a pilot, an airman. The details, the examples, and the application of the procedures outlined will benefit the new pilot, the Sunday flier, flight instructors, and even the commercial pilot. Every day is a school day in aviation, and there is something for every aviator contained in this detailed compilation.

My flying career has extended to various areas with extensive experience with general aviation operations, instructing, and the airlines. As an airline captain, I acknowledge that the lessons learned from Steve Lind resonate in my daily life and with my professional operations. Various tech and NOTECH skills are intimately interwoven into all the methodology of Steve's instruction and descriptions in this book, sometimes subtly, and on other occasions, it's direct. There is a reason for everything, and often we don't understand the "whys" of something. In this manual, the whys are explained in a way that will make anyone a better and safer pilot.

—Captain Scott M. Kennedy/Airbus A320

Preface

This book is written for less than 1/2 percent of the population. Unless you are a pilot, or at least a student pilot taking flight training, and understand basic aerodynamics and aircraft nomenclature, this flying manual will be over your head. You don't have to be able to "walk the walk" but you must "talk the talk" (pilot parlance) in order to comprehend these chapters. If you can, then this book is for you. A pilot can tell a nonpilot in half a sentence.

Any experience can be a learning one, and aviation offers ample opportunities to grow and mature as a pilot and a person. Speaking of which, since the vast majority of all pilots are male (94–96 percent), there will be more "hes" than "shes" in the content. No offense to anyone—just trying to save ink.

This manual is a consolidation of lessons learned and Sky Insights gleaned from decades of flying small aircraft (my first flight was in 1966) and teaching flight students. Charles Lindbergh said that CFIs (certificated flight instructors) teach cadets about basic aerodynamics and students teach instructors about advanced aerodynamics. This is a true statement.

My flying background (sixteen thousand hours), coupled with an aircraft accident investigation career, can provide a more complete way of understanding the piloting experience. If the game doesn't scare you at least a little, then it's not big enough. Flying is the real deal and allows *three*-dimensional freedom that is hard to replicate on the ground (actually, four dimensions, as speed kills time).

As I had worked on over two thousand aircraft crashes and claims (four hundred of which were jet helicopters), it became clear and was confirmed that almost all accidents are a culmination of a chain of events and decisions/actions made by the pilot. The goal here is to learn how to *not* forge that first link in an accident chain. The how and what to do will be explained, along with the reasons. If the topic is sufficiently important, a true story will be included to fly home the safety message.

Listen, evaluate, and decide. Learn and internalize what you want and reject what you don't. There are many tips and techniques outlined here that are designed to help you evolve into a competent and prudent pilot. People involved in flying can be classified as follows: Students/Cadets, Drivers (air-driving), Fliers (air-boating), Pilots, Aviators, Master Aviators, and Angels (my ultimate goal, and wings are provided).

Let's get something clear now: I am not an aeronautical engineer nor an A&P (airframe and power plant technician), as you will be able to easily ascertain. I'm just an ol' dumb boy pilot that's been lucky enough to fly over 150 different makes and models of aircraft and will boil this experience down to its essence. I've also had to do a few forced landings (no injuries or damage), been in a hot-air balloon crash, and have been dragged through the woods by a helicopter (for a couple hundred feet) after rappelling from it.

My expertise is in knowing that I am not an expert. The one thing I know is that I don't know and always learn something new every day and every flight. There are many better pilots out there, and *better* is the enemy of *good enough*, so the goal is to constantly improve our knowledge and skills as an Aviator. As an ardent student of human (and aircraft) movement, I have found there are limits to genius but no bounds to stupidity.

There are two kinds of pilots: the quick and the dead. We will learn how to be quick in mind and action so we can skip a premature dirt nap. This isn't basket weaving. Our objective here is to become a safe, competent, and confident Pilot or Aviator. Guns, planes, risks, and danger ain't no stranger to an Airborne-Ranger. So get smart and be hard-core. Good luck and keep 'em flying!

Introduction

There is a lot in *Small Aircraft Operations Manual* that I think pilots should know and understand, and by "small" aircraft, I mean weighing under 12,500 pounds. Read this book through the first time just for fun, as many items are more fully explained later in the text. Obviously, online-search any terms or phrases that are unclear. As mentioned in the preface, you have to bring something to the table to be able to fully benefit from these tips and techniques (some potentially life-saving).

Piloting an air machine through the world's largest ocean is the biggest thing a human being can do. Most of our planet is covered by water, but all of it is surrounded by air. We are all just lobsters walking around on our great big air ocean floor. The larger the craft is, the easier it is.

A multiengine jet pilot was filing a flight plan for a Cessna Skyhawk he was going to rent and told the briefer to write "Emergency" in the "Remarks" section of the plan. The briefer questioned this as the filer had not even taken off yet. The captain responded, "I only have one engine, no radar, no anti/de-ice, no copilot, can't climb over the weather, no Inertial Navigation, *etc*. It's an emergency!" We are the Pilot, Navigator, Radio Operator, Dispatcher, Loadmaster, and Captain all in one.

There's no Pause button here. No pulling off to the side of the road. No way out once you're in it, so study and learn. I don't pull many punches and try not to mince words. If something is repeated a couple of times, then that is on purpose, as it is important. I am not advocating you do anything unsafe or careless in this Manual but emphasize the opposite. Finally, it is said that God does not deduct from one's time on earth the hours spent flying. Fully enjoy this special ability.

Photos of some of the air/land vehicles mentioned can be viewed at stephenmlind.blogspot.com.

Mission Preparation

What to Wear and Bring

The attire best suited for flying is composed of natural-type fibers. You want to wear cottons or wools and avoid any kind of synthetics or acrylics, which could be real bad in a heat situation. Don't wear a bright-colored shirt, if you can help it, to decrease glare/reflections off the instrument panel; same for your front-seat passenger. The ideal outfit would be a flight suit, a real one made out of Nomex, or cotton, at the very least. Definitely do not get a nylon or double-knit type of flight suit. Most flight suits have numerous pockets that can store various gadgets.

I highly recommend a belt tool or a Leatherman type of tool, a signal mirror in one of the pockets (as it is the most powerful signaling device during the sunlit time), a handkerchief, a small chart plotter, and a small E6B "whiz wheel." Always carry a book of matches and a lighter to start a fire. Have some emergency "Mordida" (bribe) money (a few hundred dollars) secretly stowed in one of the pockets, along with some other spending cash. Always carry a dime, penny, nickel, and quarter, so you have four different-size screwdrivers. They could also be used for a pay phone, if one can be found.

If the craft has a V-belt-driven alternator, then have an extra V-belt stowed on board. Keep this belt in a sealed plastic bag so it does not dry out and oxidize and crack. Have a handheld luggage scale so cargo items can be accurately measured for weight and balance calculations. Carry some basic tools in a small bag along with a first aid kit and some basic survival gear. In Alaska, this also means bringing a weapon of at least a .30-caliber size. I carried an M1 Carbine with the Airborne folding stock and two thirty-round magazines jungle-clipped together. Why waltz when you can rock and roll?

One of the best devices to have in your headset bag, if it's small enough, or possibly even in the flight suit, is some type of tracking beacon or emergency position-indicating radio beacon (EPIRB). Those are expensive. However, in the event of an emergency, it would be very worthwhile to have one. The new EPIRBs and devices with GPS enhancement allow the search-and-rescue team to just *drive* to your location as it's posted that accurately.

Many times, *flying* a search mission is not required because of these new, very accurate beacons. Many of these devices are registered with NOAA, the National Oceanographic and Atmospheric Administration. They know what plane it is in, the capacity of the aircraft, who operates it, etc. This EPIRB should be worn securely on your belt. There are loops and a safety lanyard provided for that purpose. The lanyard should also be secured, separately, as a backup retention system.

This beacon and a pouch tool can be worn on your belt. The type of belt I suggest is a GI-style web belt (one-inch width) with an adjustable roller pin buckle, or any buckle that can be adjusted for any belt diameter. It can now double as a carrying strap, a sling, or worst case, a tourniquet. When you are actually flying over water, wear your PFD (personal flotation device) and have the EPIRB secured to your belt. Here's why you secure the beacon to your belt.

A student pilot made a hard forced landing and had stored his EPIRB on top of the antiglare shield. The sudden stop broke the windshield, and the beacon shot forward out of the plane and landed thirty feet ahead in a poison ivy patch (of course). The injured pilot had to crawl to it to activate it. The aircraft's ELT probably triggered, but many of those do not have the enhanced GPS reporting option.

If a device has a telescoping antenna, then always retract it by pulling it down from the bottom section. Don't put your palm on the top and push down, as the aerial will eventually fold over and break.

There's nothing like a (white) silk flying scarf in the wintertime. You can wear it inside the airplane, and it warms the back of your neck and a little bit on the top of your shoulders. In a small aircraft, that scarf will help, as the rear compartment has little or no heat and is very cold on your head and neck. I learned to fly in Wisconsin, and if the sun is not streaming in the cockpit, causing a "greenhouse" effect, it is cold enough to see your breath. You know it's cold when you check the heater control knob regularly to confirm it is all the way out and on.

Silk is less abrasive on your neck for turning around or for swiveling your head as you constantly scan for traffic. You can also use a silk scarf to clean your sunglasses and wipe your screens and instrument glass off. It, too, can also be called to serve as a signaling device (especially if surrendering), a sling, a crude filter—you get the point. As we learned in the Rangers, in survival or demolitions work, your imagination is your only limit.

Always bring a hat with a bill, a baseball-type cap. If your hat has a button or top ornament on it, remove that from the top of the hat. If a downdraft was encountered of sufficient force, and even if your seat belt was tight, you could strike the ceiling and that button on the hat could hurt the top of your head. Normally, if you wear headsets, even when you hit the headliner in the airplane, the top of the headset protects you to some extent.

The bills on caps today are curved, which has made the bill absolutely worthless for its intended function, which is to block the sun from getting in your eyes. Therefore, you have to grasp the bill and fold the curve out, make it so the bill goes straight across instead of curved or crescent-shaped. On the last half-inch of each edge, fold the edges down forty-five degrees or almost ninety degrees to block the sunlight from coming in the sides. You can now wear the hat low enough, which is just above the eyebrows. In a low-sun situation, such as morning or evening, especially if the runway is lined up with the rising or setting sun, the hat will actually keep the sun out of your eyes.

Having a sun visor down may work as you descend or roll on the takeoff, but as soon as you raise the nose to flare or rotate, the sun visor goes up with the airplane, rendering it useless, and the sun now blinds you at this very critical moment. Unless you have the hat pulled down so low you can just see under the bill and over the anti-glare shield, you won't be able to see through the windshield.

I was in a T-303 Crusader taking off from Freeport, Bahamas, at dawn when that very phenomenon occurred. The sun blinded the lawyer-pilot flying as the nose rotated up, which allowed the sunlight under the visor bottom. He actually let go of the yoke with his left hand to shield his eyes, and the nose pitched down. I was in the right seat and quickly pitched the nose back up. He did not even know he almost crashed.

The only reason I could still see was, my properly adjusted hat bill blocked the blinding light. That would be an example of an accident happening because of sun glare, and whether the investigators could have ever figured out what actually transpired, in that he did not have a hat on or the hat wasn't folded properly, is very doubtful. Have and use a flying hat and leave it in the aircraft so it's always available.

Speaking of headsets as some protection to the top of the head, headsets are highly recommended in general. Of course, the noise-canceling ones are the best. I learned to fly before the intercom system. The plane did not have a radio or even an electrical system, except for a small wood-prop-driven generator located between the main landing gear, so cockpit communication consisted of just yelling back and forth.

The normal conversation went as follows: The instructor in the back seat would yell something, and I would say, "What?" and then he would yell something again, and I would say, "What?" And that was the normal conversation in the cockpit once we were underway. Voice-activated intercom was a good invention.

When buying a headset, as in anything aviation-related, always purchase quality. I know it costs a lot, but it's your hearing. The lightness of a headset is a significant factor as you'll be wearing it for hours. In turbulence, its weight is increased, so the lighter, the better. Make sure you have the program setting inputted into the headset option switch, where the headset will turn itself off after thirty minutes of inactivity. This obviously protects your batteries from dying if the noise-canceling function is not powered down after the flight.

If you stow the headset or leave it in the aircraft, don't put it over the seat back, where the ear cushions are constantly being crushed and the clamping spring force is being sapped. Just put the ear cushions together, but don't smash them, then retract the headset arms all the way down, rotate the microphone so it's tucked up between the headset arms protecting the boom mic, and place the set in the aircraft where it is out of the sun or stow it back into its bag.

Once you take the headset out of the bag, zip the bag back up all the way; that way, anything in the bag stays in the bag. Always have everything in the cockpit stowed. You do not want anything floating around that could potentially jam a flight control.

When you plug the headset plugs into their receptacles for the intercom and radio, ensure the nuts around the plug holes are tight. If they're loose and you can reach behind the backplate of the headset plug receptacle, hold the adapters steady back there as you rotate and tighten the nut. This will prevent the nut from unscrewing.

The rear of the plug-in is held to prevent them from twisting with the nut, which would cause the wires behind the connector to become too tight and break their soldered joint. If the backplate for the headset plugs is not mounted solidly, hold the backplate as you plug the plug back in just to relieve some stress on the backplate. And of course, always ensure that the headset plugs are fully seated. The plugs are different sizes, so they can only go one way. The large plug is for your ears, and the smaller one is for your mouth.

If you have copper-type plugs for your headset or hand microphone and they become a tarnished brown, indicating corrosion, the best way to remove that corrosion is a Scotch-Brite pad. I keep one in a headset bag. Just grasp the headset plugs with the pad and rotate the plug-in pin against the pad to scrub, and it will be bright and clean. This removes the tarnish, making reception much better on both the intercom and radio. If you have a hand microphone that starts acting up, besides taking it to the avionics shop, if it is a carbon-wafer-type mic, you can tap it to try to free the carbon wafers.

One of the better ways to wear the headset is to place it on top of your head, and once the cups are over your ears, if it's that type, then make sure the adjustment is equal on both the left and right arms so the headset sits squarely on your head. Swivel the mic boom all the way down, to its lowest position, and then bend the boom arm to place the flat part of the microphone, not the edge, against the corner of your mouth, not in front of your mouth.

This way, the headset boom being down, then curved up, does not block any vision downward on that side. Also, the boom mic arm can't change position in turbulence by falling down, as it is already at that stop. Having the mic at the corner of your mouth instead of in the center also reduces the popping noise when pronouncing *P*s and reduces excited mouth moisture accumulation. Have the mic close enough to your lips that you can purse your lips (kiss) and touch it.

The boom mic has a foam anti-wind noise cover over the mic itself and is a good option. When using a hand microphone, also just touch the edge of the grill part to the corner of the mouth for the above reasons. Plus, if it is already touching your cheek, it can't chip a tooth in turbulence.

If you have an ignition key switch for your aircraft, ensure the switch-retaining slip ring is tight, by twisting the knurled slip nut clockwise (righty tighty / lefty loosey). Try to have the absolute minimum number of keys on the key ring, as an excessive amount of keys adds weight to the ignition key cylinder itself, especially in turbulence. That weight is then increased with the stress of a wad of keys flipping around and could wear and eventually fail the switch. Even worse, in moderate or greater turbulence, if there was sufficient weight on the key ring, it could swing and cause the magneto switch itself to rotate and turn off or just down to one magneto from Both. If the former happened, there would be no doubt, as your engine dies instantly.

By the way, don't just turn the switch back on. The actual, detailed technique for an ignition off-air restart is as follows: Leave the key off (you're gliding now and got everyone's attention). Place your mixture control to the idle cutoff (full aft) position, to allow all the gas to vent out of the engine. Merely turning the ignition key switch back on, with the mixture still in, will ignite a backfire (now you also have everyone's attention on the ground) from the accumulated unburned gas in the exhaust system. This will force your muffler innards to go for fresh air.

The resulting explosion will be more impressive the longer it takes to discover that the switch is "off" and then instinctively turned back on. So don't do that. Instead, place the mixture to "off," throttle wide "open" for a couple of seconds, then reduce the power lever back to the "high idle" setting position (one-half inch). Now switch the magnetos to "both," then advance the mixture slowly until a restart occurs. Leave it a tad lean and monitor the engine gauges for temperatures. As the engine warms up, advance the throttle and mixture back to the previous cruise power parameters. And you're back in the game.

This procedure is necessary because when the engine died at cruise speed, it was still loaded with fuel and also lost all its internal heat and became the new poster child for extreme shock cooling (depending on the OAT [outside air temperature]). The above procedure allows the engine to warm up before returning to a high-power cruise output. Remember, if the propeller is already windmilling, never engage the starter.

First of all, there is no reason to (the prop is already rotating), and more importantly, if the engine doesn't start and rev up, the starter will remain engaged. This is bad, because a "hung" starter increases propeller windmilling drag, which decreases glide ratio and range. Worse yet, the huge electrical draw/demand from the still-engaged starter can quickly overwhelm the aircraft's electrical/charging system, resulting in a depleted battery, an extremely hot starter, and no way to lower electrically operated flaps, and the landing gear must now be lowered manually.

Another scenario is that the magneto switch position, because of the weighted key ring swaying around in turbulence, has rotated from "Both" to "L" or "R," leaving you running on only a single mag. Unless you are really in tune with your airplane, the fact you are down to one mag may be something you miss. At cruise power, the loss of a magneto could be subtle enough, principally when being bounced around, to not even perceive it. This is why, regularly, you look at everything you "own" and check that all switches are in their proper positions. Once discovered, the mag switch can just be turned back to "Both."

So for the key ring, it would be best to just have the ignition key and the door and maybe hangar key attached, and that is all. Once I have done the mag check, if there is a ring on the key, I flip the key ring itself over the key so the weight of the key ring holds the key to the "Both" position and also prevents them from jiggling around too much and being distracting.

Have a spare set of keys in your jacket or flight suit. To finish up on keys, train your crew (family) that when they hear "We're going flying," all respond by saying, "Airplane keys!" Bummer to arrive at the airfield and discover you forgot the keys (jeez!).

It is always a good idea to have one or two extra sets of batteries for whatever devices on board require them. These spare batteries can be stowed in the glove compartment (BTW, never have seen gloves in there) or headset bags. As we know, the definition of a pilot's flashlight is a cylindrical object used for the storage of dead batteries.

Nine-volt batteries are very dangerous, as their electrical contacts are co-located and both can touch some metal object (like a headset bag zipper) and start a fire. These type of batteries come with a plastic electrode safety cover for this fire-hazard reason. Tape over this battery-safety snap strap to secure it in place as an extra precaution.

I do not recommend a kneeboard, unless you are flying an aircraft with a joystick instead of a yoke. Don't have anything on you or mounted in the cockpit that would restrict *full* flight control movement. A small RON (remain overnight) bag containing toiletries (contact lens case, toothbrush, *etc.*) is good to have on board just in case and doesn't weigh that much.

Have a pen or two on board to write down clearances and weather info. Don't have a fountain/ink-cartridge-type pen, as they'll burst at higher cabin altitudes and make a mess. A "space" pen is ideal, as they write on almost anything and are nitrogen charged and can write upside down. NASA spent a million dollars developing it; the Soviet cosmonauts just used a pencil. Also have a grease pencil, and you can just write something on the inside of a side window.

One thing to record there would be the time of takeoff so you know exactly how long you've been up. This grease pencil writing will easily wipe off with your hand, a sleeve, or a cloth.

Speaking of grease, you always have some available for light lubrication purposes, and it is the "nose oil" (sebum) that is located on each side of your nasal crease where it joins the face. Draw/wipe your thumb and forefinger down these creases, and that "grease" can then be smeared on a zipper, a seat belt insert tab, a telescoping antenna, *etc.* for lubrication purposes. It can also be used to minimize scratches in optical surfaces due to its antireflective properties (fills in the scratch). Pencil lead can be used to lubricate zippers and keys, too, and doesn't attract dust since this graphite contains no oil. Electrical and battery contacts can be cleaned by drawing on the corrosion with a pencil and then erasing off the lead and green stuff. One last, always-available lube option is the oil on the dipstick, which a drop or two may be employed to loosen a door hinge or whatever.

Reference the Pilot Operating Handbook (POH) or Aircraft Flight Manual (AFM); I assume it has been read, so now read it again and take note of all the various important airspeeds; e.g., Vr (rotation [raise nose]), Vx (best angle [most height / least distance]), Vy (best rate [most height / least time]), Va (maneuvering [can't break]), Vg (best glide [most distance / least height loss]), Vg (landing gear [up or down]), Vref (approach [over the fence]) and make a sign or plaque and affix it to your instrument panel in front of you so all the pertinent speeds of the aircraft are readily readable. Laminate this placard and mount it to a blank spot on the panel, where it can easily be seen. Do this for each aircraft you regularly fly.

Speaking of reading, know the applicable Federal Aviation Regulations, particularly the "rules of the road" contained in FAR Part 91. Learn the system; it shall set you free.

Tab/mark the page of the POH (paper clip, Post-it, *etc.*) that pertains to engine cruise performance power settings; normally, 75 percent of power is the maximum. It's based on the pressure altitude and OAT conditions (density altitude). Once arriving at cruise altitude, you have a labeled ready reference to set the power within proper parameters, to ensure the engine is not being overboosted.

If your mission is a cross-country, as opposed to a local flight, and there is to be a landing at another location, ensure you have current charts and approach plates as required. Have the current charts folded as to how you will use them in flight. Normally, only two map panels are exposed, and if there are multiple charts required for the trip, have them folded and stacked on the floor, or wherever your charts go in your aircraft. Have the charts arranged in the order of their use. Whenever a new chart or book is acquired, then "brand" it. Write your initials on it so you can always identify your property.

The approach plates (if IFR) should be reviewed to ascertain which of the various approaches will be used at the destination based on the weather, and especially the winds. Tab/mark the one you think will be used, for quick reference. Also study the airport diagram, to identify the most direct taxi route to the desired FBO (fixed-base operator), especially if going to a busy airport.

This is in addition to the electronic data that is available in the cockpit nowadays. Don't completely rely on the "magic" magenta line as, but for one solar flare or electromagnetic pulse (EMP), the electronic stuff will now display a big red X on the screen (if that). The charts and compass are much more difficult to turn off. Always have a plan B, or C, too, at least.

The way you can guarantee the sun will "come out" is to forget your sunglasses. As IFR (instrument flight) pilots, we can make the sun shine on an overcast day by climbing through it. Breaking out on top of an extremely bright undercast can "snow-blind" the human eye. You almost need "glacier glasses" (welding helmet).

I once had to fold up a navigation chart into a sun-hood for a passenger to block the painful light reflection, and made two small horizontal slits for him to see through (map hat). A vinyl see-through sunshade that "clings" to the bothersome window helps, too (have one or two). Laying a chart on your lap can keep the hot sun off your legs.

The sunglasses you purchase do not have to be expensive ones. The pilot-style sunglasses have obviously been designed for the purpose of aviating, and they would be the ideal shape. They droop down on your cheeks, allowing vision down, to the sides, and up, far more than regular glasses. The lens, as you look in the mirror buying sunglasses, should be dark enough to block you from seeing your eyes. If you can see your eyes, they're not dark enough.

The ideal sunglasses are gradient driver's or aviator-type glasses, where the top half is darker than the bottom half of the lens. This way, you can just cast your eyes down and look through the less-tinted glass to see the instrument panel more clearly. Do not wear polarized glasses (do use them by the water), as they may visually distort some windshield and instrument glass, causing a distraction and some loss of visual acuity.

The sunglasses that you wear should not have wide bows on the sides that could potentially act as blinders, like on a horse. They should be thin enough that you retain your range of vision, which in a human goes over 200 degrees (220 degrees) from side to side, and so it is very important to have that peripheral vision available and unblocked. The side bows should also be thin enough that they easily fit under your headset pads.

I actually pull my sunglasses out after I put my headset on and then sort of rest the earpieces of the sunglass bows on the top of the headset pad. This way, it does not break the seal of the headset around my ears, and since my glasses are not prescription, it does not matter that they are slightly tilted. If you have prescription glasses angled like that, then you would increase their magnification. Have a couple of extra cheap pairs of eyeshades stowed in the glove compartment for passengers who may need them.

Always dress appropriately for the season. There is no guarantee you will not spend the night on some hilltop. Always try to wear socks and pants, instead of shorts and sandals, if at all possible. For footwear, I wear cowboy or flying boots that are flexible enough for me to be able to manipulate the rudders and toe brakes or heel brakes.

If you have heel brakes, tennis shoes don't work well or at all, because they'll slip off and aren't firm enough to catch the brake tab / heel pedals. Then, for heel brakes especially, shoes should have straight edges on the sides and back of the heels, not tapered or undercut edges like on cowboy boots. If they're tapered, you can't get a grip on the corner of the heel brake tab, which is about all you can catch with your heels while you're also using the rudders, especially in a crosswind scenario.

You don't want the shoes to be bulky, as that makes it more difficult to get in the aircraft, and they get in the way down at the bottom in the foot wells. The smaller the shoe, the better. You're sort of a ballerina, pointing your machine's nose with your toes, so you have to have feeling and a grip on the pedals.

I don't like loafers (in general) or tennis shoes, as they are too soft on the pedals. Boots would be superior in a survival situation also (snakes). There are now flying shoes available, and one of their innovations is two small roller wheels partly protruding from the heel bottom back so they roll on the floor when the toes are angled up, like on the rudder pedals. Pretty neat. Wonder if they retract.

Flying gloves are always a good idea, even if it's warm out. The best are tight-fitting and unlined. At least wear a glove on the hand manipulating the stick or yolk. If you watch most pilots fly and not wear gloves (most don't), regularly they are releasing the yolk with their flying hand and wiping their moist palm on the leg of their pants. This happens every few minutes. Gloves cure that habit. The gloves don't last very long for that reason, and they wear out very quickly, but that's better than constantly drying your flying hand on your pant leg.

Also, in the event of some small fire, you could actually just reach over and put it out with your hand. Leather gloves, or better still, Nomex gloves, were designed for such a thing, besides general flame and flash resistance. I've had live wasps (five or six) drop out of the wing root air vent onto the antiglare shield. But by wearing leather gloves, I solved the situation safely.

The best gloves have gauntlets, where the gloves extend over your wrist and halfway up your forearm. Aviator gloves were designed specifically for this, and they're a combination of Nomex and Kevlar and generally have palm and finger areas that are leather-lined on the palm side. I highly recommend those, and they can be obtained for a relatively cheap price. They're available in different colors, so they can match your flying outfit. I usually just leave them in the aircraft.

The gloves in general should fit well. If they're too small, they'll wear out even faster. If the gloves are thin enough and you have enough dexterity in them, you can wear them on both hands and still be able to manipulate the radio and navigation devices. Unfortunately, the gloves have to be removed to use a touch screen, but you can always just take your flying gloves and, on whatever hand you use for that, snip off the end of your thumb and your forefinger tips, and now you have a glove on and can still manipulate the touch screen.

If the glove is a little small initially, then the fingertips will wear through anyway. Gloves are also useful in a survival situation. When it comes to flying apparel, it is function over fashion. Finally, it is best to have it when you need it. The US Army Ranger Standing Order No. 1 is, "Don't forget nothing" (written in 1756).

One final tip for keeping warm is an old Native American trick. Cover your wrists. Tennis-player-type wrist sweatbands work well. They seal a heat-loss area between a normal glove and jacket sleeve and are quite effective in keeping you comfortable. If too warm, then remove and hang them on the half of the control yoke that you're not holding. Conversely, to cool down, put ice or run cold water on the area on the inside of the wrist just below the hand crease. The blood vessels are closest to the skin there.

The acupressure point for anti-motion sickness is located in this same inner wrist area. To help prevent nausea, there is a point three fingers down from the wrist joint. Lay three of your fingers on the inner forearm measuring from the wrist joint crease. On someone else, use their fingers. Locate the point in between the two tendons there that is three fingers down from that crease. That is the acupressure point to combat airsickness/seasickness. Rub that site with a thumb to activate it. Both places (L and R) can be massaged simultaneously with enough dexterity.

A homemade device to knead this pressure point would be to slip a marble underneath the wristbands so the ball impinges at that point on your inner arm. Wear one on each wrist. These should be worn for at least thirty minutes prior to the flight or boat ride to give it time to work. Ginger is the natural way to prevent a "spun gyro," radio slang / code meaning "I have an airsick passenger on board."

Aviators avoid any tonic-water drinks. The quinine in tonic affects a pilot's inner ear (no more Tom Collinses). Before the flight, don't drink fluids with acid in them, such as coffee (or have just *one* cup) or orange juice. Have some gingersnap cookie packs and a couple of extra wristbands and marbles on hand, and of course, some "white mics" (Sic-Saks), stowed in various strategic locations. Practice grabbing these puke bags and getting them out of their paper envelope just so you don't fumble if/when it happens.

I learned as an army tank officer that the most important thing the commander could do the evening before a big mission was to get a good night's sleep. The same goes for the pilot. Some tricks to use to get to sleep is to first program your mind to have your subconscious think about the upcoming sortie. Tell it to have everything organized and available for instant use during the flight. Since the subconscious never sleeps, this gives it a "project" to work on. If you can't control your brain, you can't control anything, and your mind controls your body. Attempt to achieve *ataraxia* (it all looks Greek to me).

Once in bed, take a deep breath and sigh (like a dog or cat does before it goes to sleep). Lie on your right side and breathe through the left nostril only. When the alarm clock later wakes you, then hit the Snooze button and stretch all different ways while still in bed, and go back to sleep. You will be ready to get up once the alarm sounds again. Take three deep breaths and drink a glass of water to activate your autoimmune defense and digestive systems (I haven't been ill in decades). To remedy dry eyes, fast-blink a few times (ten). Another way is to close your eyelids for two full seconds, then open them. Do this five times to makes the eyes "water." Never rub your eyes. The above suggestions do have some scientific basis, and they work for me.

Reference the actual trip itself; once the operation has been conceived (where we are going), the ideal way to fly the trip is to let the weather pick the day of the trip instead of the pilot picking the day. This obviously requires great flexibility on your part and of the availability of the aircraft. However, that would be the ideal way. When it's the perfect day, then you go.

I always thought if I won the lottery; the ideal situation would be to have an aircraft like a Short SC.7 Skyvan, which has a rear loading drive-up ramp. I would modify the interior to be like a Winnebago-type camper containing a galley (kitchen), bunks, and a head (toilet). Because of the rear loading ramp, I would be able to load a vehicle (like my 1985 Jeep CJ-7) into the aircraft cargo cabin. I'd paint the plane in camo colors and travel to airshows as a military display aircraft. It could be both partly deductible, and the fuel costs may be reimbursed by the show sponsors. The advantage of this technique is that you have a place to stay and eat and a car for local transport too.

If you have no destination in mind, then just wait till the wind is blowing very hard one day and simply fly downwind. Now your direction has been decided for you. Then fly downwind as far as you can comfortably go. Remember, if you don't go too far, you never know how far you can go, notwithstanding your thirty-minute reserve.

Otherwise, if you do not have that flexibility, the weather apps are sufficient to look at the weather three or four days in advance, and you can pretty well forecast what conditions you will be facing. It never hurts to wish for good weather, and a tailwind, while you are at it (works for me).

When taking someone up for their first flight, just fly a normal traffic pattern with a full stop landing. If they're okay, taxi back and take back off for the planned flight. Let them know that is the plan and explain all noises and vibrations to them. Demonstrating that you can actually get this thing back on the ground relieves them tremendously. Otherwise, that's all they worry about the whole flight.

Head *into* the wind on a flight like that, so if they want to return, it will be quicker than if you initially went downwind. Explain a bumpy ride as like a jeep driving down a rough trail (good fun and a built-in massage). Tell them the sun's heat has turned on the "lava lamp." Have them put their phone on airplane mode for better pictures and videos. (It also charges faster.)

Do not take any pictures before the mission; it's an old flying superstition from Baron von Richthofen (which turned out to be accurate). Save the group-hug shots for after the voyage, when all are smiling for real.

Now let's get the craft ready to go.

Preflight

The preflight is the last step you can take before boarding to ensure the aircraft is airworthy and ready for the proposed mission. It is your last, best opportunity, and always scrupulously follow the POH. As you walk toward the aircraft, observe it as a whole and note: that it's still tied down, that the cowl plugs are in (so there's probably no bird's nest in the engine compartment), that the external rudder gust lock is in place, etc.

When walking up to the aircraft, look under the engine compartment especially and at and around the entire ship in general to see if there are any puddles or leaks. From the color, smell, or taste, you can tell what type of liquid it is.

The engine's crankcase breather tube usually makes "chocolate milk," and a few drops of it below the aircraft's engine compartment is proper. It's the moisture in the oil condensing out of the crankcase. While we're at it, during preflight, especially in the colder climes, stick the tip of your little finger up into this breather pipe to make sure it did not freeze closed. If that would happen, the engine's lubrication system would overpressurize and probably blow an oil fitting off, causing a mess on the windshield, among other things.

If you have new passengers with you, as you approach the aircraft, particularly if it is a high-wing airplane, caution them about banging their foreheads on the trailing edge wing flaps. This is especially true if they are wearing a hat with a bill that obstructs their upward view. Having someone walk into the back of the flap while attempting to board puts a damper on things before you even start.

The newer Cessnas have a built-in rubber bumper on the end of the flap for this reason. This painful impact will leave a linear diamond-shaped design across the forehead, aptly dubbed a Cessna hickey. Inform all that a NO STEP sign does not mean to step on it (seen it happen).

Unlocking the entry door is made simpler by looking at the lock and noticing the scallop or scooped-out section of the lock face that's normally at one end of the keyslot. That indicates the smooth part of the key, not the keyed/toothed side of the key, goes to that scalloped end of the slot. Many people try to put the key in upside down and have to redo it, or force it, and damage the lock.

The key can be broken off in the lock if you're strong or it's cold enough. If you find yourself forcing something, or having to slam the door even harder this time, then look and see what is wrong and remedy it. Be gentle on these lightweight air machines—they are not like cars. If it doesn't work, then you are not doing it correctly.

Be careful having a passenger or student pilot actually unlock the door, as they may turn the key to unlock the door, open it, then turn the key back, relocking the door, and then they toss the keys on the airplane seat or up on the antiglare shield and shut the door. Now you are locked out of your own airplane. (How's the lesson going so far?)

The ignition key switch slot has the same scallop where the straight or smooth edge of the key goes. It's best to have the ignition key up on the antiglare shield so you can see it through the windshield during preflight while you are checking the propeller.

Before you actually open the door, be aware of the wind direction and strength. If it is a tailwind, have a firm grip on the door. This is true while getting in, but especially when getting out, as the wind could take the door out of your hand and potentially rupture/hyperextend the door hinges. This is really a hazard with a very light aircraft, or a helicopter, where the doors are made of incredibly lightweight materials.

If the aircraft has a passenger door, you can reach across the seat and unlock it at this time so it will be open when you are on that side of the aircraft during preflight. Open the windows and doors to air out the cabin, especially in sunny settings. It gets very hot in a sun-exposed cockpit due to greenhouse effect.

Try to have a "flow" to your procedures. Here we can take our hand across the instrument panel and go over to the master switch and turn on the battery side (only) of the split master rocker switch (the red one). Check your fuel quantity. This is done now so if the aircraft has not been fueled yet, you can call for the fuel truck and can continue with the preflight instead of discovering they're empty later during visual inspection of the fuel tanks with most of the preflight already done.

Sometimes the gauge needles are stuck. You never want to tap directly on the "glass" of any gauge; instead, tap next to it. Or go to the wing tips and rock them up and down to free any stuck components in the tank (push at a rib-and-spar junction). If it still reads "empty," you may just be out of fuel (it can be stolen by hot-rodders).

Check the fuel sumps before the aircraft is refueled as the injection of new gas stirs up the sediments and dirt in the tank. They can't be drained out effectively for quite a while. It takes fifteen minutes per inch of gas for the stirred-up junk and water to completely settle through the avgas to the sump drain low point. If the craft has "rubber" fuel bladders, then twist the sump drain valve more than pushing up on it.

It never hurts to glance at the OAT gauge and note the ambient temperature. It will be used later in the "Prestart" segment. Ensure your fuel selector is "on," and if there is a "both" option, select it. Make sure the lever is fully seated or "clicks" into the "detent." Just because the lever points to "Both," or "Left" or "Right," unless it is in the detent position, the gasoline will not feed to the engine. The fuel selector is turned on so the low point of the fuel (bowl) system can be drained or sumped later in the walk-around.

While the battery is on for those few seconds, you can hear the turn coordinator (TC) gyroscope begin to spool up. The quicker and smoother it spools up, the healthier the bearings in the gyroscope are. You then turn the battery off. Listen to the turn coordinator gyroscope "spool down." The longer it takes to spool down, the better are its bearings. If it comes to a grinding halt fairly quickly, you may want to order a new TC.

Get out your preflight checklist and start. Remember, you're not gonna buy it—you're just gonna fly it. We're just making sure all the big chunks are there and everything is operating properly. It's known as a walk-around inspection, because you start where you get in the machine and walk completely around the aircraft.

Take your time and look closely, noting any wrinkles, dents, fretted rivets, or the like. Do the antennae have a silicon (RTV) seal/bead completely around their mounting bases? If not, then that piece of avionics may fail in the rain. When flying a new-to-me company Bonanza in heavy rain, both navigation radios went intermittent while on the ILS (instrument landing system). They completely failed on the missed approach. I asked ATC where the nearest PAR/GCA was. A ground-controlled approach would be the only option in that scenario. Fortunately, we flew out of the rain and they came back online after drying out.

By the tail, caution the students and passengers not to bump into the fixed rudder trim tab. It is at the top of the rudder on the Debonair, out of harm's way, but most are down at our hip level. Don't bend it or bump it with your head while untying the tail. An airplane factory began receiving complaints from new customers that their just-delivered planes flew crooked and that the fixed rudder trim tab hadn't been adjusted.

The factory postproduction acceptance pilot said they flew straight when he got through with them and the tabs were adjusted properly by him. It turned out that the factory detail-and-finish department had a new employee that thought it looked bad being bent and all. So he straightened out every tab he saw. Do not expect what you do not inspect.

Have and use a rudder gust lock, as it is highly recommended. The gust lock in the control column only captures the ailerons and elevator. The rudder is still left free and uncontrolled and, in gusty winds, can bang back and forth like a screen door in a tornado. Can't be good on the rudder assembly.

If there is a rudder gust lock device, then take it off before untying the tail. Don't set a trap for yourself. You can't go flying with the tail still tied, but you can taxi and take off with the rudder gust lock in place, and that can be, at the most, dangerous and, at the least, embarrassing.

I once saw a Cessna 421 Golden Eagle twin that was taxiing to the runway for takeoff at a remote airfield, stopped him by blocking the taxi lane with my car, and I removed his bright-red heavy-duty rudder gust lock he had obviously forgotten about. It would have caused a crash, especially in the event of an engine failure. He owes me a beer.

When the tail tie-down rope is untied, extend the rope out to the left or the right, depending on what side the pilot sits on so that when you are in the cockpit and wonder "Did I untie the tail?" you can turn and look out your window and see the rope out to the side. If you just drop the rope under the tail, it is almost impossible to see from the cockpit.

Remember, if an instructor says, "Are you sure you got everything done?" that means you don't. If you left the nose chocks in place, do not try to power over the nose chocks. They are most likely to blow along the belly of the aircraft and possibly damage antennae sticking out down there. And one of the most embarrassing moments is trying to taxi while still tied to the airport, where more horsepower is required in order to tow the airfield with you.

Obviously, you cannot power away with the tail still tied, so in both cases, you must deal with the situation and shut down the engine properly before getting out to fix everything while looking around to ensure there were no witnesses. Then get back into the airplane and start all over. Do not get out of the airplane while the engine is running. Do not make a bad situation worse. If there are witnesses, after untying the tail or removing the chocks, turn to them and take a bow. You were the show.

When unmooring the aircraft in a strong wind, leave the upwind side of the aircraft secured. Once you untie the aircraft from the earth, it is free to go, and in strong wind conditions, that last remaining tie-down rope can be released after someone is already in the cockpit, strapped in, and holding the controls firmly for the wind direction.

Leaving Cape Cod shortly after a hurricane passed, the forty-mile-per-hour winds had pinned my Debonair against the ropes so tightly they couldn't be undone. I had to start the plane and move it to release the tension on the ropes. The drooped-wing Cessna 150 I fly will start flying at twenty-eight miles per hour (IGE, in-ground effect), so don't release the plane from terra firma until you are ready to keep control of it.

Especially if this is a training aircraft, roll the aircraft forward a foot or two to confirm there is not a sanded-off bald spot on the main landing gear tires from someone landing with the brakes on. If you see any cord exposed, it is time for a new tire.

Otherwise, you are landing on the Maypop brand of tire. If you land on that same spot or used brakes on the exposed cord section, it could result in a blowout. Unless you are fast on the rudder and brakes, there will be a departure from intended ground path. There will be a loss of centerline capture and probably a runway excursion off the edge. Always reference the POH for proper tire pressure and note that the nose/tail tire normally has a higher PSI air pressure requirement.

During your walk-around preflight, step away from the aircraft while behind the right aileron and back up fifteen to twenty feet and look at the top of the wing. Observe the symmetry and smooth trueness of the wing shape and form. The human eye is very discriminating when it comes to lines and noting linear imperfections. You step back from the craft because you cannot see the forest for the trees.

During the Vietnam War, an Air Force maintenance-check pilot for a combat unit had to test-fly a battle-damaged and supposedly repaired aircraft (O-2, Cessna 337 "Mixmaster"). As the centerline twin was slowed down for a stall check, the plane suddenly snapped into an inverted spin.

The pilot's seat belt wasn't tight, so he was pinned to the ceiling and therefore was unable to reach the rudder pedals. Both engines then went quiet. He managed to recover the airplane. He was chalk white and shaken but returned to base. (He told me near-death has a sickening, sweet smell.)

If the pilot had stepped back from the plane during the pre-flight, he would have seen the slightly warped/bent wing deformity that resulted from an antiaircraft shell that had burst under the wing, which caused the snap upset and the rapid and harsh departure from the expected flight path. Step away from the aircraft so you can see the big picture.

Under each brake, look for puddles or drops of "cherry juice," the red hydraulic brake fluid, indicating brake line or coupling leakage. After you have walked around the tail of the plane, bend and look up underneath the belly of the beast from aft to forward to detect streaks or smears of liquids there. If the mess is brown or black, it is oil; if it's red, it is hydraulic fluid; and if it's blue, it is avgas.

Ensure the rod end bushing for the aileron and rudder nose-wheel steering are loose and not binding. Be careful during the pre-flight to not set a trap for yourself. As you walk by the cowl plugs, you say, "I'll do that later"; as you walk by a gust lock, you say, "I'll come back to that." As you walk around the aircraft, look where you are and remove things you could forget and not see or remember later, especially if distracted, items that could make for a more difficult, self-inflicted, and completely unnecessary situation.

I have sun-protective covers on the tires. Pertaining to them, the rule is, when the main tire covers are removed, we immediately remove the nose tire cover also. We don't leave it for later. That is something you cannot see once mounted in the cockpit and would prove to be highly embarrassing and possibly expensive if you begin to taxi with that nose tire cover still strapped on. At the very least, the tire cover will be destroyed, along with your reputation (that's how nicknames are born).

I don't normally lower the flaps, especially when it's cold out. Besides saving the "cycle," I'm saving all the battery voltage for the start attempt. My small Cessnas don't require flaps for flight, and the Super Decathlon doesn't even have them (you slip it). The flaps are lowered later during the pre-takeoff check. If the flaps are lowered on battery power, then only raise them after the start and with the alternator functioning and charging the battery.

It amazes me how some planes still start after the flaps have been lowered and then raised, and then the pilot slowly checks all the lights (including the landing lights) during the walk-around, all while on battery power only. Good battery. Checking all the lights is not as electrically critical nowadays since the new LED lights draw a fraction of the amperage that the old landing light bulbs did.

As far as setting traps for yourself, a tow bar is the worst culprit. It is stowed, or in your hand, carrying it to or from the nose gear and when you put the tow bar in place to move the plane. Never leave it attached to the nose gear, unless you are holding it.

Also be careful when attaching the tow bar to the nose gear and try not to damage the paint there. Never drop the tow bar onto the top of a fiberglass nosewheel pant, as it will bounce and crack the wheel pant and chip the paint. Once the aircraft is moved, then take the tow bar off. If you are going flying, *never* leave the tow bar on the nose gear and say, "I'm going to get this later."

I have heard an airplane start with the tow bar still attached, and it makes a horrendous *clang clang clang* noise. I was in the next-door hangar, and what I actually heard was, "Clear!" *Clang! Clang! Clang!* It was a brand-new Mooney that the family was going to fly in for the very first time. They finally got to go five months later, after a new engine and propeller were installed. As a former aviation insurance claims manager, I can say this occurrence would be paid for, as the policy sometimes covers stupidity. The tow bar is always in your hand or properly stowed. Clear?

Closely inspect the nose gear, as it is unable to take as much punishment as the main gear can. Ensure the shimmy damper is tight and secure and all connections have their cotter pins installed in the castellated nuts. By the way, the nose gear is just used for taxi and the takeoff and landing rolls. It is technically not part of the "landing" gear, which are called the mains. The mains or the actual landing gear (not the nose gear) are the sturdiest item on the machine. You never land on the nose tire; it would be like a bird landing on its beak.

If you can get your head under the engine area and the ventral (lower) cowl is open enough to see, then look up in there. You are looking for any leaks or loose wires, hoses, or clamps. Take your time, be like a robot, and be methodical. After you have opened the cowl access panel to check the oil or to drain the fuel from the fuel bowl, give that opening the "sniff test." You should just smell warm/hot if the engine has just been run; otherwise, sniff for any fuel, oil, or electrical fire odors.

When checking the 710 dipstick: 710 is OIL written upside down. The only accurate oil check is before the first flight of the day, *or* after the engine has rested for a few hours. This allows all the oil to drain back down into the oil pan at the bottom of the crankcase.

When checking the oil level, be consistent with the position of the nose gear oleo strut. There is a difference of half a quart in the dipstick reading if my Debonair's strut is fully extended nose-up, as compared to being pulled/compressed down as far as the strut will allow. Do not exceed the maximum oil level amount. Only fill it to capacity for a long, nonstop, cross-country flight.

One-half of the maximum amount on the dipstick is the absolute minimum quantity. Below that level, the oil pump will aerate or suck air instead of liquid (which it can't). This stops oil circulation and results in engine failure.

When the oil level is brought to the max, which you may do for a long, cross-country flight, the first quart or two will eventually find their way along the bottom of the fuselage. Have a higher oil level in the summertime, for the extra cooling. Oil cools almost more than it lubricates. Conversely, a slightly lower oil level in the cold temps helps to keep the engine a little warmer.

When adding oil, be like a surgeon and drape the patient. Cover the areas where you could spill. Use a clean funnel. Try not to spill *any* oil on the engine or in the compartment and wipe it up right away if you do. At the very least, a spill will make a mess and a smell. Always shake up an oil container to mix all the additives that may have settled to the bottom while sitting on the shelf.

This is especially important for turbine oil, as the antifoaming additive has a higher specific gravity and will settle out and stay on the container bottom if not mixed/shaken up. This was discovered when a jet helicopter's engine fleet history showed an upward trend in oil foaming problems. The immediately issued mandatory service bulletin read, "Shake up the oil bottle/can before adding." This solved the foaming problem. By the way, don't shake up a gas container; leave any sediment in it undisturbed and pour the gas off the top.

Most people crush the O-ring gasket that is located at the top of the dipstick cap above the screw threads. On some small-piston engines (Lycoming), if the pilot screws the dipstick in too tight (remember, the threads are designed to tighten themselves up as the engine operates), then the dipstick becomes even tighter as the power plant functions. At the next preflight, the pilot will have difficulty removing the dipstick from its plastic tube housing.

Say the dipstick was not even screwed in at all. The oil access door would still hold the dipstick on board as it is blocked from coming out by this door. Because the plastic oil tube housing that the dipstick is in goes all the way down to the top side of the engine crankcase, only an oil mist would vent out the top of this tube to merely make a mess inside the engine compartment. It would not cause the engine to stop operating.

When the dipstick is screwed in so tight it's too hard to release, then what happens when you attempt to unscrew it is that the oil dipstick plastic tube housing safety wire breaks at the bottom of the tube where it is secured into the engine crankcase. If that tube safety wire breaks and the tube turns and loosens and unscrews itself there, then the oil will vanish quickly, as will the thrust.

Only snug the dipstick in so that its O-ring is *just* compressed (squished). Do not crush it. If you find the dipstick is twisted in overly tight, then hold on to the dipstick tube housing with one hand (to stabilize it) while unscrewing the dipstick *only* with your other hand. Use a flashlight to look down the outside of the tube to ensure its safety wire to the engine crankcase remains intact. If not, have it replaced before you fly. During each preflight, you should always grasp the dipstick housing tube itself and turn it clockwise to ensure it is snug. Do not overtighten (it's just plastic). If it was very loose, then the wire has snapped, and it's a good thing you checked it.

Look at the cockpit door hinges to ensure they are in good working condition. You do not want a door coming off in flight and striking the tail. If you are ever locked out of your airplane, you can unscrew the hinges from the airframe and remove the door to gain access (to the keys that are locked inside). If your aircraft maintenance shop is on the same airfield, then borrow their keys for the mission and return them afterward.

Look up inside the exhaust pipe/s to see the interior color. Light brown is the ideal shade (bromide residue). This means the engine has been operated (leaned) properly. If the exhaust stack interior is black and sooty, it has probably been run too rich. This dark color could also indicate an oil consumption (piston ring or exhaust valve) problem.

Now note the condition of the windshield and if it needs cleaning. Do that after the preflight check has been completed. Inspect the front of the aircraft to ensure the upper and lower cowl halves are secured to the cowl nose bowl and that all screws are present and secure. After engine start, there is a lot of vibration up there, and if enough of those screws fell out, the "hood" could open at speed.

I was in a Bonanza when the pilot did not properly latch the upper (dorsal) engine cowling door halves. After rotation, they "stood" right up and (thankfully) stayed there. We slowed and started coming back around. From the right seat, I could lean forward and see the engine in operation and commented on how that was a nice option. The left-seater said, "Shut up!"

The cowl doors were obviously designed to suffer such abuse. Nothing like a Beech or a Boeing! As the plane touched down and derotated upon landing, the cowl doors closed themselves and no one was the wiser. We didn't have to take a bow but did have to shut down, get out and lock them down, and restart a very hot and confused engine.

The power plant ran much hotter with the engine compartment doors open, by the way. Most pilots would guess otherwise. These engines are "velocity" cooled. The air that streams though the cowling inlets into the engine compartment is captured by the upper cowling and then forced to turn downward to flow through the cooling fins of the power plant's cylinders. The hot air then comes out of the bottom of the "stove" and gets sucked out past the underside of the firewall. The aft/ventral flange that is located there creates a low pressure area that accelerates the internal nacelle airflow (hence, "velocity" cooled).

This will not happen if the hood is off or open, as the air merely flows along the top of the engine and away, doing no good. It isn't forced to turn to cool by the internal cowling baffles (air dams). Engines are often run-up with their cowls off. This is poor technique and damages the engine. The A&P will say, "The temps were still okay." But there is no probe in between the jugs (cylinders), where it is the hottest. At least bungee a sheet of metal over the engine to make the cooling airflow more correctly.

Once again, always caution students and passengers about staying clear of the propeller arc path. Walk softly around the big stick. How the engine was shut down (covered later) makes a big difference as to how well the "revolver" is loaded to actually fire a cylinder and cause severe damage.

So remind the passengers and yourself to always remain clear of the propeller/knife tip-plane path. If a P-lead wire has disconnected from one of the magnetos, then the ignition system could still be "hot" even though the key is off and out. This is why you leave the prop alone or only move it opposite the direction of normal rotation, so the impulse coupling can't fire a potentially "loaded" engine cylinder. One cylinder firing will swing the prop with sufficient force to inflict serious harm. Messing with the prop is like playing Russian roulette. Remember, a knife is always loaded.

Always check the propeller for any nicks on the leading and trailing edges. If they are severe enough, have the mechanic "dress out" the nicks. Look specifically at the spinner and ensure all screws are present and that the spinner backplate is not cracked. A spinner flying off in flight can strike and damage or break the windscreen (bring goggles?).

Rotate the propeller backward, the opposite direction of operation, to align the slot in the bottom of the spinner, where the propeller blade exits to drain any water in the spinner left over from a rainstorm. When there is cold weather anticipated, have your propeller positioned vertically for a two-blade prop, or if a three-blade, with one of the blades straight down so the propeller exit slot in the spinner will allow any precipitation to run out and not be captured inside.

If the spinner cannot drain, water can accumulate in it and then freeze and act as an asymmetrical weight. This will shake the aircraft violently upon engine start. It would be challenging to discover the source of that vibration. Once this ice weight inside of the spinner has been discovered, it has to be removed. A heated hangar would take a while, so you'd need a hair dryer or heat gun to melt it. Instead, position your propeller so precipitation can drain out of the spinner.

When planning to leave the airplane, if you have a square-tip propeller versus a rounded-tip propeller, don't put the propeller exactly vertical, as a bird will land on that perfect perch and make a mess down your blade. This crap contains acids that will chemically damage what they touch. Leave the square-tipped blade at a slight angle to make it uncomfortable for the bird to perch (it will still drain). It seems birds are uncomfortable perching on a round-tip propeller, so that type of prop can be left exactly vertical.

In general, if you are parked on a busy ramp, have the propeller canted sufficiently low so that if a high-winged aircraft taxies too close, their wing will clear your propeller tip and pass over the engine cowling. Even if only your propeller blade is struck by the wing of a taxiing airplane, it is still a bad news deal.

If an aircraft comes with a spinner by design, then it must be flown only with one in place. If the spinner is removed, the airplane cannot legally fly unless allowed by the POH / Type Certificate. One of the primary purposes for the spinner (besides making the aircraft look cool) is to split the air to smoothly flow into the cowling air inlets located on each side.

Look into those cowling air inlets at the top of the engine to ensure there are no bird's nests. Always use cowl plugs if the aircraft is parked outside, especially during nest-building season. The Cessna 152 has a slot in the tail cone, allowing access to the aft fuselage, where we once found a two-and-a-half-pound mess of a nest (plus all the acidic bird droppings).

Some aircraft are designed to be more resistant to pest invasion—there aren't any openings where a bird can get in. The Cessna 150 does not have this tail cone access slot and therefore never has this problem. Plug these holes and slots but attach a red streamer so they can be removed before flight. The worst thing that can be done to a machine is to not use it. The longer the aircraft sits undisturbed, the more it becomes a wildlife refuge. It's not lions and tigers and bears but birds and insects and mice (oh my!) that are the potential safety and environmental hazards to your conveyance.

Any cabin air inlets on the aircraft should be inspected closely to ensure there are no wasp or insect nests inside these ducts. As mentioned, I've had wasps "rain" onto the antiglare shield while in the initial climb phase. They were very alive and quite unhappy. This is when leather gloves come in handy and why the plane is always perfectly trimmed.

If there is an insect nest in there, get a stick and knock it out. Most planes have a membrane material in the air inlet to prevent insects like that from entering the cockpit, but older aircraft do not (put some in there). During the wintertime, you can duct-tape those inlets closed to prevent cold air from entering the cabin of the airplane, allowing it to stay a little warmer.

While standing in front of the spinner, hold on to the propeller for balance and use your foot to compress the nose gear tire to test for its air pressure. Since most of the weight of the aircraft is on the main gear, the nose tire could be underinflated and yet not look so. By stepping on it, you can tell. Kick the tires and light the fires.

Look at your landing light, if you have one. Check the filament on the bulb to make sure it is intact, if it is not a LED bulb. We used to try to mount the landing light so the filament was vertical rather than horizontal, which could potentially extend the life of the bulb. Horizontally, the heat would cause the element to become ductile, and a firm arrival could break the element, extinguishing the light.

Check the air filter, either foam or paper, to ensure it is unblocked and serviceable. If an air filter in a carbureted engine ever becomes blocked in flight by a bird strike or by heavy rain or ice, then turn the carburetor heat on. This will bypass the blocked air filter, allowing air (albeit unfiltered) to continue to flow to the engine, keeping it running. There will be a slight loss of power (10–15 percent). This power drop is due to the influx of less-dense, heated air. Hot air is unable to burn the same amount of fuel as the cooler ambient air, therefore, less power. If the carb heat is to be left on, then lean the mixture some more.

Now, walk straight ahead of the aircraft twenty or thirty feet. Stand so the spinner point lines up with the vertical stabilizer. Look closely to check, inspect, and observe the symmetry and trueness of the airframe from dead-on in front. Any dissymmetry of shape or trueness should be investigated. Back off from the trees to see the forest.

To confirm if the craft is sitting unevenly, or low on one side, stand next to the wing tip (low wing), or under or next to the tip (high wing), and mark its position on your body. Go to the other side and compare. Now you know for sure if the craft is canted. If the main gear has oleo struts, check the symmetry of their exposed chrome.

The same as with a nose gear strut, there should be at least a couple/three fingers' width of strut exposed; otherwise, it should be serviced. Never taxi or even tow a plane with a completely flat strut. Since there is no longer *any* shock absorption at all, a bump or dip encountered while moving could permanently deform the airframe and/or the engine mounts.

While walking back to the aircraft, look down for any foreign object debris (FOD) on the ground. Look along the predicted taxi route as well and remove any FOD and dispose of it properly. FOD consists of stones, rocks, ice, and snow chunks or anything that could damage the propeller. Being an air machine and all, the blades should only touch air, as anything else could cause harm to the thrust-making thing.

Let me make a paramount point at this time. The most important things on or in the aircraft are the power plant, which makes power, and the propeller/rotor blades, which convert that energy into thrust or lift. This dynamic duo drags the plane down the runway until it's going fast enough to lift off. But for the engine, you're not going flying, or if you *were* flying, you are now gliding or autorotating.

Always take care of the "stove" first. The order of priority of attention is thus:

1. Take care of the engine/prop first.
2. Next comes the aircraft.
3. Then take care of you, the pilot (the one that is holding everyone's life in one hand).
4. And then the passengers. When the first three items are in order, the self-loading cargo is in good hands.

The fan (propeller) is just there to keep the pilot cool, because If It stops, watch him sweat.

Check the area beneath the propeller with extra scrutiny, looking for any loose rocks or sand or even water puddles. Clean it off, brush it away, or move the aircraft to ensure a safe, clean start-up area, away from any damaging FOD. Anytime you can see the air, watch the air. If you observe an aircraft idling in rainy conditions, watch the interaction of the water with the propeller tip as it rotates.

A propeller speed below one thousand revolutions per minute will create a tiny vortex (mini tornado) of swirling waterdrops. This vortex will stop just short of the propeller blade tips (under one thousand revolutions per minute). If small rocks were there too, the same vortex would form with the fingertip-size rocks swirling around just below the tips of the blades.

Once the RPM is increased above one thousand, the vortex will then rise (get sucked) high enough for the rotating propeller tips and blade-leading edges to then strike the top of that tiny tornado. As any seaplane pilot will tell you, even just water can erode away metal propellers.

If the FOD vortex consists of harder stuff, the propeller tips will then strike the rock as it rotates, and ding, or nick the leading edge of the blade. This or a fellow rock will also then be propelled, with uncanny accuracy, into wing-lift struts, the leading edge of the horizontal stabilizer/stabilator, the aerials on the belly of the fuselage, or wherever additional havoc can be most readily wreaked.

This is why it is important to make sure there is no FOD beneath the propeller tip area before start-up. Even chunks of ice can have a deleterious effect on the propeller blades, as the tips, even at a low RPM, are moving at a great angular velocity. There will be further discussion on this subject later.

However, an advanced (and tricky) technique, prior to a flight check-ride, is to "seed" this area with some FOD (little stones). Then "discover" this danger during your thorough preflight. Make a big deal of removing the FOD that you found, possibly adding the explanation, for the examiner's benefit, of why it is important to have this area clean and clear. There's nothing like good, aggressive cheating.

Most pilots over-rev (greater than one thousand revolutions per minute) their engines on the start. Especially during a winter start, it's almost impossible not to exceed one thousand. Once over one thousand revolutions per minute, whatever FOD was there has now been sucked up into the blades and has done its damage. While we are on the topic of propeller-propelled projectile damage, always look behind you if the engine is to be started or revved up, to ensure a clear path downthrust of your propeller efflux (wash) path.

Continuing the preflight inspection, we are now on the other side of the nose of the aircraft. We can inspect the nose gear fork and scissors from that side. Ensure all castellated nuts have their cotter pins inserted and are properly fastened. Be careful not to snag or cut yourself on these protruding cotter pin ends, as they're sharp and rusty.

Check the rudder steering shaft rod end bushings for movement. These are similar to the aileron bushings and must be loose and not binding. At some point during the preflight, you will ensure the Pitot-static vent openings are clear. We, of course, know to never suck or blow on the static vent openings or the Pitot tube. This could damage the instruments (ASI, altimeter and VSI) and looks weird.

Check the door hinges on that side of the aircraft too. During the preflight procedure and according to the POH instructions, we will come upon the fuel tanks and will check cap security after visually ascertaining the fuel level. While you have the fuel cap off, look at its sealing gasket or O-ring to check its serviceability. If it's dried up and cracked, it will not properly seal, and it will be unable to keep precipitation from entering the fuel tank and the aircraft's fuel system.

If necessary, just to get home, and as a temporary fix, take a little hydraulic fluid from the brake system if there is access to the brake fluid reservoir. Then smear some "cherry juice" on this gasket or O-Ring. This will cause the rubber-type material of the gasket to swell, and it will provide some temporary additional sealing.

Besides internal fuel tank wall condensation, leaking fuel caps are the primary cause of fuel contamination from water. Technically speaking, it is basically impossible for a properly certificated, inspected, and operating fuel facility to pass any water in their product into the aircraft fuel tank. (More on that later.)

Many aircraft have a bonding chain or cable/wire connecting the airframe to the fuel cap. Make sure this chain is not overly twisted and then replace the fuel cover. Ensure the cap is tight. Many times, the twist ears on the top of a screw-on cap will line up with the relative wind-flow direction. Now give the cap "one twist for Mommy and one twist for the kids" to confirm it is completely sealed. Both hands must be employed to completely tighten the Super Decathlon's gas caps as that plane can stay in powered inverted flight for two minutes. Since the fuel caps are then on the bottom of the fuel cell, they must seal very tightly, and so both hands are needed to screw them on entirely to their stops.

A technique for Beechcraft-style fuel caps is to have the flipper operating lever facing aft for flight, but if the aircraft is to be parked outside, then reverse the cap direction so the flip lever is facing forward, toward the leading edge of the wing. With the arm of the cap facing forward, any water that would pool in the cap from precipitation will now be away from the center pivot point of the cap, where it can cause corrosion from being trapped there, and also seep into the fuel tank.

Turn them back around for flight, if you'd like. For any aircraft, if there is water by the fuel cap or in it, then dry this area before moving the cap. Blow it away with your breath to ensure no water enters the fuel tank upon cap removal.

Always, if possible, supervise the refueling of your aircraft and confirm that the proper product is being pumped into your tanks by looking at the fuel-type label on the tanker or pump (1203 is avgas [blue] and 1863 [black] is jet fuel by DOT code). Advise the fueler person to actually read the affixed placard next to your aircraft's fuel tank opening, as rubber or bladder tanks should not have the fuel nozzle inserted into the fuel cell more than three inches. This prevents the end of the fuel nozzle from nicking or cutting the bladder, causing a fuel leak. This decal also specifies the type of fuel (avgas or jet).

The fuel nozzle tube should touch the side of the fuel tank opening at all times to prevent a gap across which a spark could jump through the gas fumes that are present. Not good. Also instruct the fueler not to put excessive sideways pressure from the nozzle tube against the round opening of the fuel tank inlet. This could potently crack the neck between the cap screw-on area and the fuel tank itself, resulting in a costly repair.

The aircraft should always be connected to the refueling point with the bonding or grounding cable. As the first item of business in refueling, connect the bonding clamp to some nonpainted point on your aircraft. Disconnecting this cable will then be the final task after refueling. So the bonding cable is first on and last off.

An advanced technique is to actually touch the fuel cap with the fuel hose nozzle tip end prior to opening the fuel cap. This action will dissipate any potential static spark without any fumes being present. Merely dragging the fuel hose across the ramp surface to the aircraft can build up a static charge. Depending on humidity conditions, this dragging, and even the fuel flowing through the hose on a very dry / low-humidity day, can cause a static charge to accumulate. The wider the temperature/dew point spread, the drier the atmosphere.

If you get a static shock getting out of your car, be warned. Try not to wear a nylon jacket or any synthetic material, especially while self-serve refueling. These materials are more spark-prone and are dangerous under heat. Do not use a plastic, straw-type fuel level dipstick either. Unless it's labeled "static-free," it, too, can cause a spark when there are gasoline fumes present. I've been the safety officer at an FBO (refueling facility) for decades, and basically the goals are thus: don't spill a drop and don't make a mushroom cloud.

No one should be in the aircraft while it is being refueled, and all electrical switches should be turned off, with no radio or cell phone use during the gassing operation. If you need to walk under the wing being refueled, go from wing tip to wing root; do not walk aft of the trailing edge or allow anyone to stand there. If the fuel tank is overfilled, the fuel will flow down the top of the wing and waterfall off the trailing edge.

Anyone standing there or downwind, if the fuel "geysers" straight up from being overfilled, will be drenched with one-hundred-octane avgas. Afraid of a little lie, scarecrow! (Sorry.) Assuming no spark, the good news is, the avgas will quickly volatilize (evaporate) off you and your clothes. Stand and rotate in the breeze and try not to inhale the fumes (same with tear gas). A gray powder residue will remain (the lead additive). Wash this lead off your skin.

Jet fuel is worse. Kerosene will not evaporate away and will chemically attack the skin. You'll need a shower and new clothes. Wash jet fuel off your skin ASAP. Be aware of the wind direction and where you are to avert a gasoline baptism. Jet fuel is just diesel fuel without the oil additive.

Watch the fueler's control of the hose itself. Any touching of the hose to the fuselage or leading edge of the wing could cause a black scuff mark. My Super Decathlon has matching nicks on the wing main lift struts from the fueler's ladder. The nicks were painted out, and clear "wear" tape was applied to that area to try to protect it. The fueler is now warned about hitting the plane, or I just position and remove the ladder myself. The fueler should not be wearing a metal-type belt buckle either, as this accessory lines up precisely with a low-wing leading edge right where the fuel tank opening is located. My Debonair also has matching scars from Billy Buckle, Uncle Ladder's nephew.

Unless the aircraft is going to be flown right away, the gas tank fuel levels should be left down an inch or two for possible expansion of the fuel, especially if the fueling operation is being done on a cool evening and the flight won't be departing until the next day in the hot afternoon.

If the tanks are topped off, the fuel will expand and drain from the tank vent tube, causing a waste of money and damage to the ramp, where the fuel will puddle and eat through the surface. If anticipating a short flight with an asymmetrically balanced payload (i.e., three people in a four-seater), then put less fuel in the heavier side and more in the lighter-side fuel tank.

If your aircraft is parked where one wing is higher than the other because the ramp is not level, then the fuel selector should be set on "Left" or "Right" if you have that option, as opposed to "Both," as "Both" will not prevent a cross-feeding of gas from one side to the other. Most missions only last one or two hours, so the aircraft does not have to be topped off.

On a canted ramp, the higher-wing tank can be almost filled, and if you don't have a fuel selector with the "Left" or "Right" option, then the higher-wing fuel will then self-cross-feed from gravity into the lower wing. If the lower wing was also filled, the pressure from the higher wing to the lower wing would cause the gas to drain out from the fuel tank vent but now, because of hydraulic pressure, head force instead of heated fuel expansion. If the check valve in the fuel vent tube fails, then the entire fuel load could siphon out onto the ground. One reason not to be smoking when entering a hangar.

I have two training Cessnas (172M and 150L) parked on a slightly sloped ramp, and unless planning on a cross-country flight, I fill only the higher-wing tank. No gas leaks out of the low tank, the fuel vent is on that side (port/left), and eventually, the levels equalize. This doesn't waste gas and doesn't damage the environment or airport infrastructure. Avgas will emulsify (dissolve) asphalt.

A way to see if your avgas is contaminated with jet fuel is to do the following: Put a couple of drops of your aircraft's gas on a paper bag or piece of cardboard. Let the avgas spot volatilize (dry) and see if anything remains. If there is an oily ring around the dried spot, then there is kerosene in your fuel. Good catch. As the Pilot in Command, we are the final safeguard in preventing a misfueling incident/accident. Be present, look at the tanker labels, and study the receipt to prove the proper petro was pumped.

If you have parked the aircraft on a transient ramp, or it has been out of your sight, then at the very least, walk around the machine to make sure it has not been clipped by a fuel truck or whatever. Most importantly, there could be an airworthiness issue. Additionally, if this damage is not discovered at that time, and you fly away and then later discover the harm, you will not be able to prove it happened at the location of the incident.

One time, while parked as a transient, I had a Bonanza "touched" by a tanker but luckily caught it in the perfunctory walk-around. I measured the damage height above ground on my body. A tanker was then located that had some damage to it at the same height. A bonus was, there was actually a "paint swap" at that site matching with my plane's paint color.

The FBO manager was found and was very politely invited to see something. After viewing the evidence, he conceded liability. In such an instance, they will pay for your deductible, and the claim occurrence won't go on your insurance record. Remember, when dealing with anyone airside, be a "Sky Knight." As my dad said, "Sell, don't tell," and as my wonderful wife (the proofreader) says, "Because nice matters."

Some insects, like bees and wasps, are attracted to the smell of avgas or something in it and will actually build nests in the fuel vent tube. Always check the fuel vent openings, both the forward and aft ventral drain holes, to see that they are clear of nest-building materials. The same goes for the Pitot tube, although there is a cover for it that will prevent infestation.

Some aircraft, like the Bonanza, have fuel vent tubes that are at a specific forward-facing angle (ten degrees). Ensure they are properly slanted and not bent incorrectly. There is a small hole on the back/aft side of those fuel vent tubes; make sure this hole is open. This is the anti-ice vent hole that will allow the fuel tanks to breathe (inhale) if the primary vent opening facing forward ices shut.

If air can't be put back into the fuel tanks as the gas is consumed, then the fuel tank could collapse from vacuum. It's like sucking your cheeks into your mouth. This could stop the fuel from flowing to the engine. Also, be careful when crawling around underneath a low-wing airplane so one of these vent tubes isn't struck and bent or broken off (done that—damn!).

If you are ever parked on an inclined ramp, remember to always chock or tie down the machine, as it *will* roll downhill. Even though it seems to be sitting there just fine, a wind gust can jostle it sufficiently, and along with gravity, this shaking can overcome static inertia. Once the craft starts to roll downhill, this two- or three-thousand-pound airplane will take some effort to bring to a halt. If left unattended, it will eventually roll downhill, seeking the most expensive damage it can find. A very embarrassing insurance claim.

I learned this, almost the hard way, someplace in Ohio, when the company's Bonanza went coasting by the line guy and me. We ran after it, got in front of the F-33, and being highly motivated, stopped it after about fifteen feet of effort, about ten feet away from a building wall. Jeez! You're not done until it's chocked and locked.

The remainder of the preflight is now completed pursuant to the POH; this will be the last opportunity for the pilot on the ground to ensure the aircraft is fit for flight. During your preflight walk-around inspection, be especially mindful of any missing screws or fasteners and also check the continuity of any bonding cables connecting the control surfaces to the airframe.

The electrical "bonding" or, as some call them, "grounding" cables are important to protect the aircraft in the event of a static charge buildup and, more importantly, if a lightning stroke (channel) is inadvertently flown through during a T-storm. The airplane does not actually get struck by lightning, but it flies through the lightning stroke that is already occurring (bad timing). This is because the airplane is obviously not grounded while in the air and therefore can't be "targeted" by lightning.

By the way, this is why they are technically called "bonding" cables, not "grounding" cables. The cables do not go to the ground but instead bond the aircraft control surfaces to the rest of the airframe or bond the refueling point to the aircraft. An example is when one shuffles their feet across the carpet in the winter (low-humidity conditions) and then electrically sparks/shocks someone. This electrical discharge would not happen if there were a bonding wire connected between the two people.

If your aircraft has static wicks, the little hairs or fibers protruding from the ends should not be trimmed off, which I have seen, but should be left that way (it's like unbending the rudder trim tab). Any airframe-built-up static ion charge dissipates electrons back into the atmosphere via these static wick tips located at the primary control surface outboard extremities. An aircraft flying through precipitation (especially dry snow) is like dragging your feet across the carpeting in low-humidity conditions.

As an inexperienced dumb-boy pilot (now I'm an *experienced* dumb-boy pilot), many decades ago, while I was flying though moderate to heavy snow at one thousand feet in a Piper Cherokee, a bright-blue static spark about the diameter of a thumb jumped aft out of the radio panel. It turned and hit the windshield. This mini lightning strike spread into a "Tesla fingers" shape along the inside of the windscreen as it passed through the Plexiglas, or wherever it went.

It made a loud cracking noise when it happened, and there was a very strong smell of ozone. I might have spotted. Properly functioning static wicks and bonded control surfaces would have prevented this phenomenon, the consequence of which was a fried radio and a very unhappy rental aircraft owner.

Returning to any missing screws, if there are any missing, also check the opposite symmetrical side of the aircraft to see if that screw is missing as well. The airframe goes through many harmonic vibrations as the engine starts, stops, and changes RPM in between.

Watch an airplane's wing tips and tail shake and wobble at the very end of propeller rotation during a shutdown. The airframe actually emits a shaking noise at that time. This shaking is also why the sun baked plastic trim pieces on the tail plane crack and have to be regularly stop-drilled.

This is why it is important to have the engine at its lowest idle RPM before pulling the Mixture to idle cut-off. This reduces the number of harmonic vibrations transmitted through the airplane.

This is especially noticeable at the wing and elevator tips. The higher the RPM at shutdown, the more nodal frequency ranges the aircraft is subjected to, and the longer it is harmonically "excited" and shudders.

If you discover any screws on the ground or in the cockpit, make a special effort to discover from whence they came. Once the missing hole is discovered, then also check the security of any other screws in the area. After maintenance is performed, and especially following the annual inspection, it is a good idea to go around and check the security and tightness of all inspection plate screws and others. Even if only a couple of screws were loose out of the eighty you checked, it was worth it, if just for the peace of mind of now knowing all is well.

Have a small plastic Ziploc bag in the glove compartment to store any extra screws you find. That way, if you are missing any other screws in the future, there is a collection available for replacement. If you cannot figure out where this errant screw came from, put it in the Ziploc bag and show it to your mechanic to see if he can locate where it belongs. After all, the screw was serving some purpose before it fell out.

Look at the tires before you get into the aircraft, and if there is a possibility they could be frozen to the ground, then give them a scuffing kick with the bottom of your foot to the top of the tire and break the ice free. Also, if the aircraft tires are parked in a crack or depression, then go ahead and push or pull the aircraft out of that hole so that it will taxi away with less engine effort.

If the main tires are in a crack in the pavement, then excess RPM (2,000 or so) will be required to start the aircraft moving out of that depression. This should be avoided with a just-started, cold engine. Many of the larger engines are RPM-limited until the oil reaches a certain temperature. For example, the IO-470K engine must be kept below 1,200 revolutions per minute until the oil temperature has reached at least seventy-five degrees Fahrenheit.

If I'm parked in a hole, I have to sit there for ten minutes or so (on a cold day) before the engine can be revved up high enough to get out of the crack, to even begin the taxi phase. This time could have been spent moving to the runway while warming up on the way. Use manpower instead of horsepower to position the craft so it's ready to roll.

If you are going to push or pull on a high-wing aircraft that has multiple lift struts, always push or pull on the larger strut, not the smaller strut. The small strut is usually located aft of the main strut, with both connecting the bottom of the fuselage to the underside of the wing, forming a triangle. The larger/forward strut is the stronger one, so use it.

If you must push or pull on the propeller, which should generally be avoided, then grasp it as close to the hub/spinner as possible and never outboard toward the tips. Better still, use the tow bar—that's why they made it.

As stated, if there are gusty wind conditions, then the upwind wing should be left tied down until a pilot gets in the plane and can hold the flight controls properly based on the wind bearing. After there is a crew member on board and ready, the wing can then be untied. We normally hold the flight controls fairly lightly; however, in high-speed wind conditions, maintain a firm grip on the yoke or stick of an airplane. Otherwise, a gust can snatch the controls right out of your hand (now be white-knuckled).

Untie the remaining ropes. Technically speaking, this is called unmooring. Once the airplane is untethered from the earth, it is free to go downhill or downwind.

While building flight time as a banner tow pilot, I had missed the pickup rope with the grappling hook and had to land to replace the rope back on the catch poles. This was in Kansas, where the wind blows hard enough that they don't have a wind sock—they have a log on a chain. I taxied the Super Cub across the grass infield to the pickup point and shut down the engine and dismounted. When I finished with the tow rope and turned around, the plane was *gone*.

I mean not in sight, and in Kanzania (the heartland of the Soviet breadbasket), one can see a very long way. Finally, it was spotted one thousand feet away, nuzzled up to the airport perimeter fence. Because of its castering tail wheel, it had rolled/sailed downwind until it was eventually corralled by the boundary barrier. Fortunately, no damage was done except to my brain, which ground to a halt upon not seeing my horse where I had left it. Engage the parking brake or chock it when in doubt. (I didn't know it even had a parking brake, duh!)

Before you get into the plane, take one last look around to make sure it is completely untied, the oil access door is closed, the lid on the ramp storage box is secure, and your car dome light is off. This entire preflight procedure only takes about six minutes. Try not to be distracted during the process. Be here now.

Cleaning the Windows

This section will pertain to the cleaning of aircraft transparencies. Looking at another pilot's windshield once, I asked, "Did you clean that with a Hershey bar and a brick?" Some don'ts on cleaning the "glass," the windshield and side windows: never use paper towels or anything that could scratch the Plexiglas. Aircraft transparencies are actually *not* glass and not like automobile windows at all. There are specially designed cloths for aircraft window cleaning (such as DuPont Sontara wipes).

Another don't is to never use any type of normal glass cleaners that have alcohol or, even worse, ammonia-based chemicals in them. These chemicals and solutions will "craze" (make tiny cracks) the plastic glass and cause striations, which will produce sunlight refractions in the glass. This crazing, at certain sun angles, makes it difficult or impossible to see through the window. Use only aircraft-approved products for the view ports.

Unless the commercial product application is done precisely as directed, streaks are left and are difficult to locate and remove. Shake the heck out of the spray can before you use it. Water is the universal solvent, and of all the various products I have tried over the years, water is the best. If the windshield is cleaned after the flight, it will be easier for you to clean off the bug debris and air grime. They have not had a chance to bake onto the windscreen from the sun.

It is critical all transparencies are clean on the outside if an airframe/window protective cover is to be used over the fuselage. Putting a cover over a dirty windshield literally grinds the grime into the glass. This scratches the Plexiglas, and scratches are very hard and time-consuming to remove. The wind blowing and fluttering the protective cover lying on top of the windscreen also adds mechanical sanding action to the mix if the glass is not already very clean.

As for removing bugs from the leading edges, it is easier to do postflight than it is five days later during preflight. When cleaning the windows, water and a bare hand can work best and not scratch the glass. Some helicopter owners actually never touch the transparency with anything but water and air, as anything else could potentially scratch the canopy bubble. They will run water on the glass and blow it off with a low-pressure air hose, thereby leaving it untouched by human hands.

When rubbing on the glass to remove deposits, never use a swirling or circular motion. Use straight back-and-forth strokes. An advanced technique would be to use straight strokes going in the direction of the relative wind.

With that in mind, for the outside of the windshield, you would go from top to bottom and from bottom to top in straight strokes— no sideways strokes. A terry cloth towel and a microfiber cloth is best for drying, and once again, the drying strokes should be lined up with the relative wind direction. On the inside of the windshield, use straight strokes again, but going from left to right and then right to left. This way, any streaks that remain on the windshield can be identified as being on the outside (vertical strokes) or on the inside (horizontal strokes). This will make it easier to locate and remove the streak or smear.

On the outside of the side windows, the strokes will still be in the same way as the relative wind and would be from forward to aft, and then aft to forward. On the inside side windows, the cleaning and drying stroke direction would be vertical, from bottom to top and top to bottom. Once again, from the orientation of the streak, you know where to go (in or out) to clean a blemish that was missed.

Some furniture spray wax products also work well to polish the Plexiglas, and you are also left with a fresh, lemony smell. This wax also fills in some of the scratched minicracks on the windshield surface, thereby reducing refractions and reflections in the glass. Use the same direction of strokes as mentioned.

Except when using water to wash the windshield, do not touch any of the glass with your fingers. This also includes the cockpit instrument glass. There are salts and oils on your fingertips that will leave a smeary residue. This is another reason that you tap *next* to a sticking instrument gauge and not on the glass itself. Don't touch a landing light lens with your fingertip, as this "oil" could burn it out (not LED).

Clean transparencies are important, especially the windshield, as a bug spot at the right point on the glass will routinely catch your eye as a potential traffic hazard. Every time you look though that spot, you believe for a split second that it's an aircraft (and "jump" a little).

As mentioned before, a clean windshield is very important during times of low angle sun, morning, or evening, where the upsun (into the sun) landing or takeoff can be difficult or impossible to see through a dirty windshield. This increases the level of difficulty unnecessarily.

This is why on a calm-wind day, you should take off and land downsun (the sun on your tail) instead of in your face. The same option is available if there is a *direct* crosswind, so use the runway direction that best suits the sun angle or departure terrain. Always make it as easy on yourself as you can. Eliminate all the handicaps that you can by taking your time, thinking, and doing it right.

Washing and Waxing

As an aside, when the aircraft is to be washed, place tape over the static ports so water can't get in. Take another piece of tape and stick it on the control yoke / joystick handle. Of course, the best way to dry an aircraft off after washing it is to fly it. The piece of tape on the yoke is there to remind you to remove the tape from the static ports and Pitot tube cover. Lower each aileron and the flaps to dump out any wash water present, which could freeze at altitude and cause a flight control imbalance or flutter.

Don't wash (or wax) any machine while it is exposed to bright sunshine (do it when it's very cloudy or in shade/indoors only). "Particularately," if the liquid wash water is "hard' (test it). The various minerals and elements in hard water can leave a residue deposit, a chalky white ring around the edge of a drying wet spot and can quickly become almost impossible to remove. Dry off the darker paint-job colors on the sunny side of the craft ASAP. Otherwise, that spot edge ring will be sun-welded to the paint forever, or so.

The wax protects the paint, and the paint protects the machine's skin, which is what protects you and yours. Invest in an in-line garden hose RV type of water softener/filter to ameliorate the hard water's effect.

During a moderate rain event, go down to the hangar to do a free and "green" wash job. Pull her out and let the rain soak it. If it's warm enough, go out in the rain (Ranger sunshine) and wash the thing mechanically (elbow grease). No soap is necessary; just swish the wet around with a towel (use two towels and both hands). If it's too cool out, put it back in the hangar and wipe it off and then pull it back out for the rain-rinse job.

Place the machine back under cover and dry it off. If you timed it "perf" and the weather is now VFR (visual flight rules), then simply fly it to dry it. As learned before, dump out all the accumulated liquid moisture in the flight controls and flaps.

Use a polymer-finish-coating type of paint-protective product, as this type does not break down under UV sun exposure like a wax does. It also doesn't bead up the rain/dew drops as much but instead "sheets" the moisture, which then flows downhill and off the aircraft skin's slope. A beaded bubble of water functions like a magnifying glass in the sunlight and focuses/concentrates a burning sunbeam at one point on the surface and compromises the wax there. A polymer type of coating (Rejex) will prevent and resist that sunlight damage, as it actually cures and becomes stronger in the sunlight.

Mounting

We are now ready to get into the aircraft. As I used to like to say in the Tank Corps, "Mount up!" As mentioned, on a light aircraft or helicopter, be aware of the wind direction before you open the door. If the wind is from behind you, have a good grip on the door when opening it so that the wind does not take it out of your hands. A door caught by the wind can hyper-open and strain or damage the door hinges.

On a light helicopter, the door may nearly break off. My helicopter instructor would remind us before a door was opened by saying, "That door costs $487!" This was back in the seventies. They probably cost a bit more now. Look inside to check for any charts or papers that could be sucked or blown out of the cockpit or merely fall out when the door is opened.

Be careful while getting into the aircraft. As I tell my students, "Watch your big clobber feet." Particularly on older aircraft that are parked outside, all the plastic trim pieces have become quite brittle and fragile and are easily cracked and broken. Once you are in the seat, scoot your bottom aft against the seat back and sit up straight and tall in the saddle.

If there is a possibility your breath could "fog" the windows from its condensation, then breathe through your nose and point your head down when talking or cover your mouth when speaking. If the windshield interior fogs up, you'll have to open the side windows and maybe the doors also to cool/dry the whole cockpit out. The "defroster" function on a small airplane has no blower fan (like a car does) and really only works when the aircraft is flying.

Adjust the seat backward or forward and be able to push one rudder pedal to its stop with a slight bend remaining at the knee.

Students have a tendency to sit too close. However, don't be back too far, as you still must have the ability to move your flight controls all the way to the stops. You are sitting too far back if your toe-tips on the rudder pedals' tops are required to push it to the stop. This means that side's toe brake is now engaged.

Landing in a heavy crosswind in this configuration will cause the downwind tire to be brake-locked upon touchdown. If you need to sit further forward, or higher up on the seat, have cushions or chair pads available to use to adjust your position for comfort and flying safety.

Make sure you are squarely in the center of the seat and directly behind the control yoke or stick. Once the forward/aft position of the seat has been set and confirmed, double-check that the locator pin in the seat track rail is properly and fully seated. While pushing down on the seat adjustment lever, scooch back and forth to confirm this locking pin is completely in its seat rail hole.

We want to prevent a seat slip-back scenario. This normally happens at rotation. As the nose rises, inclining the flight deck angle, you seat-slide downhill/aft at a very unpropitious moment. If that ever happens, pull back on the throttle and *never* pull back on the yoke. This is why you hold on to the throttle (like a gun) during the initial takeoff roll and ensure the seat is always locked in.

You want to be sitting high enough so that you are at the proper "design eye height." On larger aircraft, there are actually sighting points or markers (little white balls) that have to be aligned to ensure your eyes are where the aircraft's designers meant them to be for optimum visibility out the windows.

To establish proper eye height, you can make a fist and stand it up on top of your head. It should just touch the ceiling's headliner. If you are sitting too low, landing will be especially difficult. Once again, obtain a pillow or cushion to raise your eye height. The higher you sit, to a limit, the easier it is to see at rotation and during the landing. You can still see over the nose, even though it is pitched up during the flare.

Once everything is adjusted, put your lap/seat belt across your hips, not your thigh tops or lap, double-checking that the belt itself is not twisted. A twisted seat belt would cause more damage to your body than a straight one and is also weaker.

Make sure the buckle is fully secured and pull until the seat belt is tight like "Moby Dick in a footlocker" (how paratroopers wear their chute harness straps). You and the aircraft are now one. You have put the machine on, like donning your very own set of wings. As in the movie *Avatar*, the seat belt clicking shut is like the rider and the air dragon joining together.

Tuck the loose end of the lap belt under the seat belt to properly stow it. This will prevent the seat belt end from flapping around in turbulence, especially in "negative G," which could be distracting. And in the unlikely event of a ditching, when the cockpit fills with water, the end of a loose seat belt would start swaying around in the current and you would think, "Oh, good, and there're snakes in here too?"

A properly stowed seat belt end also won't get caught in the door when closing it. One of the worst things that a loose, flapping seat belt end could do is flick you in the eye. Chance favors the pre-pared mind (and cockpit).

Put on the shoulder harness if it is separate from the lap belt. It should be worn loose enough so that all panel items and the fuel selector on the floor can still be reached. Snug it up for takeoff and landing and make it real tight if you're going to crash. Ensure that it's not twisted and snap/lock it into the seat belt attach point.

If it won't click in, the female end of the lap belt may be rotated, thereby preventing shoulder harness attachment. This Murphy-proof design feature won't allow the harness tab to engage in the retention slot because it indicates that the belt is twisted. I've seen students attempt to hook on to this upside-down seat belt slot twenty times in a row (oh, boy), with the same result (the definition of insanity). If something doesn't click right away, or the door won't close, and the like, there is probably a reason. Look and find out. The solution is *not* trying it again for the twenty-first time, or slamming it even harder.

If it's cold out, start the engine and then get the headsets out and hook them up while the engine warms up. If it's not cold, the headsets and charts can be set up before the start. Always be in your seat with its position adjusted before messing with the headsets. I just had a student that got out his brand-new $1,200 headset before he even got in the plane. As he adjusted the seat forward to the flying position, his headset cord was rolled over by the seat and captured between the floor track and the seat track roller front wheel.

Despite our efforts, we were unable to remove it at the moment, so he had to wear some old, musty headset we had lying around. Good lesson. Taking the headsets out after the seat is positioned and the belts are on prevents this cord-capture possibility. Perform the required items in their most logical sequence. Ralph Waldo Emerson said, "There's always a best way of doing everything."

Before closing the door, look specifically to ensure that nothing is hanging out of the door opening. Closing the door on the seat belt damages the webbing and cuts or breaks the headset cord wire. If there are backseat passengers, make sure their fingers are away from the doorframe. Slamming the door on their fingers makes for a bad ride.

Never let a passenger latch or lock a door, as if this is not done correctly, it will pop open (surprise!) at rotation. The aircraft's weight transfers from the tires to the wings as the craft starts to fly and the stress on the airframe changes. This is usually when the improperly latched door will "explode" open (keep flying the plane, by the way).

It's no big deal for most planes. The Debonair cabin door will not close in flight. Land, close it, and fly again. Have your passengers actually practice unlatching their belt and shoulder harness and opening the door. Just because they *say* they understand means nothing.

Once you're in the aircraft, get out the prestart checklist and use it. At the very least, "read the book." Imagine the instrument panel as a page in a book. Start "reading" from the top left of the panel and look at each gauge and instrument in a row from left to right. Then drop down to the next row/line and check each in their respective order. Don't skip a "word."

Do this row after row until at the bottom of the panel on the far right side. Now all items have been set correctly. Use the checklist to confirm. "Reading the book" is a good, methodical way to locate everything on the panel when preparing to fly an unfamiliar aircraft.

Make sure the primer is locked in (a half-turn from the "unlock" slot) and rotate the cockpit interior light rheostats to their full on position, then back to off. This light-switch-twisting exercise cleans some of the green corrosion off the rotating rheostat contacts, and the lights are now confirmed to be off as well. These instrument panel night-lights could be on and wasting away and you wouldn't even know it in bright daylight. This way, when the lights are needed, they will probably work, because they have been exercised regularly and weren't left on to burn out.

Once the battery rocker switch is on, look at the overhead dome light to ensure that light is off too (some are hot-wired). The dome light in the Debonair was accidentally knocked on, and it got so hot it warped and discolored the plastic lens cover, making it a potential fire hazard. Look around and see everything.

A way to keep the cockpit a little cooler in the summertime is to pull out the firewall shutoff (red) knob to seal the cabin off from the engine compartment, where some heat can leak into the cockpit. If your aircraft has this option, then have this control lubed so that it works, and by adjusting that knob, the temperature can be regulated without having to use the heater. The firewall cutoff must be disengaged (pushed in) for the heater and defroster to function. It should be engaged if carbon monoxide poisoning is suspected or there is a fire up front.

Get everything else in the cockpit organized for flight. Place the charts and plates, already arranged in their order of use, into their stowed location. Hook the headsets up and close the headset bag zippers to keep everything inside. Open and adjust the air vents. As a rule, I don't have any charts or papers or anything on top of the antiglare shield. Take a look around outside and get ready to start. Note whether there are any children or pets present on the ramp. A spinning prop is a mutt magnet.

Normal Start

The initial portion of this section will pertain to carbureted airplane and helicopter piston engines. First, get your feet up on the rudder pedals, where they will live. If your feet are flat on the floor, then you're a passenger, not a pilot. Earlier, we noted the OAT, and for a normal first start of the day, try the following procedure. Put the key in the ignition switch and turn it to "Both." Now you know you have the correct key. You don't want to prime the engine for start with the luggage door key in and then have to exchange it for the correct one on the ring.

Place the mixture control to the "full rich" position. Sometimes it is set up so the mixture control knob doesn't go in all the way to the panel but leaves about a quarter-inch gap or so. This indicates that the mixture cable is at "full rich" and has been fine-tuned that way by the A&P on purpose. Don't mash it in that last bit; just advance it until it stops moving.

Next, set the throttle to low idle with it open only about one quarter of an inch. We don't want to over-rev the engine during the start, because during the first few seconds, there is no oil pressure/lubrication. A higher-than-necessary RPM after start causes additional dry metal scuffing engine damage. The high school student who starts up his fancy car after school lets out and revs it up right away is trashing his engine.

After you get to know your engine, you will know how much prime it needs depending on the OAT. The colder it is, the more priming will be required, as this cold, dense air needs more gas to start. The engine can be primed using the throttle by quickly pushing it in an inch or less and then returning it to the low-idle position. Only do this when the engine is turning over; otherwise, the gas just falls out of the carb, creating a potential fire hazard. If using the primer, ensure it is fully seated and locked in after use. A partially closed/unlocked primer will cause a rough-running engine (too rich).

Once primed, then turn on the battery side of the split-rocker master switch. Leave the alternator side off. Having the alternator on unnecessarily wastes voltage that could be used by the starter to turn over the cold engine.

Yell, "Clear?" It's meant to be a question, by the way, not a command, and actually look around for a second. If there is someone by the knife, give them a second to get clear. Before pulling the trigger on the main gun of a tank, the Gunner yells, "On the way!" then waits one second for the crew to brace themselves for the recoil of the 105-mm cannon. The purpose of this forewarning is defeated if he gives the alert and then immediately fires.

Down South they say, "Y'all clear here?" then start the engine. Hold the brakes (the parking brake can be used) and the throttle and engage the starter. Count the number of blades as they pass, and if it doesn't start within five or six blades, release the starter. Never re-engage the starter if the prop is still moving, as this will cause damage to the starter and/or the engine ring gear teeth. If everything were set up properly, it would have started. An engine is like a machine gun; if set up right, it will fire. Give it another shot of prime and try again.

Grinding on the starter for ten seconds or more causes unnecessary wear and tear, so do something different. This little starter motor is turning over this great big engine and gets very hot very quickly. If the start is unsuccessful initially, then reanalyze the situation and let the starter cool off. The POH will recommend a minute or two at least. Time it. Time is relative, and that two minutes can seem like forever, but excessive cranking, especially without a cool-off period, will fry the starter.

However, if all has been done properly, she'll fire right up. Control the RPM right away and keep it as low as you can without killing the engine. During the first few seconds after start, an engine at 800 RPM will suffer half the dry-scuffing wear and tear as one at 1,600 RPM. The start is when the most wear-and-tear damage to an engine occurs. My engines regularly make it to TBO (time between overhaul) plus 10 percent, and a good start technique has a lot to do with that.

Once the engine starts, move the carb heat to the on position and then "lean" the mixture back one inch. Turning on the carb heat will suck any backfire in the carb air-box back into the engine, where it belongs. If there is black soot in the air-box, then there was a fire in there at some point. Then turn the carb heat off and check to see if there is oil pressure indicated. In very cold conditions, this could take as long as sixty seconds. If there is still no oil pressure, then shut down the engine before it eats itself, and investigate further.

Adjust the RPM so it runs smoothly, but keep it below one thousand. Once running smoothly, then turn on the alternator and check to see that the "low voltage" light is extinguished and that the amp or volt meter indicates it is charging properly. If not, then turn the alternator switch back to off and try again. These master rocker switches, like anything, do wear out. If it takes a couple of attempts to get the alternator online, then have the switch replaced. If a night mission is planned, the electrical charging system now becomes the second most important thing on the aircraft, right behind the engine/prop.

The reason the alternator is left off during the start sequence is to save voltage for the starter's use. The alternator does draw power when turned on, as it takes some voltage/amps to "erect" its electrical field. Additionally, if the RPM fluctuates dramatically during the actual start, an engaged alternator has no choice but to spike and surge the aircraft's charging system. Having it off reduces this stress on the voltage regulator.

Hot Starts

For a carbureted engine, this is a piece of cake. Give it a little (one-eighth to one-fourth inch) throttle and hit the starter; count three or four blades then release the starter and she'll go. However, it can be very tricky to restart a big fuel-injected stove that just has been recently run and then shut down.

Mostly on hot days, you try to get her to go before the battery gives out while twirling the prop. Study the POH for the recommended hot start technique and follow it. There are also some ways to cheat, such as installing a Slick Start type of product or, ideally, an electronic magneto (Electroair). I had an E-mag installed on both of my fuel-injected engines, and the hot start difficulties are essentially resolved.

When you hear the engine fire (*pop pop*), then release the starter and let it start. As soon as it does, hit the boost pump with a quick burst to purge any remaining boiled fuel vapor. Pump on, then pump off. If a fuel-injected power plant starts and dies and the prop is still rotating, then hit the boost pump and leave it on until it starts again, then turn the pump back off. Generally, Continental engines like gas, and Lycoming engines like air for the start. Have the Continental throttle one-third open for the hot start. After a Lycoming starts, then push the mixture control in slowly so as not to flood it.

If it won't hot-start and you've been cranking on it, then stop and let all, especially the starter, cool off. The initial hot start method is to fully open the throttle and run the boost pump with the mixture in the idle, cutoff position (make sure). My POH says for thirty seconds, as we're trying to purge the hot gasoline from the injection lines that lie above the hot stove. I can only handle about thirteen seconds of that pump action and then turn it off. Hope you have a good battery.

Now push the mixture all the way in and give the engine a one-second burst of fuel pump boost to put cool, fresh gas in the injector lines. That's the theory, anyway. Leave the mixture rich and reduce the power lever to a high-idle position and go for the start. Keep it running by turning the boost pump on and off, as required.

If it still won't start, then wait the cool-off period again and try this desperate scheme. At this point, we don't know if the engine needs more gas or not. Is it flooded or too lean? If we knew, then we would know what to do, but we don't here. So let's flood the heck out of it. Now we know for sure.

Throttle wide-open and mixture-full rich and turn on the boost pump for four to five seconds. If the avgas is running out of the bottom of the cowling, then it's flooded. This is a dangerous situation now. This will now be a flooded engine start and can be employed anytime you think the power plant is too rich on gas.

Pull the mixture back to idle and keep the throttle full in. Hit the starter and hold the brakes, hard. As the engine turns over, it becomes more and more lean until the perfect fuel/air mixture (14.7:1) is ignited by the spark plugs and explodes to life. Don't dally on reversing the engine controls. The throttle is at full blast. Three hands are really required for a hot start, so move your two to reduce the power and advance the mixture before the RPM gets too high. At least we got the darn thing running, but stay ready with the boost pump and leave the RPM at high idle (1,000–1,200) for now. Lower the RPM to normal idle only after the power plant is running smoothly.

As an electrical aside, when the alternator is turned on after all this, it will show a huge charge rate on the gauge. So turn the avionics and other electrical equipment on to help absorb this extra alternator effort and don't make the battery take all that juice by itself, as it were.

Something called residual heat is the additional handicap in a hot start scenario. Even on your gasoline-powered car, look at the exact location of the engine coolant temperature needle right before shutdown. The engine is very warm, especially on a hot day, but under control and well within parameters.

While the car engine is operating, so is the water pump and the oil pump, and the radiator fan is spinning too. All these things help cool the big metal stove. After carefully noting the temperature gauge reading, turn off the engine and wait a couple of minutes. Leave the hood closed. Now rotate the ignition key to the "accessory" position; don't start the engine.

Once the instruments come alive, watch the temp needle zoom past where it was when all the cooling devices were operating. When the oil and coolant liquids stopped circulating and the radiator fan stopped spinning, it got rather hot under the hood with all that heat still trapped in there. The same test can be done on the plane. After shutdown and then after waiting a couple, three minutes, flip "on" the battery side of the master and note the oil and cylinder temperatures. An air-cooled aircraft engine is even worse for residual heat accumulation than a car is.

The following method is brilliant, and I wish I could take the credit, but some very smart CFI came up with it. The hot start problem stems from the fuel left in the fuel injector lines after shutdown. These lines are sitting above a very hot engine, and the gas in them is cooking. The avgas boils and is no longer a liquid. This creates the "vapor lock" situation. Instead of shutting down the engine with the mixture control, turn the fuel selector to off. After a minute or less at idle, it runs out of fuel and stops.

The benefit of this is, now there is no fuel left in the injection lines to get hot, so no vapor lock. To restart, turn the fuel selector back on and prime the engine to get fuel back up to and into the injector lines like a normal start. And then start. Voila! It works. Having the craft parked with the fuel off makes it a little safer too. There are fewer places for gasoline to leak from, particularly if accidentally rammed.

Also helpful for an anticipated hot start would be to park the plane facing into the wind for additional free natural cooling. Once the plane is stopped and chocked, move the prop (correctly) so the blade cambered curves on the "back" side (the front of the blade) direct more wind into the cowling air inlets of the engine.

Explaining further, on a normal "tractor" (not "pusher") propeller-pulled airplane, what's called the face of the propeller blade is actually the flat-surfaced, flat-black-painted, noncambered side (where all the dead bugs are). This face is also called the thrust/working side of the prop. This thrust side faces aft, toward you in the pilot seat. That is actually the "face" of a propeller blade and is the section that pushes the air back while the rest is just busy screwing itself into the ether. The actual "back" side of the blade faces forward. Technically speaking, this is proper propeller-producer phraseology.

For enhanced ambient cooling, have the right tip of a two-bladed prop at the four thirty position, which makes the left tip at the ten thirty location (as viewed from the pilot's seat). Once the propeller is positioned so, more prop blade-directed breeze blows into the cowling air inlets, aiding engine compartment cooling.

Open the cowl oil access door and unscrew the dipstick and pull it out enough to keep the access door open. Also open the oil-add cap, too, if available. This lets additional heat out of the engine compartment and allows the moisture in the oil to "steam" out. It really condenses out, as you can't actually see steam. But you can sure see the water vapor from the oil rising out of those openings.

Make sure you don't set a trap for yourself in doing this and try to restart the engine with the oil-add cap off and the dipstick still out. Reseal the dipstick and oil-add cap once it's cooled off, or it will just suck the moisture back into the engine. Don't leave it open overnight.

One of the reasons we start the engine with the headsets off is to hear a still-engaged starter ("hung starter"). It will make a loud growling noise as it is turning a lot faster than it was designed to due to its gear ratios. The amp/volt meter should return to its normal position soon after a good start, as the battery is now charged back up. If the amp meter still indicates a heavy electrical draw, then the starter Bendix has not disengaged from the start gear. Shut down the engine normally and investigate.

The reason the mixture is pulled back one inch is that most airplane engines run excessively rich at idle RPM. Some of the unburned gas can leave lead deposits on the spark plugs, and this excess lead actually bridges the electrode gap so no spark can jump across to ignite the air/gas mixture; 100LL avgas has four times more lead in it than the old red 80/87 aviation gasoline.

Ironically, the "LL" stands for "low lead." Originally, there was the green 100/115 avgas, which had six times more lead than 80/87. So the blue 100LL was invented to lessen the problems caused by all this lead in old engines that were designed for 80/87 usage. Some pilots add a lead-scavenger type additive to the avgas to help combat this excess lead situation. Having the mixture leaned one inch when the RPM is below one thousand eliminates this spark plug lead-fouling problem. Always make it full rich if revving up to move (full rich above one thousand revolutions per minute) and then relean the mixture one inch once underway.

Aircraft Exterior Lighting, Day and Night

Before you start the engine, especially at night, turn on the red flashing beacon, except when it is very cold out. Otherwise, turn it on after the start, in order to save battery power for the start. I call the red beacon the knife light; once or before the propeller is spinning, it should be on. Leave the strobe lights off. Having them on in the daytime is just a nuisance to all on the outside and a waste of juice on the inside.

Lights like that are turned on when pulling onto a runway and turned off after landing and pulling off the runway. There is no requirement to have the strobes or anticollision lights on while on the ground, anyway.

Pre-Taxi

Now that she's running and charging, it's time to turn on the radios and other E-gear. If there is an avionics master switch, then be careful turning an individual radio switch to off in flight. Since we always use the avionics master switch, the On/Off switch for each individual radio is never exercised/used, so there may be enough corrosion in that switch itself that once it is turned off, it won't turn back on, due to that residual internal electrical resistance.

Look around the cockpit and ensure all is stowed or set up—headsets, charts, plates, etc. Enter the ATIS or AWOS/ASOS frequency in the radio and listen over the speaker. Leave the headset on the floor for now. You want to be able to hear the engine as it warms up. Normally, the RPM will slowly increase by itself. Hear and see that on the tach and reduce the RPM back to eight hundred.

Concentrate on hearing and understanding the weather information. It's easy to have the ATIS play through four times, and you still don't know what the temperature / dew point spread is. Don't have noise going on in your ears that you are not listening to. Bad habit. Say out loud the phonetic letter of the ATIS three times (e.g., "Kilo, kilo, kilo") so that it is harder to forget when ATC (air traffic control) is eventually contacted.

The wind sock that you've been glancing at the whole time has shown you the proper runway, but the ATIS provides important safety data that you also need. Look at the Kollsman window on the altimeter to confirm it's close to that announced on ATIS.

An altimeter trap can be set, as it is possible to set the "hundreds" hand to the field elevation, but the "thousand" hand is off by one thousand feet (oops). Glad we caught that little killer mistake, as we could be flying one thousand feet lower than indicated. That could be a non-habit-forming experience at night out in the boonies. To eliminate this type of error, simply reset the altimeter to zero-zero (hands at twelve o'clock), and then dial in the field elevation.

Normally, there's a slight discrepancy between your Kollsman barometric pressure reading and what is reported. The published airfield elevation is the highest point on the airport property and has, of course, been surveyed and is therefore extremely exact. Bulldozers didn't come in last night and change the MSL (mean sea level). Note this two- or three-hundredth-of-an-inch difference and apply that math to the rest of the flight as ATC gives barometric updates.

After returning, note the accuracy of this technique. When you set exactly what ATC gave during the flight, your indicated altitude could be off by sixty feet or more. But as you look around, everything still looks the same. No hill or hole in sight, although the altimeter says there is.

Carefully note the temperature and the dew point and do the arithmetic to get the spread (difference). If the spread is less than five degrees, think about the time of day. On average, the temperature increases as the day goes on, with 2:00 p.m. being the warmest. Normally, dawn to an hour after dawn is the coolest time of the cycle (sun equals heat).

Also note the spread trend. Is it getting bigger or smaller? Leaving the aerodrome in the late afternoon with a closing temp / dew point spread is asking for scud-running problems. Remember that once the spread gets to be only a couple of degrees apart, the air is getting water-moisture-saturated. Any cooler and some of the water vapor will condense to droplets/clouds and fog, reducing visibility and ceilings. Some local environments are notorious for this type of hazard.

ELTs and Guard

Now that we understand the ATIS data, let's dial in the emergency locator transmitter (ELT) frequency (121.50) into the number 2 comm and turn the squelch off (pull the volume knob out or select "test") to hear if there is a transmitting ELT on the airwaves. If you can hear an ELT sweep tone with the squelch on, then it is probably yours or the next-door-neighbor aircraft. The ELT transmitter wattage is so low it can't "break" squelch unless very close. During the late 1960s and 1970s, I flew quite a few search-and-rescue sorties in Wisconsin and Kansas tracking down active ELTs.

Some were hooked to a crash, unfortunately, but most were just inadvertent activations from rough handling. Note the time when you hear one while flying, as an ELT can be tested from on the hour to five minutes after the hour, with a maximum of three audible sweeps allowed. Otherwise, notify ATC with your location and altitude, as for an ELT to have overcome your radio receiver's squelch means you just flew right over it. It is very near.

If there is a second comm radio available, I highly recommend having this "Guard" frequency tuned in and set on "receive only" (listening silence). Select to listen over the speaker and check the volume.

It could keep you out of a TFR incursion rap. I've heard the USAF broadcast a warning on 121.50 to an errant aircraft, and it sounded like this: "Aircraft 20 west of ABC at 2,200 feet on a heading of 110 degrees, turn around. You are five miles from entering a restricted area. This is the United States Air Force." The next two calls went distinctly downhill from there. Having Guard tuned in also provides entertainment. I was checking my location, altitude, and heading, like all who were ear-witnesses to that military order of "Turn around!" I almost did a 180 myself, just to be doubly safe. Anyway, guard, Guard, if you can.

This is now the time to complete all navigational radio setup tasks. Double- and triple-check all frequencies, bearings, radials, etc. Be careful of transposition, where the numbers are input in reverse. This is the most common number-usage error. Garbage in, garbage out. Up until the time ground control is called, you are on your own schedule. Ensure everything is done before that radio conversation is initiated. Take your time; think about what you are going to do and say. You really have to know only two things in flying, or in living, for that matter: what you should be doing now and what needs to be done next. As we say in the Rangers, there's "nothing to it but to do it."

Radio Communication

After everything is ready and set, we can go ahead and call ground control. Ensure the avionic audio control panel is set correctly, check the frequency again, and always pull the squelch off for a second to adjust the volume level, then re-engage it.

Watch the amp/volt meter needle "flick" to verify that various items of electrical equipment have activated. If the amp/volt meter needle doesn't move at all when an electrical switch is engaged, then that item is inoperative. To confirm, disengage the alternator side of the master switch. Now look at the electrical system charging needle (BTW, it's showing a discharge state now) and see if it moves at all when that switch is engaged again. It is dead if there is negative movement, but at least now you know. Depending on what is not working (e.g., inop Pitot heat/IFR flight) may force a scrubbed sortie decision. Good catch, huh?

If there is an extraneous noise coming from the speaker, then check the volumes of the navigation radios to see if that is what is causing the noise. If not, then turn each light switch off, one at a time, to isolate the noisemaker. The flashing red beacon on my Skyhawk "talks" to the ADF with a series of clicks every time it flashes. If it bugs you and you don't need it, leave it off.

The first communication with any ATC facility is the most important one and sets the tone for the rest of the conversation. It's easy to forget you turned the volume down/off while briefing the passengers or while just talking in the cockpit.

When you first call, ATC can hear you on the radio, but you can't hear them respond. The ultimate radio error is to inadvertently "step on" (transmit while someone else is already talking) an ongoing communication with your initial transmission because you can't hear them due to your speaker volume being set too low.

Ground control responds to your initial call, but you can't hear it, so you transmit again. Once again, they respond and you miss it. Now they are annoyed, but at least the rest of the radio net audience is amused. Hopefully, the problem is discovered and rectified, but the damage has been done and you must now eat humble pie, especially if you stepped on someone. Always check the volume and that you are on the correct radio and frequency before transmitting.

Think about what you are going to say. Practice out loud and say *no* "Uhhs." The trick is to completely communicate your message in the least number of words and syllables while sounding cool. By the time the radio PTT (push to talk) button is released, ATC has you sized up. Be precise and succinct.

Basically, it's

1. who you're calling,
2. who you are ("This is"),
3. where you are,
4. what info (ATIS) you have, and
5. what you want to do (intentions).

Even though you have a very good idea of what they are going to say, still pay close attention. People hear what they want to hear. Pilots have to hear and understand what was actually said.

Use the full call sign for ATC and your aircraft in your initial call-up. Leave out the "November" part, unless in foreign airspace or if you have a short call sign. We say "November Six Zero Hotel" (N60H) for that plane in order to skip the "Is that your full call sign?" question. Once commo is established, we can revert to our nicknames. Call them only "ground" or "tower" and just use the last three characters of your call sign. There is no need to state your N number at a nontowered airfield. Just state what type of aircraft and maybe color, "Red Cessna." Saying your N number just wastes airtime for no reason and needlessly provides evidence.

You must say the current ATIS phonetic letter to prove you have it. By the way, the letter *Q* is pronounced as "kay-beck." *F*, or *foxtrot*, can be abbreviated to "fox," and *P* is either *papa* or just *pop*. The number 3 is *tree*, and 9 is *niner*, so as to not be confused with the German word for *no*. To obtain the exact time from ATC, ask for a time "hack." They will provide the Zulu time to the second.

There are twenty-four time zones on Earth, and each is labeled with a letter. The letters *I* and *O* are not used, as they could be confused with 1 and 0. That leaves twenty-four letters. Beginning at the first time zone to the west of the zero-degree longitude line (prime meridian), each time zone has a corresponding letter in alphabetical order. After going around the planet, the last time zone letter is *Z*. That's why Greenwich mean time is referred to as Zulu time.

Pre-ATIS days had the control tower telling each aircraft the winds, barometric pressure, and runway info when they called in. If you heard that data given to another aircraft, then you would tell ATC, "I have the numbers." This way, ATC would not have to say it all again. This is incorrect radio technique for the ATIS, as the current letter must be read back.

When ground responds, or anytime ATC gives you a clearance, merely repeat back exactly what they said and end the transmission with your call sign. Until you are practiced, trying to paraphrase them will usually go wrong and ATC will have to clean it up (it's being recorded). You say your call sign last as you can't forget it, since it is written on the panel right in front of you. Repeating back their lines is easier when done right away. They're speaking English, so you can understand it.

If there is any doubt as to what they want you to do, or how to do it, then ask for clarification. If you hear a miscommunication and ATC didn't catch it (poor hear-back skills), then make a blind transmission and say, "I don't think that aircraft got the message correctly." We're all in this together, and precise communication translates into safety for all.

Always listen to the other aircraft transmissions to build your situational awareness (SA) as to who else is around and where they are. You are aware of what is happening in front of you by looking and what is happening behind you by listening to the radio.

When the radio comes on during an ongoing cockpit conversation, be quiet for a second to see if they are calling you. If not, you can return to the cockpit talk but still listen to the transmission to set that aircraft's position and intentions in your mind. Hearing an "inbound" to your departure runway alerts you to a potential traffic conflict, and once airborne, you are now extravigilant and know where to look, even before ATC tells you.

This is why it is always important to be exact in reporting your position. I am over or on the position I report. However, many can see what they are reporting and say they are there but are actually still a couple of miles away from there. When someone reports a position and I can't see them there, then I look upstream from where they are approaching and see them two or three miles farther out than what they reported. This is why it is always important to be exact in reporting your position. I am over or on the position I report. When you look there, you'll see me.

Don't just say "Downwind," "Base," etc., but always add the "Left" or "Right" part so we truly know where to look for you. I can't assume you're on left downwind unless you say it. Be exact and sound like a professional on the radio.

ATC is going to insist you read back certain items such as assigned headings, altitudes, and hold short instructions, so do it the first time and save the airtime so others can use it. Your goal is the fewest radio exchanges to accomplish the task.

Listen to the frequency before you push to talk so as not to jump into the middle of an ongoing conversation. If ATC has just given a clearance or asked a question, then wait for the other party to respond and that conversation to be finished before you transmit. Be sensitive to the sound of the radio when it breaks squelch, and if you hear that as you get ready to push the PTT, then don't. Someone else has just pushed their PTT. Otherwise, there will just be a squeal while both are transmitting, with no communication happening and airtime wasted.

It's amazing that a frequency can be completely quiet for the longest time and then two will transmit at the same split second. Weird. When you hear a perfectly "blocked' transmission, both stations started and stopped their transmissions at the same moment, then those parties are not aware they made no communication. So advise the net by blindly announcing, "Blocked!" If you are the one that just transmitted, then either talk immediately or wait a couple of seconds to let the other station talk. Otherwise, you'll both just block each other again.

Be polite and professional on the air at all times, as it may be recorded, and that's how you *should* speak on the radio. Never get into an argument over the radio. Have that conversation on the phone after you land, if necessary. Concerning an on-the-air argument, there's no percentage in it; it's a losing proposition and is poor form as a pilot. If there is an issue and you think you've been wronged, then tell ATC to "mark the tape." Then later, request a copy of it (for your lawyer, if need be). Admit nothing, deny everything, make counteraccusations, or merely say "Roger." PS: If you ever say "Over and out," you should wash your mouth out. That's just Hollywood crap.

When you actually transmit, speak clearly and enunciate. Don't mumble or trail off at the end. Modulate your voice that you hear over the sidetone of the headset and make it sound pleasant. Hit the PTT before you start talking and don't let off until after completely finished transmitting. If you're too quick on the PTT, the first and last words of the transmission are clipped off and not heard.

If the radios ever stop working for some reason, then check the following items. Are you "breaking squelch" with the PTT? Is the "transmit" light illuminating when the PTT is pushed? Physically push the radio back into its holding shelf to see if it came loose. Try the hand microphone and listen over the speaker. If the radios were working and now they aren't, then you have something misset.

Check the audio control panel to ensure *all* switches are correct. Check the "squelch" intercom adjustment as it might have been accidentally moved too high. Mess with everything that pertains to the radios and then everything electrical.

While I was ferrying a newly purchased plane to its new owner, the intercom stopped working in flight (with no audible sidetone on the radio either). After checking all the "radio" stuff with no luck, I then moved all the various electrical switches. When the panel night-light rheostat knob was rotated, the intercom and radio sidetone came back online.

You never know, especially when it comes to electricity. Finally, if you can't transmit but can receive, then ATC communication can still be accomplished by using the "Ident" feature on the radar tran-sponder. Squawk 7600 and "flash" the ident button. When ATC says, "Aircraft squawking 7600, if you can hear me then squawk Ident," now you do that and you are back in the commo game.

When talking on the radio, take your time and get it right the first time. In communication, you always have time to say the right thing the first time. When ATC tells you to do something, then comply/move and then talk. It's "aviate, navigate, and then commu-nicate." Especially in a situation like a go-around, don't drop the airplane to fly the microphone.

We now have our taxi instructions and are ready to move the aircraft to the launch position. In real life, this whole preflight/start segment takes less than fifteen minutes. Once you know *what* to do, it doesn't take long to *do* it. Most take longer and didn't check half the stuff we did.

Taxi

The term *taxi* stems from WWI RAF flight training jargon. The students were given clipped-wing aircraft that could only stay aloft while in ground effect (IGE). Ground effect is defined as being below one wingspan (or rotor diameter) above the surface. Since they really couldn't fly away, the cadets would drive their "bus" or "taxi" around the airfield for practice. Hence the name.

Look around before you move and get your eyeballs ahead of the machine. On the ground, look at least a football field ahead. Look behind to ensure your breakaway power prop blast won't affect anything. Overcoming static inertia takes even more power if pointed upslope. "Enrichen" the mixture fully before exceeding one thousand revolutions per minute. Add power smoothly until the aircraft begins to move, then reduce RPM to control your momentum with power and not brakes. Touch the brakes at the very beginning of the taxi to confirm that they work. If they don't work, or are asymmetric or mushy, you can shut down the engine and coast to a stop and not have far to push it back to its parking spot.

It's amazing to me how some have it all revved up and are therefore having to "ride the brakes" to check/slow their taxi speed. That's just sucking around for a brake fire as well as wearing them out unnecessarily. This poor air-cooled engine has little cooling air, and the higher the RPM, the more heat there is in the engine compartment. Take it easy on the stove.

Do you drive your car with one foot on the gas and the other on the brake? Inexperienced pilots do this, as I guess it gives them a feeling of more authoritative control, but it is a damaging and unacceptable technique. My CE-150 just came out of annual with no discrepancies after a year of flight training. That's your goal. Operate the machine as it was designed to be, and by doing that, it will just keep doing that.

Relean the mixture control back one inch once underway. If the plane has been sitting for a while, the tire bottoms will have taken on a temporary flattened "set." The tires will thump around until they become round again. To help the airplane start moving, push and pull on the control yoke. The up-and-down elevator in the prop blast will rock the plane in pitch and help it to overcome static inertia and start to roll.

This won't work on a T-tail, as the pitch control surface is above the propeller efflux. Not much will happen on modern-design composite low-wing airplanes either, as their elevators are so small and the tail arm so short they have little pitch-changing effect at low speeds.

While underway, S-turn the plane a little and confirm that the compass and directional gyro (DG) swing, that the turn coordinator (TC) tilts, and that the ball moves (skids). The attitude indicator (AI) should not move, as there is no pitch or roll movement, just yaw while taxiing.

Before and then once moving, and this is a major point, hold the control yoke all the way back/aft. Your taxi speed plus the prop blast hits the up elevator and pushes the tail down, raising the nose by slightly extending the nose gear strut. This extra couple of inches of propeller tip-to-ground clearance makes all the difference in protecting the air knife from nicks. Obviously, the ambient surface winds will change our technique as their velocity increases, but that will be addressed later. Here the conditions are twelve knots or less.

By merely doing this (holding the yoke full back), my propellers very rarely get nicked or rock-dinged. Run your fingers down a flight school plane's propeller and feel the imperfections. The propeller blades on all four of my aircraft are literally pristine.

When the blades have to be dressed out with a file to blend in these stone scars, metal material is also removed from the blade. If this happens frequently, the blade/prop may have to be retired due to insufficient dimensions remaining. Holding the yoke back would have avoided these expenses. So it makes monetary sense to do it.

More importantly, the prop-leading edge stays sharp and smooth (the way it was designed) and therefore more efficient compared to a dull one. Watch the ground in front of you and avoid FOD. Try not to go through puddles on the way back *in* after a flight, as the water could rust a brake assembly and such. On the way out, it's no big deal, as all will dry off in the slipstream after takeoff. If there is a section of gravel/rocks on the taxi surface, then increase your taxi momentum enough so the power can then be reduced, allowing the plane to coast across that rocky patch at idle RPM.

To move an aircraft that is stopped over gravel and the like, begin the roll very gradually with minimum RPM. If it stays below one thousand, then the rocks are merely agitated. Once moving, power can be added as the rock vortex is being left behind.

The most important reason the elevator is held full aft during taxi is that a sufficiently damaged propeller blade tip can come off in flight. In four years of airplane accident investigation for a major propeller manufacturer, I learned why this happens. Prop blades endure tremendous stress in tension. The stress lines flow from the hub to the tips due to centripetal force. At tach redline, the tip speeds are transonic. That's why all the noise.

A nick/crevice on the leading edge, toward the tip end especially, can become a stress concentrator. A stress flow line can't jump across the nick and is forced to flow around it. This concentrates with other diverted stress lines of force and begins a high-cycle fatigue crack at the bottom of the crevice (which looks like the Grand Canyon under a SEM [scanning electron microscope]). This cracking of the prop blade propagates until there is insufficient blade structure to support the load, and part of the blade tip goes for even fresher air.

Your world has just changed, and you have about five seconds or less to do the right thing, or *bang*, you're dead. Even if just a small portion of the tip separated, the imbalance across the prop disk is in the *tons* of force magnitude.

I knew a pilot that had a blade separation in a Cessna 206. He said the shaking was so violent that he had a hard time seeing (human eyeballs un-gimbal [blur] at 12.5 Hertz of vibration). The rivets on the cowling top stood up out of the paint and hula-danced. The engine was breaking its motor mounts and started to flop around. He immediately switched the ignition key to off and safely landed on Interstate 70 in Kansas (the world's longest runway).

There are only three times you shut down the engine by turning off the magnetos, and this is one of them. If not, then the rest of the scenario has the engine releasing itself inside the engine compartment with only the cowling skin holding it in, but not for long. When the power plant's four hundred pounds or so is subtracted from the weight and balance calculation, there is an extremely noticeable CG (center of gravity) shift aft. Like I said, *bang*.

The only survivor of this scenario that I'm aware of is a PT-17 pilot that "lost" an engine (it left the airframe) and pushed the stick full forward and dived the plane toward the ground and flared at the last moment. Raising the nose was easy but had to be well timed.

The drill is this: If you ever see the cowling rivets stand up, then switch the ignition off immediately. Like a gunfighter move. Practice it. By the way, you now see the distinction between "I lost power to an engine" and "I lost an engine." Big difference.

If the engine is killed quickly enough, the mounts may remain intact and you can just glide down and land (I've had to do six forced landings). If only the sheet metal of the cowling is holding this still-windmilling monster in place, we have to stop the prop because this tin cowling won't contain it for long. Carefully raise the nose and slow down.

Once slowed sufficiently (around stall speed), the engine piston compression overcomes the relative wind force and the flopping propeller rotation will finally cease. A stopped prop will significantly improve your glide ratio as a bonus, and the plane still has its center of gravity and remains flyable.

All these problems can be avoided by merely holding the yoke back during Taxi operations. Also, more of the airplane's weight is focused on the main tires, where it belongs. This also reduces stress on the nose gear assembly during taxi. All positives and no negatives. Few do this yoke-back taxi technique, though.

The winds are now above twelve knots, and the trick is to get to the takeoff position without getting flipped over. When the winds are howling, you'll need to use advanced crosswind countering techniques or leave it tied down. My little drooped-wing-tipped Cessna 150L will fly at twenty-eight miles per hour in ground effect, so high-wind taxi methods must be employed.

Small planes with their tricycle gear are just that, tricycles. And tricycles can tip over to the forward left or right. Depending on the wind strength, once it starts to tilt too far, it cannot be stopped until the plane is over on its back.

You are now doing your "bat impersonation" by hanging upside down from your seat belt. How's the mission going so far? Since we're inverted, we need to do a couple of things right away. First, turn off the master switch. The engine has already shut itself down. The master is off because of the leaking fuel—we are upside down, after all. Don't just release the seat belt, as landing on the ceiling after the fall from the seat can cause serious neck damage. Most people are not strong enough to hold their body weight with only one arm. Actually, most can't with both arms.

If you are not solo, have the passenger hold themselves off the ceiling with both hands as you release their belt. This should cushion their impact sufficiently. Then have them release you. If solo, then tuck your chin against your chest as hard as you can and release the seat belt and twist to land on a shoulder, not just your neck.

So how do we avoid all this? The wind sock only depicts wind speed up to thirty miles per hour or so. If it is standing straight out, do you really need to go flying today? Are you experienced enough to handle it? I have recently had a couple of close calls due to high crosswinds in turbulent conditions, and that we didn't damage or just smash the airplane was only based on instinct, experience, and luck.

There are two kinds of missions, "Wanna go" and "Gotta go." Only the military and MedEvacs are "Gotta goes." If we don't wanna go, we don't have to go. Leave the plane tied down and launch later, when it's more favorable.

A boater can see his water ocean and note how rough the waves are and therefore decide to leave his vessel moored that day. We can't see our air ocean, except for the wind sock, and must surmise what the conditions will be like from prior experience. If someone popped a bunch of smoke grenades so that we could see the air and how turbulent it really is, then we would know not to go. High-wind flying is something you work up to.

Flight schools that cancel the lesson every time due to these wind conditions (because they don't want to scare the student and thereby lose the customer's money) are doing a disservice to the client. Students need to be shown why they should not go up in conditions like that as a low-time flier. If they are never exposed, then the first time they are, as a newly licensed pilot, may be their last time. So if the sock is standing straight out, really consider your "go" or "no-go" decision. He who runs away lives to fly another day.

If you are on an airfield that has a mix of large and small airplanes, be very wary of the jet engine and rotor wash hazards. Be careful even when you are going to taxi behind another small airplane that is in its run-up spot and perpendicular to your path. Look at their prop. If the individual blades are indiscernible, then they are performing the mag check and producing significant prop blast. As you approach to pass behind, bias to the far side of your taxiway to increase the distance away and tightly hold the flight controls so the aileron is down on the side nearest the other airplane.

At Washington National (now Ronald Reagan) Airport, we were taxiing my Debonair behind a parked Boeing 737 with a ground guide properly signaling the 737 to "hold position" (X). The ground guide's primary job in this scenario is to ensure there is no one behind the jet, as the pilots can't see back there. For a large airplane, especially a loaded airliner, to start moving requires a tremendous amount of power. They may have to "stand up" the throttles just to get going. Depending how close to the engines it is measured, the jet blast velocity can be well over one-hundred-plus miles per hour. We were passing about 150 feet behind the 737 when the stupid ground guide gave the signal to the airliner to begin to taxi.

A Beech Baron had recently (at that time) been flipped over at O'Hare by a 747, killing all four in the light twin. Jet aircraft with low engine mount configurations are especially dangerous to small airplanes. Jet engines that are mounted high on the tail will mostly blow over the top of a small plane. The engines on a Seven-Three are very low-mounted. Depending on the direction the large aircraft turns after rolling, the blast will remain aimed directly at you and prolong your exposure to it if you are moving too.

The genius ground guide was indicating for the jet to turn left, which was the way we were moving too. So we stopped. Otherwise, the blast would start by hitting us from the nine o'clock position, transitioning to the seven o'clock if we had kept moving. By stopping, we would only get hit at the nine o'clock position (port wing), and then the blast would harmlessly travel to the front of us as the jet turned.

I held the aileron toward the jet engine efflux full down, and the elevator too. Even with the brakes firmly held, the blast skittered/skidded us sideways about twenty feet. WTF! I wonder, if the Baron pilot had held his controls like that, could they have survived? By the way, I believe the ground guide did it on purpose as he looked right at us before giving the airliner the "go" signal. Him, I'd like to meet some day (payback is a MedEvac).

So as you taxi along, look ahead, and if there are large aircraft parked that you will be taxiing behind, then note the following for each plane in line. If the air stair door is closed, the tail red beacon is on, the chocks are removed, and there is a ground guide in front, they are getting ready to move. Look at the ground guide.

A competent one will signal the jet to hold position and signal you to pass behind and get out of the way. The way to acknowledge a ground guide's signal is to move your ailerons up and down a couple of times (most linemen don't know this). Twist the yoke, then quickly comply with the signal. Jet engines at idle/residual thrust are fairly benign. If the wind is blowing from the jet toward you, then you will smell kerosene exhaust as you pass.

A flight school Skyhawk (complete with CFI) was going to taxi obliviously behind a running executive jet, but the alert ground guide caught it and did not give the "go" signal but gave the "hold position" signal to the jet. He then gave the arm-and-hand signal to the Skyhawk to go. The CFI just sat there, almost exactly behind the jet, with the guide frantically signaling go. I don't believe they even had a clue as to what was going on at their three o'clock position.

Just doing the lesson, I guess. Amazing! Talk about "up and locked." Anyway, the jet got tired of waiting and tipped the Cessna onto its left wing tip, complete with a prop strike (on a brand-new engine, of course).

Similar hazards are present with helicopter rotor wash. Stay at least two or three rotor diameters away. Really note the surface wind direction. If it is blowing from the helo to you, then point your controls toward it. It may take a few seconds for the wind to carry the rotor wash to you, but it's coming. If the helo weighs, say, seven thousand pounds, then the rotor is blowing down over seven thousand pounds of thrust (you weigh two thousand).

If a blast of wash is heading your way, and sometimes you can see it (e.g., on snow, mowed grass), then quickly point your nose into it, like a ship into a wave. The airplane is designed to take high wind speeds from the front. Compared to your mere 1,800-pound weight, the wash will move you unless prepared. If the surface wind is blowing the rotor wash away, then there will be little wash effect.

When a helicopter (fling-wing) "air-taxis" behind the back of a line of parked airplanes (frozen rotors), with the wind blowing from the helo to the planes, the rotor wash will hit those planes with enough turbulence to bash each airplane's rudder back and forth against the stops. If I'm standing on the ramp and I see that scenario developing, I will run to hold my rudder from the outside to prevent possible damage.

Whenever you're outside by a rotorcraft or thrust-vectored machine in air-taxi mode, remove your hat and button it inside your shirt; otherwise, it will be gone. I did a lot of work with Huey helicopters in the Rangers. As their landing rotor wash approaches, turn your back to it and tightly close your eyes. It's called a dust-off for a reason.

Scanning techniques aren't just for inflight operations but must be used on the ground too. Most taxi and fly with their heads up and locked. When in an army vehicle carrying a swivel-mounted machine gun in the "travel/carry" position, the barrel is pointed up and toward the front and locked into that straight-ahead position so it can't swing around while maneuvering and hit you. Don't be up and locked. Have your head on a swivel, looking around all the time. Most students act like they're driving a tank, which only has a small four-by-six-inch vision block to see through. My rule is, you get five seconds to stare straight ahead (what are you looking at?). Look around and see what needs to be seen and avoided, thereby preventing potential problems.

Another of these potential problems is taxiing in front of a plane that is parked but running. Normally, that pilot has his head down, doing cockpit things, and does not realize you are approaching. They may release brakes, start moving, and then look up to see their prop hit your wing. I stop before passing in front of a running plane, until the pilot sees me, and then I move.

Be very careful when moving from behind a blind corner, like at the end of a hangar row. Slowly stick your nose out until you can see the other traffic getting ready to whiz by. When someone taxis by way too fast, I announce on the radio, "Rotate!"

Be aware of air traffic operating on a nearby active runway. Moving down a taxiway that is parallel to the runway in use exposes you to aircraft that are launching and landing. Be prepared to ground-maneuver to avoid should an errant craft start heading your way. Pull onto the grass or wherever is necessary to evade this approaching danger, whatever it takes. If ever crossing from a hard surface to a soft one in a tricycle gear airplane, then cross the boundary at a forty-five-degree angle. Have the nose gear and one of the main tires drop off into the grass/soft simultaneously.

We were earlier speaking of the decision to "go" in these high-wind conditions, and since we have decided to go, we will apply the following techniques to keep us safe. Taxi slowly in windy conditions, walking to crawling speed only. Avoid sharp braking, sharp turning, and bursts of power as a general rule. It is imperative that the flight controls be held properly and firmly (white knuckles) to counteract the wind. When taxiing, hold the controls to "climb" into the wind when it is from the front half of the plane and "dive" away when the wind is from behind.

If the wind is on the nose, then hold the yoke straight aft. If the wind is strong enough, the nose tire will come off the ground, allowing a "wheelie" taxi. Release some yoke back pressure and leave it on the surface. If the wind is from the left front, then also twist the yoke that way, and the opposite twist for wind from the right front.

As the airplane turns exactly sideways to the wind while negotiating the taxiways to the runway, put the controls (elevator and aileron) to neutral, and when the wind is from behind, then "dive" away. As we all know, this tricycle is most vulnerable to flipping over with a strong quartering tailwind. When the wind is from the left or right rear, then always have the tailwind-side aileron down. Down, all the way, like to the stops, but no further (don't force it). The elevator will also be down as the yoke is forward (diving). Smoothness really counts when the wind is from the four to eight o'clock position. This is where any sharp or abrupt taxi maneuvers could upset the apple cart. The above strong-wind flight control placement technique is generally known but rarely practiced, at least from my observations.

Let's address elevator deployment in a tailwind. I learned to fly in an L-4 tail-wheeler (WWII Piper Cub). News flash: If a conventional-gear airplane has a tire in the back, it is called a tail-wheeler. If there is just a tail skeg stick back there, then it is correctly called a tail-dragger. Anyway, in a conventional-gear-type design, the elevator is normally held full up/stick aft. This keeps the tail on the ground during taxi operations and enhances control of the machine while moving on the surface.

In both types of airplanes, tricycle or not, we are holding the elevator up in winds of twelve knots or less. Here's the math: Assuming a twelve-knot wind while on a downwind taxiway leg at a taxi speed of ten knots, there is only two knots of relative wind blowing from behind the plane. Now into the mix put the prop wash blast blowing at ten knots across the elevator from the front, and the relative wind flowing over the elevator is eight knots from the front. That's why it's still held up.

This is why you should hold the stick back all the time in light winds while moving in the taxi phase. If going to stop with the tail into the wind, then move the yoke/stick forward and lower the elevator while sitting there.

Lower the flaps all the way on a downwind taxi leg in a high wind. They act like sails as the wind from behind pushes on them and provides some free taxi thrust. Power can be reduced, but the speed is still maintained. This will also provide some extra stability in a strong downwind taxi scenario too. Don't forget to raise them before takeoff.

An additional way to stay safe in these conditions is to take advantage of the taxiway surface "crown." Most road surfaces have a double-slope design, the middle part of the road (the "crown") being the highest point, and sloping down on both sides to the shoulders to promote water drainage. In a crosswind taxi, bias the airplane to the upwind/downslope side of the taxiway. Don't be on the yellow line unless the wind is blowing straight down the taxiway or you are on a crowded ramp.

Assuming the taxiway is wide enough, place the downwind tire on the yellow line or a little upwind of that. If the wind is from the right, then have the left tire on the yellow line or a little to the right of it. You can stay in the middle of the upwind half, but don't go off the taxiway edge. Being positioned in this manner tilts us a couple more degrees to help counter the crosswind. The wind is now striking the top of the wing more than the side.

The opposite, for comparison, is a plane taxiing on the downwind side of the taxiway, where the wind is now hitting the bottom of the wing, causing a lifting action. The upwind taxiway side provides supplemental stability, and so why not do it? When given a taxi "clearance", you own the whole taxiway, so use it. No one's going to say anything, and so what if they do? You own it for now.

When transitioning from one taxiway to another, think about which is the upwind side on the new taxiway and smoothly turn to that side at the intersection while also moving the elevator and ailerons to their new proper positions, depending on the wind direction. I've been in forty-five- to fifty-mile-per-hour winds in a Skyhawk (Goodland, Kansas), and only by using every trick in the book was I able to safely do it. We crawled to the runway but were under control. The passenger/copilot should help hold the yoke, as a strong gust can rip it right out of your hand, just when you need it the most.

As an aside, if your Pegasus has a castering nosewheel design (e.g., Grumman, Cirrus, Colombia), then in normal wind conditions, always taxi on the right (starboard) side of the solid yellow taxiway line. Our American planes want to pull to the left due to engine/propeller torque. These nonsteerable nosewheel planes use differential braking to taxi, as you can't directly control the nosewheel. If the free-castering nose gear is on the yellow line/crown, then when it trends left, it starts downslope on that side because of the grade, requiring even more right brake to stop the turn and keep it going straight. The more power used while in the taxi mode causes more torque/left turning tendency, and therefore more right brake dragging occurs.

There are instances where this overuse of the right brake caused it to catch fire. The burning brake then caught the wheel pant on fire, which ignited the wing and burned up the whole airplane while on its way to the runway. Impressive! Don't become a reverse Ace by destroying five of your own aircraft, as you won't be able to afford the insurance premiums.

This can be avoided by traveling on the right side of the taxiway. The slight upslope the nose tire now faces (toward the crown) chiefly cancels the left torque effect, greatly reducing the need for right brake application. If the throttle is used to control momentum (less RPM), instead of the brakes, there is reduced left-turning tendency, eliminating the need for right braking almost entirely. This should be in the POH for those type airplanes. Use gravity and the taxiway crown slope to your advantage.

Inspect the surface of the chosen run-up spot to guarantee no contamination is present. Pick a clean, unspoiled position to park on. If there is room at the end and you are not ready to take off immediately, then don't block access to the runway, if at all possible. Tuck yourself in the corner and out of the way. Leave the runway accessible for others that may be ready to go. Be considerate, because nice matters, right?

If a plane is blocking access at the end and there is another access taxiway close by, then hold short of it. By bypassing that last exit point, you lose the option to request that location for takeoff should you become ready to launch first.

Students can take a long time completing the pre-takeoff check-list, or an IFR (instrument flight rules) aircraft has to wait for its Release so that taxiway can be blocked for quite some time. Also, if you pass up that last taxiway access point and another aircraft pulls in behind you, you're now trapped. Otherwise, you can still use the full runway length from the alternate access point by simply requesting to "back taxi, full length."

As we approach our run-up spot, we anticipate a possible brake failure. Always test the brakes before you need them. One hundred feet from where I plan to stop, the brakes will be smoothly "touched" to confirm they operate. If they don't work, there's still time to use the parking brake if available or shut down the engine and coast to a stop. The doors can be opened all the way (while S-turning [don't fall out]), to help slow down and steer onto the grass, if need be. If this brake failure is discovered too late, it could result in a collision with something.

The second occasion to kill the engine with the magneto/ignition switch is if you're going to hit another aircraft or something else bad like that. In driving, if you are going to hit something, make it *soft* or *cheap*. In flying, really limit yourself to hitting air only. Therefore, always anticipate brake failure and verify their function prior to needing them.

To make a smooth stop, as the airplane is almost halted, slightly release some brake pedal pressure so the brake-dipped nose won't jump up at the end. A smooth stop won't spill the coffee in the back and is the sign of a pro driver.

Always have the nose gear pointing straight ahead at the stop, as it takes more power to move a cocked nose tire. Park at a for-ty-five-degree angle to the runway, especially if in a high-wing air-plane, so you can still see the final, base, and downwind traffic legs for your takeoff strip.

If there are high winds, then line up into them if able, or just hold the controls. A tail wheel or a castering airplane can simply swing around, but ground control may not appreciate that maneuver. With ATC, always get permission first, if in doubt, not ratification later. If you ask for something that makes sense, they'll usually say, "Approved as requested."

Never point your plane at another aircraft for the run-up and be aware of one that is directed at you. If you can move so they are no longer aimed at you, then do so. A friend of mine was doing her run-up when another plane doing his run-up at her four o'clock accidentally released his brakes. His prop started by eating her right aileron, actually more like shredding (think one-inch julienne fries) and was almost to the topped-off wing fuel tank when the engine had had enough and stopped slicing. Don't let them point at you, and don't point at them either.

Also, be very aware of your aft prop-blast area and always look behind you before revving up. If lined up on the taxiway with others, then angle the plane forty-five degrees so your efflux goes off the taxiway shoulder and doesn't blast the aircraft behind you with surface grit. As an aside, never prop-blast an open-door hangar space, as the mechanics inside will chase you with large wrenches. You just blew debris into the open/exposed engine they were working on. Oops! Situational awareness (and security) is 100 percent of the time and 360 degrees of the area.

Pre-Takeoff

If there is limited room and you have to do the run-up by the hold short line, then don't pull right up close to it. Leave a little wiggle room just in case the plane inches forward at some point of brake application inattention. Most don't realize they are slightly rolling. If the brakes are making little noises, you are not holding them firm enough. When it comes to runway incursions, the tower is "vulture's row" (aircraft carrier argot), just watching and waiting (FAA MOR [*mandatory* occurrence reporting] program).

Set the parking brake for real. Some apply it so it holds at idle, but not enough to restrain the plane at the higher magneto check RPMs. Read the POH; some small planes (Pipers) can't apply both the toe brakes and the parking brake simultaneously. Use caution setting the parking brake if the brakes are hot. As the brakes cool and contract, you may not be able to release them, and now no one can move.

Now that the aircraft is stopped by the runway, switch to the tower frequency so you can listen to the ongoing game in the air and start to become SA. Select "squelch off" to ensure the volume is turned up enough. Our headsets are still on the floor, by the way. Don't put them on before you have to, as you are more receptive to the ambient ground noise surroundings with them off.

Now, read the book. Like prestart, start at the top left of the panel and look at each gauge in the row, one after another, and confirm all is proper. This is a touch/feel exercise, not just a look-at-it deal. Are the interior light rheostats really off? Is the fuel selector actually clicked into its detent? Is the door closed and locked? Double-check all frequencies and radials and route programming, especially for the initial departure leg heading and altitude. Lower the flaps and look to confirm flap symmetry, position indicator operation, and that they are both raised or in the desired takeoff setting. Look and listen for any binding or grinding as the flaps operate.

Going back to the pre-takeoff checks, the primary flight controls are now confirmed to be free and correct. Feel for any binding or resistance. The "correct" part of "free and correct" is extremely important, especially if the aircraft is just out of maintenance. It is possible to hook things up backward. Hold the yoke with both hands and point both of your thumbs straight up. Twist the yoke to the left and say, "Up thumb, up aileron." Your right thumb is pointing at the left (should be) "up" aileron. Then twist the yoke the other way and look and say it again. Most would not be able to cope with *reversed* aileron control after liftoff.

Check the elevator and rudder movement while turning around to look, if you can see them. Slowly move all the controls to their stops to see if they "catch" or interfere with each other; they shouldn't. Look at the elevator trim tab. It should be lined up with the trailing edge of a neutral elevator. Move the trim wheel to check for correct operation. For a "servo" trim tab, a "nose-up" trim wheel movement moves the tab down and vice versa.

A light twin was picked up from maintenance and crashed on the test flight. The elevator trim tab was hooked up backward. The aircraft was there for that maintenance specifically. What can I say?

Flaps

Some observations about flaps in general follow. Up to half-flaps (twenty degrees) add more lift than drag, and over that adds more drag than lift.

Both of my old Cessnas have forty degrees of flaps available. The reason the manufacturer limited the new models to only thirty degrees is that my planes won't climb in a go-around scenario with full flaps deployed. If left fully extended, there is too much drag for the engine thrust to overcome and the plane will just fly level. When you see the birds jumping out of the trees at the end of the runway and the stall horn chirps if you pull back the slightest bit on the yoke, then glance at the flaps, and if they are still down, raise them to twenty degrees.

Don't raise them all the way, though, as the "bottom will fall out" because the retracting flaps are reducing the wing area too. Most flaps travel aft as they also deploy downward. This aft travel increases the wing area, making it easier to carry the load at slow speeds.

The flap handle go-around operation should be practiced in the cockpit numerous times. Do cockpit muscle-memory flow exercises so that you can perform the control movements necessary for different maneuvers (like a go-around) "with your eyes closed," or at least do it sufficiently so you don't have to look down except for maybe a quick confirming glance. More on go-arounds later.

My Cessna flap lever must be continuously held to move the flaps up or down (unless completely retracting them). Extending the flaps while flying takes three seconds for each ten degrees of down deployment. The flap handle is shaped like a flap so only touch and maybe a quick glance will confirm you are operating the correct control. It takes only five seconds to go from forty degrees to twenty degrees. It takes less time going up as the relative wind slipstream is helping them retract and is opposing them on extension.

Flaps decrease takeoff ground roll distance (with up to twenty degrees maximum extension), but they reduce the climb rate (by adding drag). In the Debonair, I raise the takeoff flaps after the gear is completely retracted. Follow your POH. Flaps should not be used for a short field takeoff as they add drag (unless POH required). They should always be used for a soft field takeoff, though.

To establish the optimum "lift over drag" flap setting angle for your specific airplane, twist the yoke to lower one aileron all the way. Now extend the flaps to match that down-angle of the aileron. Normally, about eighteen degrees or a little less (the 50 percent flap selection option). This aileron full-down angle was designed to give the most lift for that wing.

Use this established setting for soft field takeoffs and for slow flight in general (e.g., sightseeing, photo shoots). In slow flight, add power before raising the flaps. The safest way to raise the flaps is to "milk" them up. Raise them a few degrees and then stop and wait a couple of seconds. Repeat until they are completely stowed.

Only operate the flaps in a wings-level attitude. If there is an asymmetric movement of the flaps, or one moves but the other doesn't, then the plane will roll toward the side with the lesser down-angled flap. If in a wings-level flight attitude, this roll can easily be counteracted by opposite aileron and rudder. Raise the flaps (if you can) to eliminate this condition. If you were already in a banked turn when the flaps went asymmetric, now the plane is getting close to being inverted, which is bad at seven hundred feet AGL (above ground level) while on the base to final turn. Only operate the flaps when the wings are level.

Religiously observe the Vfe (flap extension) airspeed or the white arc on the airspeed indicator (ASI). This aircraft is trusting you to keep it within its design envelope. Lowering the flaps with excess velocity can structurally damage the wing.

Run-Up

Close the windows and check behind you one more time and "enrichen" the mixture to full rich. Always ensure the mixture is set that way before going above one thousand revolutions per minute. Double-check that the oil temperature is above the yellow line, if applicable. Most small airplanes are warm enough if they run smoothly as the throttle is advanced. If they falter or hesitate, then they need more warm-up time.

Once it's warmed up, gently advance the throttle to the prescribed run-up RPM and listen to the engine. Go to the magneto switch and click it two notches to the left. Don't go three clicks, as the engine will die, as you just selected off. If that happens, then leave it off and let the engine stop. Don't turn it back on at that higher RPM, as even after only one second, there will be a loud backfire from the unburned gas left in the exhaust system.

Turn off the alternator and avionics master switch and restart the engine as usual. Turn everything back on. We have established, though, that the ignition switch off position works, confirming the P-lead wires are attached to the mags (grounding them). Usually, we perform that mag switch-off "test" at the lowest idle RPM, where quickly turning the switch off and then back on causes no backfire damage.

You go two clicks left, then back to "Both," and then one click to the left and back to "Both," so that you now know it is set on "Both" magnetos. I took off in a little Ce-150 once with a hefty passenger and noticed degraded engine performance on the initial roll. I glanced at the mag switch and then reached down and turned it to "Both," solving the problem. Self-inflicted wound.

Look at the tachometer as each mag is checked and note the RPM drops to confirm they are within parameters. If there is no RPM drop, then the timing is too advanced and should be properly readjusted before flight.

Because we've had the mixture leaned one inch during the taxi phase, there should not be any lead fouling of the spark plugs and each mag side should run smoothly. If there is a rough-running one, then a plug or two is fouled. If it is minor fouling, it will clean itself up on takeoff with full power application. If it's really rough, then we must try to cure it now. Put the mags back on "both" and rev it up to a couple thousand RPM. Then lean the mixture a little and let the lead melt out of the plugged spark plug gap.

By the way, the engine really doesn't like a long run-up period in general and definitely doesn't like what you're doing to it right now, so make it snappy. "Enrichen" the mixture and rev it back down to the run-up RPM and check the mags again. If still rough, then try it again. Otherwise, the offending plug or two (usually the bottom ones) will have to be pulled and the gap mechanically cleaned. Having the mixture leaned during the taxi time completely avoids this hassle.

After the mag check, come to the right across the lower sub-panel and engage the carburetor heat. Look at the tach and say, "See the drop, hear the drop" (RPM and noise). If there is no RPM drop, then you are not going flying right now.

Unless the temperature / dew point spread is very wide, the carb will eventually ice up, especially in humid air. Remember, the temperature inside the carburetor Venturi plunges as much as 90 degrees Fahrenheit. No matter if it is 100 degrees outside and 114 degrees in the cockpit greenhouse, it is still well below freezing within an air-flowing carb throat. No carb heat is a "deadline" item (tank talk). No carb heat, no fly. Be careful pulling on these controls too hard, as once a student actually pulled the carb heat control cable completely out of the panel. Mongo strong.

Once the mags and carb heat are checked, look at the engine gauges, the fuel tank levels, and see that the amp or volt meter is charging and the suction/pressure gauge is inside its green arc. Now smoothly reduce the power to a high-idle RPM and relean the mixture one inch again. The spark plugs can still load up while waiting to launch.

Confirm all has been done with the checklist and *now* put on the headset and turn off the overhead speaker and flick the audio control panel lever to "phone" (i.e., headphone). Make sure you are on the correct frequency, and double-check the volume setting. This whole process, from engine start to takeoff, only takes about eleven minutes in the winter (mostly waiting for the engine to warm up) and less time when it is warm out. Takes way longer to read.

Normal Takeoff

If not already able to see if someone is on final, then move the plane so that you *can* see. There's no reason to call the tower if an aircraft is on final within a mile or two, as the tower will probably order you to hold short. Skip the radio call and wait until the final leg is unoccupied and the just-landed craft is clearing the runway (three thousand feet is the runway separation requirement). Whether at a towered or nontowered airport, your first takeoff call should state the runway number and which way your first turn will be after takeoff and in what cardinal direction you will be heading (e.g., "Runway 33, left turn, west"). If remaining in "closed traffic" (the pattern), then say so.

Always make this call even at a remote airfield. A family's four-place bush plane was departing from an austere strip out West on a beautiful early Sunday morn. The CTAF/Unicom radio frequency was dead quiet, and so the pilot, which was parked midfield next to the runway, hidden under the trees, decided not to make a "blind" transmission of his intention to back-taxi on the runway. Meanwhile, back on final was a bush plane approaching to land on this very same runway. That pilot had also been monitoring the very dead-quiet frequency too and made the same decision to remain silent.

That's understandable, as it takes a lot of effort to make a radio call. About wears me out. The very happy ending was, the landing plane's wing tip flashed by the nose of the one that was just pulling out. There was only ten feet of clearance. Woah! I bet both those lucky pilots make all their calls now.

As you proceed to cross the hold short line, check flight control freedom (in case you picked up a jamming rock or stone) and say out loud, "Lights, camera, action!" Now turn on the strobe lights and the like (in the daytime) (lights) and ensure the transponder (camera) is on the ALT mode (C) and that the squawk code is correct. Always advance the mixture to full rich (action) for takeoff (unless high). If you smell "hot engine" with full power applied during the takeoff, then check the mixture position and "enrichen" it if you forgot.

If told to "line up and wait," then don't line up on the center-line, but stop at a forty-five-degree angle so you can still see the final leg. And always look high and low on short final before pulling out. Don't blindly trust the tower, or anyone (except your Ranger buddy). Look, then move. I've been cleared to go and glanced to see a plane in the flare getting ready to streak past me. Good thing I looked. If ATC or the mechanics goof up, they still get to go home.

The rest of that story is that I slammed on the brakes and stopped just as the tower broke squelch to yell, "Cessna 204, *stop*." Seeing me stop, they released the push-to-talk button and the frequency remained quiet. I didn't say anything either (boy, do they owe me one). Since I'd already been cleared for takeoff, I waited until the just-landed airplane cleared, and then went. The tower tape was clean. Trust, but verify.

Once given clearance to go, then *go*, and use the whole runway. Many pull onto the runway and have already left one hundred feet of it behind before they "give it the gun." The runway behind you, the air above you, and the fuel left in the tanker do you no good (one of the few times you can have too much gas is if you're on fire).

Don't stop on the runway and *then* go, as it is less efficient to accelerate from a complete stop, and that practice uses more runway than an airplane that continues to roll for the takeoff. Keep your power under control while pulling onto the runway.

As you pull onto the runway, actually look at it, full-length. During the pre-takeoff check, if I can see the runway, just like the wind sock, I'm noting it. Look all the way to the very end, if it can be seen, and then bring your eyes down the length of it to in front of you. Look specifically at the end to see if another plane is going to take off the opposite way. Been there; having a plane departing toward you can easily happen on a calm (and direct crosswind) day.

"Nordo" aircraft don't have radios, so they can't hear your calls. This plane doesn't have a radio!

Closely inspect the runway for things as small as turtles, ground-hogs, and other varmint types. Most people look, but they do not see. Pilots must actually see. Now quickly sweep back up one side/shoulder of the runway (fifty to one hundred feet to the side) and then back down the other side, searching for other aircraft/airport vehicles, which are hopefully continuing to hold short.

Look for deer herds, geese gaggles, *etc.* that are also "holding short" but waiting to dart out, uncannily, at exactly the wrong time. If they do and you're going too fast to stop but too slow to fly, turn your taxi/landing light on and off irregularly to try to break their hypnosis (same with car headlights; I learned to drive in Wisconsin). The last resort before impact is to pull back on the yoke and raise the nose (a car can't do this) and hit them with the belly of the plane or pop/zoom over them (and hope they're not big-antlered bucks). This prevents windshield entry or misses them altogether. If you miss them and are still airborne, then stay in ground effect (at least ten feet, to be above the wildlife [higher in Africa]) to accelerate to Vx. If the plane lands after the zoom/stall pop-over, then continue the takeoff run or just abort it.

If operating a fuel-injected low-wing, then really know where the emergency fuel boost pump switch is located. If the engine dies quickly at the wrong time, then flick that boost pump switch on and hopefully keep going. The older Beech Bonanzas have that switch positioned so that with your hand still on the throttle, your fore-finger can reach down to the lower right an inch and flick it like a trigger, and you're back in the game. Normally, it is the engine-driven fuel pump that fails. If this happens, you will have to use the mixture lever to control the excess fuel flow when power is reduced, as the boost pump provides the maximum TO GPH (gallons per hour) fuel flow only. It has two speeds, full blast or shutdown.

If the fuel tank level is less than full, then make a gradual, slow turn onto the runway. A quick change of direction could shift the fuel load enough to "unport" (uncover) a fuel inlet in the selected tank, causing a bubble of air in the fuel line. Power plants attempting to run on air or water make *no* noise. Conduct a nice, easy turn onto the runway (particularly at low fuel states). Most use way too much power pulling onto the runway and are riding their brakes. Yes, we are excited, but let's wait to apply all that power until we are actually on the centerline.

Our job now is to keep the aircraft lined up and going straight as we roll down the runway. Many "S-turn" down the strip by pushing the rudder pedals back and forth. If under hostile fire, then by all means, serpentine, serpentine. Otherwise, it's hard on the tires and causes unnecessary drag, slowing acceleration.

If flying a tandem-seating aircraft (seat in front and back) and the windshield has a center post or split screen, then don't hold your head in the middle for takeoff and landing. Figure out if you are left- or right-eye-dominant and look out that side of the windshield. My left eye is the one, so I lean left to see around the center support post from that side.

Keeping the plane straight uses less room and looks and feels better to all. Be able to put and keep the craft where you want it. We are now going to take time to understand the left turning forces that are going to happen during the launch and after. These items must be understood, as they happen every single time and can be used to our advantage.

Torque

Torque is a force that is opposite to the direction of rotation of the engine/propeller. American engines rotate clockwise, as seen from the cockpit. The whole airplane wants to roll left because of this torqueing force. Torque begins as the engine is cranking to start and ceases when the engine completely stops. The more power, the more left rolling/twisting force. If you look closely at the left tire of a plane doing a run-up, you will see that tire appears flatter than the starboard one.

A Cessna Centurion was being hand-propped (a real bad idea for a big six-cylinder stove), and of course, it immediately started, with the throttle wide-open. Fortunately, the "pilot" got out of the way as it went shooting past and the plane pulled to the left (no pilot to hold right rudder) and crashed.

The engine/propeller assembly departed the airframe and continued running for a couple of seconds. Amazing! The prop was spinning, and the engine was too. Together the RPM was 2,700, with the propeller rotating at 1,350 and the engine rotating in the opposite direction at 1,350 RPM. A graphic but expensive double demonstration of the force of torque.

I built a seven-foot-long helicopter model (Huey AH-1 Cobra) in the mid 1970s (one of the first "drones" in the Midwest) and attached it to an anchored vinyl record player turntable to "track" the main rotor blades and to adjust the antitorque tail rotor (eleven-inch diameter) yaw trim. When the 0.61-cubic-inch engine was started and was just idling, and without the main rotor even being engaged, the machine affixed to the movable turntable immediately and magically began to rotate/yaw.

If a real single-rotor helicopter was started up on glare ice or on floats on the water, it would rotate/yaw opposite the direction of the main rotor revolution even though the antitorque tail rotor pedal is being held to its stop. Not until the RPM increases sufficiently to produce enough sideways tail rotor thrust will the uncontrolled rotation finally cease. For that minute or so, the helicopter is completely at the mercy of torque (and the wind/current).

Since the airplane can't roll (a longitudinal axis-type roll) much while stationary on the ground, this force translates itself into a left-yawing motion once the plane begins to move forward. As the power lever goes forward, so does the right rudder foot, especially at low speeds and high power, to counteract the increasing torque effect.

A "torque roll" was demonstrated while I was in a P-51 Mustang that we slowed down, and when the power was increased, the plane would eventually begin to roll left, notwithstanding full right rudder displacement. We don't have a 2,250-HP Merlin V-12 engine (regrettably), but this same uncontrollable roll can occur if we don't correctly use the right rudder when it is required.

The loading of the airplane can help to counteract the torque effect. Bias the cargo load to the right side in the compartment, for example. For the people-loading part, if you are seated two on one side of the plane with only one on the other side, then the plane is laterally imbalanced. If just carrying three people in a four-place plane, leave the left rear seat unoccupied.

This added right-side weight automatically dampens some of the left-rolling torque effect once airborne. This condition would also allow some slight reduction in right rudder pressure, which makes for less control surface displacement into the slipstream. This reduces drag and increases performance. Another reason to have the back seat pax in the right rear seat instead of behind you is that you can "monitor" them more readily. It is very difficult to check on the passenger seated directly behind the pilot, to gauge how they are managing.

Another left torque-opposing trick pertains to airplanes that do not have the fuel tank selector option of "Both." If the plane has the

"Both" option, then that fuel selector position must be chosen for takeoff (and landing). For those craft that only have the Left or Right tank alterative, then select the Left-side fuel cell for the takeoff and climb portion of the flight. This makes even more sense if flying as the sole occupant and sitting in the left seat.

The pilot-only-load scenario laterally imbalances the airplane (nontandem seating); however, with the engine drawing fuel from the left side, the lateral imbalance effect is diminishing every second. My Debonair is flowing avgas at twenty-two gallons per hour to the six-cylinder beast up front. This is reducing the weight on the left half of the craft at a rate of 2.2 pounds per minute; a 22-pound difference in just ten minutes. Additionally, all the weight still remains on the right side, as that fuel tank remains untapped. The longer the climb continues, the more the right rudder displacement can be released, as the plane is slowly "immunizing" itself from the torque force and coming into lateral balance, with only the single pilot on board. Don't fight the various forces but understand them and use them.

P-Factor

Suffice it to say that whenever the relative wind is striking the propeller disk at any angle other than straight on, P-factor is happening. When the relative wind comes straight at the prop disk, like at the beginning of a takeoff run (except a soft field TO or a conventional-gear plane), the propeller is generating equal amounts of thrust from both sides of its rotating circle. Equal propulsion is being generated on both the left (ascending) and the right (descending) halves of the propeller disk. It is pulling straight ahead.

When the nose is raised at rotation speed, the relative wind now strikes the disk from a few degrees below level. Due to the resulting difference of propeller blade angle versus relative wind angle, the right half, or "descending" half of the propeller disk, is taking a bigger bite of air and generating more thrust than is the left/ascending half of the propeller circle. Your rowboat now has different-size oar blades and will pull crooked. P-factor is a yawing force. It can be a left or right yaw, depending on whether the plane is in a climb or a descent attitude (relative wind angle).

P-factor is a major issue with a twin-engine airplane. Unless the engines are counterrotating, then the left propeller power plant (number 1) is the "critical" engine. If flying with only the right-side engine (number 2), then the descending propeller blade of that engine causes even more left-yawing effect as its outboard blade thrust is more off-center than number 1s. This makes it harder or impossible to keep the plane from yawing/rolling left (onto its back).

Twins have twice the number of engine failures as single-engine aircraft (makes sense) but four times the fatality rate due to losing power from the critical engine at a slow speed (takeoff and initial climb) and having this asymmetrical P-factor force exceed the rudder's capability to control the craft. Chop number 2 and force-land or roll over and crash.

A horrible example of using P-factor is WWII Luftwaffe gun-camera footage showing attacks on four-engine bombers. The fighter pilots only shot at the two left (critical) engines (number 1 and number 2), as the bomber can't maintain altitude and still be under control with only the two right engines (number 3 and number 4) pulling.

So when the nose is lifted at rotation, also add some additional right rudder to continue to track the runway centerline. P-factor starts as the nose gear oleo strut extends, and continues all the way through the climb. P-factor ceases after the nose has been lowered to level off. P-factor starts when the nose pitches from level, and stops when it goes back to flat. Nose goes up, more right rudder in, due to P-factor.

Propeller Slipstream (Corkscrew) Effect

The third left-turning tendency is the horizontal vortex swirl that is created by the whirling propeller, and it surrounds the fuselage, especially when high enough to be above ground effect. When the airplane is on or near the surface, this corkscrew of air is blocked from twisting around under the belly.

The part of the swirl we care about is the airstream that starts from the right aft side of the propeller disk and turns under the bottom of the fuselage between the main gear and twists up along the left side of the aft fuselage and then pushes on the vertical stabilizer from the left side. This left force on the vertical stabilizer swings the tail to the right, which yaws the nose to the left.

This helix phenomenon begins as the plane climbs out of ground effect and continues until higher speeds are gained. Once the plane is going fast enough, this corkscrew airstream is outrun and reduced to negligible. This prop slipstream effect is a left-yawing force that is, once again, counteracted with additional right rudder. The more power and the slower the speed, once above ground effect, the greater this left-yawing helix force becomes.

In cruise, and while in the descent, when the power is reduced and the plane is going faster, this force disappears. During the approach and landing phases, the power is so low that the force is nil. So hold a little more additional right rudder as you climb out of surface effect and keep holding it until leveled off.

Gyroscopes and Precession

This effect pertains to rotating objects that exhibit a "rigidity in space" characteristic due to their mass spinning on an axis. Close enough for us; we're just pilots. Our gyroscope here is the propeller. When an input force is directed at a rotating mass, the output force manifests or happens ninety degrees later in the direction of rotation.

When the nose/prop is raised or pitched up by pulling back on the yoke, then that force inputs from behind the prop disk at its six o'clock position. With the propeller's clockwise movement, this force results or manifests itself at the nine o'clock location, ninety degrees later, in the direction of rotation. This yaws the airplane to the right, but only for a second or the amount of time it took the nose to stop rising. The force then disappears. It only occurs when the nose is changing direction. Up, down, left, or right.

This right-yawing force starts the same time that P-factor initiates and helps to temporarily counteract it. A tail-wheeler has P-factor happening just sitting there, as the prop is angled up all the time due to the tail sitting on the ground. During its takeoff roll, the tail wheel is raised to level.

When this happens, a force is then put into the prop disk from behind, at the twelve o'clock position. This force results/outputs at the three o'clock location and yaws the nose to the left and then ceases once the tail is level. P-factor stops now also as the prop is hitting the slipstream straight on. P-factor will kick back in when the climb begins, and so will gyro precession, at least temporarily.

The intensity of all these forces can be lessened to some extent by smoothly adding power and gently changing pitch. These forces will happen every single time, and that's some of the beauty of flying.

Physics is physics. By using constant, steady, smooth pressure, the forces can be kept under control.

These forces were so great in a WWII fighter that the student pilot would line up on the far right edge of the runway and try to get airborne before the plane ran off the left side of the strip. Right rudder, right rudder, right rudder.

Act like your right rudder has a built-in ratchet. When the rudder pedal is pushed in a little, it "clicks" and stays in that position (by you holding it). This is how to use the rudder on takeoff. As the throttle is advanced, we know the airplane is going to pull to the left, and we can be ready to push the right rudder pedal *in* one click.

If it is pressed too hard and the plane goes to the right, merely release some right rudder pressure and keep adding power and let the left torque energy pull it back to the centerline. Don't give it left rudder, as it will be too much correction and you'll be heading toward the left edge of the runway. We can't stop these forces, so learn how to utilize them to your benefit.

At rotation speed, add another click of right rudder as the nose pitches up. This will cancel P-factor. As it climbs above twenty-foot AGL, give it one more click to counteract corkscrew slipstream effect. Check that the ball is centered and hold the right rudder continuously in the climb. If there are clouds, you can see if the nose is staying at one spot or if it is yawing (don't need to see the ball).

At your cruise altitude, release one click of right rudder as the nose comes down to level, since P-factor is gone. As the speed increases, let off a couple more clicks as corkscrew effect is left behind and torque decreases as the power is reduced to cruise power. At cruise power and cruise speed, no rudder should be necessary to fly straight.

Otherwise, adjust the fixed rudder trim tab. Write a note to yourself in flight, or it will be forgotten until the next crooked flight. Bend the trim tab opposite to the way you want the rudder to move. If, for example, at cruise speed and power the ball is out to the right side, then bend the tab to the left. The trim tab moves the control surface, and the control surface moves the plane.

The airplane spends most of its flying time in cruise flight. To reduce pilot workload, there are certain "tweaks" designed into the airframe to overcome all the previously mentioned forces while the plane is in cruise mode. There is a pilot-adjustable elevator trim tab to stabilize pitch forces while in flight.

Additionally, the engine mount is angled slightly down and to the right. The dorsal fin is affixed to the top of the fuselage slightly off-center, and many times the left wing has a slightly higher angle of incidence (one-half degree) too.

These tweaks let the plane fly straight and true at cruise. During the climb, when there is less speed and more power, the tweaks aren't enough and must be assisted with additional right rudder. In a descent, especially in a high-speed letdown with low power, the tweaks are now too much. The plane yaws to the right, requiring left rudder pressure to keep it going straight and the ball centered. Right rudder on the way up, and left rudder on the way down. Every time.

Gyroscopic precession effects are also the reason the brakes are normally engaged before the landing gear is retracted, once a positive rate of climb has been confirmed. The spinning wheels/tires are the gyros, and they are trying to maintain their rigidity in space. On airplanes, where the main gear retracts by swinging inboard (normal way) or outboard (e.g., Beech Sierra, BF-109), the axis of wheel axle rotation swings from horizontal to vertical (ninety degrees). The spinning gyroscopes (wheels) are resisting this movement the entire time. The wheel bearings and their races are being subjected to unnecessary sideways friction and brinelling wear.

Some airplanes have even more retracting geometry happening (single-engine Cessna RGs, Curtiss P-40 Warhawks, etc.), which makes the wheel-bearing wear last longer, as there are more wheel axle plane-of-rotation transformations. The main gear first rotates ninety degrees and then travels another ninety degrees up into their wheel wells.

Two additional reasons that the brakes are used before retraction is that a seventy-mile-per-hour spinning tire has an increased circumference and could rub against items in the wheel well (e.g., brake lines, wires) and sling dirt and debris into this space too.

The nose gear can't be stopped with brakes, obviously. This doesn't matter, though, as most airplane nose gear retractions are merely swinging the gear forward or aft. The axle axis of rotation remains in the same plane and causes no extra wear. Landing gear retraction is another example of why you must understand gyroscopic precession effects.

Adverse Yaw Effect and the Coordinated Roll

As we have learned, it is imperative to fly the aircraft straight and precisely to maximize performance. This is also very true when we are rolling/banking the airplane. We have to efficiently roll into a bank when making a heading change. This may have to be done right after liftoff, so we will cover adverse yaw effect next.

Any sloppy airmanship during the launch phase will diminish the machine's performance and reduce the safety margin. The primary reason we make heading changes is so we don't have to fly all the way around the world to return to our base. Heading changes can be rudder-only skidding affairs like a boat, or we can act like we're driving a car and simply turn the wheel and slip and slide to our new heading. However, we are flying a three-dimensional aircraft: a super (not *sub*) marine.

When you are sitting in the aircraft, always stay lined up with the plane, like riding a motorcycle around a curve. You stay lined up with the bike. Don't lean opposite to the turn to stay vertical with the horizon. Keep your back straight and tight against the seat back, with your head held erect. As the aircraft rolls back and forth, your posture and body/head position should not move at all. Be a part of the machine.

The way the plane was designed to roll or rotate about its longitudinal axis is to simultaneously display the ailerons and rudder proportionately, so the inclinometer ball (turn coordinator) does not move from inside its two reference lines. Adverse or opposite yaw effect is why the rudder has to be deployed with the ailerons.

To bank the plane, one wing tip goes down and the other goes up. The one going down is being aided by gravity. The upward-moving wing has to generate lift to overcome gravity. The aileron that is now down has increased the camber of that wing section, producing additional lift, thereby raising that wing. As we know, lift also induces drag. Drag caused by making lift is called induced drag (as opposed to skin/parasitic drag). This extra drag on the ascending wing also retards or drags back that wing, too.

Without rudder, the craft rolls one way but yaws the other. A floatplane during water taxi provides a vivid demonstration of adverse yaw effect. While weather-cocked or pointing into the wind, move the yoke/stick to the aileron displacement stop; the seaplane will yaw fifteen degrees to the down aileron side. Twist it the other way and it will yaw fifteen degrees in the other direction (a thirty-degree-swing).

The lift-generating down aileron is causing induced drag, which yaws the plane. If we were parked on a windy ice ramp (no friction), even in our land airplane, the same phenomenon would occur. Full aileron displacement creates ample induced drag, requiring substantial rudder to cancel any adverse yaw effect.

Ailerons are the reason we must always coordinate with the rudder when we roll the airplane into or out of a banked attitude. A helicopter pilot merely moves the joystick (cyclic) and does not have to move the (antitorque tail rotor) pedals to roll into or out of a bank, because a helo doesn't have any ailerons. Airplanes do, so as the yoke is twisted, the rudder on that side is also pushed in. Both controls on together, and both off together. Don't lead with rudder, as it's not needed until one of the "little wings" (that's what *aileron* means in French) starts to create lift and therefore induce drag.

If you just use a small amount of aileron, then just use a small amount of rudder pressure; a whole lot of aileron, then a whole lot of rudder. Normally, more rudder will be required when rolling to the right (fighting torque also). When rolling to the right or rolling back to the right out of a left bank, use more rudder. More rudder when you roll to the right.

Perform aileron/rudder coordination (Dutch?) rolls by selecting a landmark on the horizon and roll back and forth with the nose locked onto that reference mark. Don't pitch the nose up or down. Just roll (twist); don't pull or push. Many climb when they roll right and dive when rolling left. Roll, then pull. Bank, then yank. Pretend there is a taut cable running from the horizon mark through the spinner and out the tail. Only roll about this axis without allowing any pitch or adverse yaw movement. The ball should stay glued in the middle. This ball displays the quality of your flying ability. Try not to dent it.

Practice these "Dutch" rolls until they can be done back and forth, using full aileron/rudder displacement. Now the craft can be operated to its maximum potential, and this is sometimes essential when avoiding air traffic or performing a B-1RD avoidance maneuver. BTW, *never* fly *under* a big bird as its escape move is to roll inverted and dive. Go to its side, or better, Climb OVER it. Always! Being able to deftly roll/pitch away could save the day. Maneuver to avoid (an aerial burial).

Many airplanes have an interconnected aileron/rudder feature that provides some proper rudder application automatically if the roll into a bank is mild and shallow. Twisting the yoke also moves the rudder all by itself, and stepping on a rudder pedal will also deploy some aileron by design.

The purpose of this option is not so you can fly with your feet on the floor but so you can fly with your feet only. This frees up your hands so they can fold charts, adjust navigation screens, etc. What can your feet do anyway but to tap-dance on the pedals?

Once perfectly trimmed for level flight in calm conditions, the wings can be kept level with slight rudder usage only *and* the cruise pitch attitude can be maintained by moving your feet fore and aft on the floor (really). Slide your feet off the pedals and back on the floor as the nose goes down a little, then put them back on the pedals when the nose starts back up (very subtle).

That slight CG weight change of your foot and leg position can keep the nose level in smooth flight conditions. Show a passenger how to move their feet forward and aft to control the pitch (air-surfing). It gives them something to do, and it's entertaining to watch the rug dance.

When rolling in for a turn, once the desired bank angle is achieved, then neutralize both controls. Some airplanes may want to overbank, so hold sufficient opposite aileron to keep it from banking further, but don't roll back out. With the bank angle established, check the ball and keep it in the middle by "stepping" on the ball. Constant, steady, smooth pressure.

For example, if the ball is displaced to the right, add more right rudder pressure to return it to the centered position and maintain that rudder pedal force to hold it there. If the ball is out on the downside of the airplane while banked, then it needs more rudder or less aileron. If the ball is located uphill, then more aileron or less rudder is mandated.

Pilots embarrass themselves when they properly roll into a bank, especially to the left, and then realize they didn't clear their turn for traffic. When they quickly roll back to the right, it is evident if using the rudder is an ingrained habit or not. The roll back to the right and then back into the left turn is sloppy at best and wastes energy. So more rudder when rolling to the right and keep the ball in the middle.

Once an aircraft is banked, its nose wants to drop. To make a level turn, *don't* let the nose pitch down at all. Add sufficient yoke back pressure to maintain the level altitude. The steeper the bank angle, the more back pressure is required (a sixty-degree bank equals 2Gs of pitch pull). The performance of a level turn should be practiced until it becomes instinctual. Don't drop the nose in the turn. Roll, *then* pull.

Understanding these forces and effects and being capable of keeping everything going straight optimizes our chances and marks us as skilled Pilots/Aviators, not just drivers or fliers who merely go air-boating.

Normal Takeoff (Continued)

We are now on the runway, smoothly advancing the power to the firewall. Take four seconds to do this. When you hear a prop over-speed on full-power application and then quickly reduce its RPM (an unmistakable noise), then the throttle was shoved forward too fast.

The propeller governor couldn't keep pace and was unable to prevent the overspeed (which exceeded redline), and then it catches up and governs the RPM back down to where it belongs (redline). Take your time going up to power and coming down from power. Remember, the engine and propeller are the most important (and expensive) mechanisms on the machine.

As your power came in, so did some right rudder; try to keep it going straight. I don't want my students on the centerline; I want them on the *center* of the centerline. Always strive for this type of artistry.

While listening to the engine and glancing at the ASI, say out loud, "Airspeed's alive," when the speedometer needle moves. If there is any noise, vibration, smell, or variation whatsoever that doesn't seem proper, then abort the takeoff *now*. Smoothly reduce power, apply max brakes, and get "cold" (slow enough to safely turn off the runway) and investigate while still safely on the ground.

Maximum braking consists of depressing the brake pedals to the point where the tires just begin to skid and then immediately let off a little pedal pressure, but hold that pressure until almost stopped. Many runway overruns are the result of the pilot releasing the braking rate, perceiving he had slowed sufficiently to be under control.

Only as the runway end approaches is the higher velocity realized and the brakes are then slammed on, but too late. Look at the end of a shorter runway and see the skid marks in the middle section of the runway, where the brakes were initially slammed on after a high/fast final approach. The pilot then releases the braking effort, but not until he is forty feet from the end does he realize the plane is still moving too fast, and slams the brakes on again. At the runway end are multiple black-lined memorials for not staying on the brakes until "cold." (More in the landing section later.)

But now, all sounds and feels are proper here on our current departure takeoff roll. Glance down at the engine gauges to quickly check their readings. The oil pressure will be high (top of the green), and the oil temperature low (bottom of the green) on the first flight, but that is normal.

As the power is advanced, the yoke/elevator is relaxed to its neutral position. Let it go where it wants. After pushing the throttle full forward, open your hand and make sure the mixture is full rich and the carb heat is in/off too. Hold all three engine things forward (throttle/prop, carb heat, and mixture). If there is a throttle friction lock, then lightly engage it to hold the "gas pedal" all the way in.

Normally, never take off and climb with less than full power. For smooth engine running the mixture will have to be leaned a little at higher density altitudes; otherwise, it's "balls to the wall." Less than full power reduces the horsepower, but not as bad as it reduces the GPH fuel flow to the engine. This piston stove is air- *and* fuel-cooled. At the slower Vx (best angle) speed, there's not much cooling air available, so the extra fuel that is dumped into the engine at full throttle can't burn, because there is no O_2 (oxygen) left to ignite with. This unburned fuel and its lead additive absorb combustion heat and whisks it out the exhaust system. This helps to fuel-cool the engine right when it needs it the most.

Thinking you are "babying" the engine by pulling the throttle back, especially that first inch, is having the opposite effect. If you have engine-monitoring instruments, then watch the EGTs (exhaust gas temperature) and CHTs (cylinder head temperature) get hotter as the power is slowly reduced. Balls to the wall for launch!

The old airplane power plant quadrants had different-colored balls on the top of the engine levers so the sharp handle ends wouldn't hurt your palm and the different colors marked the use of each control (black, throttle; red, mixture; blue, propeller). The "wall" is, of course, the firewall. At less than full power, your climb rate is reduced also. The B-737 that bellied into the Potomac River shortly after takeoff had the power held back so they wouldn't damage the engines. Have it wide-open for takeoff. Full speed ahead!

As the airspeed increases to rotation speed (Vr), pull back a "little bite" on the elevator/yoke (one-half inch) and hold, then one more little bite and relax slightly to hold the raised nose so it just covers half of the remaining runway (not the whole thing/end). Don't "hog" it off. Don't force the plane into the air. It may climb until above ground effect height, and then settle right back down, wasting runway (too much induced drag).

Instead, hold that small five degrees or so of a pitched-up attitude, and she will accelerate to find her own flying speed and lift off. When the plane takes off by itself, it will keep going. If you're heavy with a density altitude problem, use this technique of letting the plane fly off instead of forcing her to rise. It's ironic that as pilots, we don't fly the plane most of the time so much as we let it fly. After all, it was designed to aviate—we weren't. And if the air machine has become airborne by itself and has made it this far, it will keep going because every second we fly, the aircraft weighs less (burning fuel).

If the door was not closed properly (never let a passenger close and lock a door), it will pop open with a loud report at rotation as the wings create lift and pick up the weight of the craft. Wing lift generation changes the stress points in the airframe and shifts the fuselage enough to release an improperly secured hatch.

At this critical point in the takeoff, if a door bursts open, or there is a fuselage-slapping seat belt, or you are flying through little birds, or whatever, don't *even flinch*. Fly the frigging aircraft. Get up to a safe altitude and then analyze the situation. Always fly the plane. Distraction is the biggest killer. Stay on target.

A large four-engine turbo prop airliner leaving Reno, Nevada, had an "air start" access door left open, and the harmless (it turned out) noise and vibration it made occupied the crew sufficiently for them to accidentally crash onto a local street a mile away. Fly the plane no matter what. Get up in the air, where you are safe and have time to assess. No one has ever collided with the sky.

At Vx speed, pitch up (ten degrees max) and hold that until the obstacles are cleared. Glance at the ball and step on it to keep it in the middle. Right rudder, right rudder, right rudder. Do not climb at a speed that is less than Vx (mushing). If you need to accelerate to that speed after liftoff, then relax the back pressure on the yoke and keep the plane in ground effect (IGE) until Vx is achieved, and then pitch it up to climb.

The closer the craft is to the runway, the greater the reduction in drag, and therefore the quicker the acceleration is to Vx. Up to 40 percent of the drag is shed deep/low in ground effect, but you can only *tie* the low-altitude record. Keeping your tires four or five feet above the runway is sufficient. Don't get fancy and recontact the surface.

Once the trees/wires have been cleared, adjust the elevator trim to hold the nose at the Vx speed attitude. Adjust it for real, not just close. Better is the enemy of good enough. Normally, the pilot's goal with trim is to be able to let go of the yoke/stick and nothing changes. Once trimmed, note the specific position of the trim indicator tab or pointer now to see if it is on or near the placarded TO position index "mark." If not, then set the trim to this new position for takeoff the next time instead of using the factory mark, and see if that's a better elevator trim setting position. Mark a new index or just remember where it is.

If flying a single-engine complex airplane, there are two basic methods as to when the gear is retracted after a normal takeoff. The safest way is to delay the retraction until the remaining runway disappears below the nose. If the engine quit, the gear is already down for the forced landing.

The other is to raise the gear once a positive rate of climb is confirmed. We do our maintenance, the preflight and run-up indicate all is perfect, so everything should work and keep working. Hit the brakes before initiating the landing gear retraction sequence. As the gear is rising, reduce the constant-speed propeller RPM to 2,500.

Shift into second gear, as it were. We are moving at one hundred miles per hour already.

Bringing the RPM back a little after takeoff has two positive benefits. If the analog tachometer is not completely accurate and is showing a lower RPM than what is actual, then the prop/engine may be overspeeding, which could unbalance and damage the engine. A digital tachometer is accurate to 1 percent, but an analog (steam) tach can be off by 10 percent (have yours checked and labeled). By bringing the prop, not the throttle, back a little, exceeding the power plant's redline limit would be moderated.

The second, and most important, RPM reduction benefit pertains to noise abatement and flying "friendly" for the benefit of the neighbors who live by the airfield. Moving the prop control from 2,700(?) RPM to 2,500 RPM diminishes your noise "footprint" by a significant one-third fewer decibels (or so). At redline (or above), the propeller tips are traveling so fast that they are at transonic/compressibility speeds.

That is what causes the screaming racket that gets everybody's attention on the ground. This slight RPM decrease converts the cacophony from a really annoying nuisance to a more locally friendly and tolerable noise level. This is particularly true for seaplanes operating at a residential lake. Noise-abatement practices keeps all happy and quiet (no noise complaints).

The fliers that leave their propeller RPM all the way up during the whole departure time are making a lot more maddening sound than is necessary. The same goes for the approach, when they advance the prop lever too soon, at too high a power setting, and now come screaming in for all to hear. Wait until on final and the power/RPM is below prop governing speed to advance the prop lever forward, for a possible go-around (that's why it's done).

Once the gear is up, then the flaps are raised. Never raise the gear and flaps simultaneously. Take it easy on the charging system. Also, never reverse the landing gear switch position while the gear is midcycle in transit.

Depending on which way the nose gear "tucks in," a retrim is necessary, as the center of gravity just shifted forward or aft. The

Debonair nose gear swings toward the rear, which shifts the weight of the wheel/tire assembly three feet further aft and slightly pitches the nose up. Two notches of nose-down elevator trim is added during the retraction cycle.

By *trim*, I mean the elevator, rudder, and aileron trim, if all are available. Have it set up, as much as possible, for the aircraft to hold the climb attitude all by itself. If elevator trim is the only option, then you will have to hold right rudder, especially at the lower Vx speed.

At a couple hundred feet AGL, glance down and, from left to right, confirm that the primer is in, the mags are on "both," the gear/flaps are up, all engine instruments are good, there's fuel in the selected tank/s, we're charging, and the vacuum pump is working. If not, we can return; otherwise, away we go!

On a low-wing airplane, look at the fuel caps to see if they are siphoning avgas. Some older Beech fuel caps could be secured slightly cocked and would leak gas. Bernoulli's theorem is very visible as the blue gas sucks out of the leading edge cap and rises to about a foot over the top camber of the wing while heading for the trailing edge and the soon-to-be blue-dye-spotted tail plane surfaces.

On a high-wing plane, look at the trailing edge of the flaps and see if there is any "sparkling." Even at night, the flashing beacon may make a leak visible. That could be a leaking fuel cap and your range and endurance are being quickly reduced. You are losing weight, though. This problem will not be noticed unless you turn your head and look for it.

Maintain the Vx speed or slightly higher all the way to five hundred feet AGL. Don't just stare straight ahead, tank driver, but look around and bank the wings to see left and right, especially if there is traffic in the pattern.

At five hundred feet AGL, reach down, not look down, and give it a couple three notches of nose down trim. We now want to set up for a Vy, best rate of climb. The nose will come down to around five degrees, improving forward visibility and airspeed. During the climb, and even before this point, lower the nose and/or bank left and right temporarily to see what is in front of you, then put the plane back where it belongs. Look where you are going. This completes the normal takeoff technique discussion.

Short Field Takeoff

Utilizing the previous advice provided, this is a way to do a short field takeoff. Pull onto the runway as close to the end as possible. Have your tail off the end and over the grass and your flaps up (follow POH). Hold the brakes firmly and advance the power right up, confirming that all "feels," looks, and sounds appropriate.

Right before reaching full throttle application, release the brakes. Be ready with quick right rudder to keep her straight and do not touch the brakes at all. Heels on the floor. Hold the tail slightly low of level to reduce strain on the nose gear and to make the least amount of induced drag. Accelerate and do not let it take off yet, as we are in ground effect and as low as we can go. We are the most efficient as we can be, located at this low altitude.

While rolling, never push the yoke too far forward, especially on a tricycle gear airplane. If the main tires lift off the ground (called wheelbarrowing), thereby making the nose tire the new equilibrium pivot point, good luck. The plane is inherently unstable up on its nose tire, and you *will* lose control. Keep the mains of the plane on the plain.

If at any time, in accelerating for takeoff or slowing after landing, there is significant vibration in the airplane, it is probably the nose gear in "shimmy" mode (someone probably clobbered it on landing). Release forward pressure, if any (there shouldn't be), and add some back pressure on the yoke to raise the nose slightly and relieve some of the weight on it. Having the elevator always positioned properly alleviates this shimmy problem, as by never landing on the nose eliminates it.

A way to tell if you are actually going to be able to fly out of this short field or be able to stop in time if you can't is as follows. We are assuming the pilot has scrupulously performed the POH performance calculations for the ambient density altitude conditions, obstacles, and field length.

Weight (or lack thereof) is all important. Some passengers actually answer the "How much do you weigh?" question by saying what they would weigh if they were on the moon (1/6 G). Actually weigh the cargo/baggage (I don't mean the people)—don't guess.

A transport airplane had to fly a "milk run," literally. The loadmaster did not know how much the thousands of gallons of milk (cargo) weighed. So he used the weight of water (8.34 pounds per gallon and is most dense at thirty-nine degrees Fahrenheit), which turns out to be a little less than what whole milk weighs. The transport aircraft was therefore sufficiently overloaded to run off the end of the short runway and creamed in (sorry, no tears, please). The crew survived and were very popular with the local cat population.

Time your departure for the cooler morning or evening hours, which offer thicker air, thereby improving performance. Do not underestimate high-density altitude conditions when operating a small aircraft at high weights. After the calculations are done, then add another 20 percent fudge factor. The POH performance charts are "enhanced" by the marketing department to improve competitiveness.

These figures are based on the perfect plane with the perfect test pilot in perfect conditions, and that is the absolute most that machine can do. How perfect are we and our machines? Add 20 percent to the takeoff distance, both ground roll and distance, to clear the proverbial fifty-foot obstacle, which really might be eighty-plus feet.

If this is a grass field, how long is the grass? If up to the axle of the tire, ground drag will be increased significantly. The longer the grass, the more rolling resistance there will be, which slows the acceleration rate. Worse yet is wet grass, which clings to the gear and adds another 20 percent to the required ground roll distance.

Look at the runway and note where the halfway point is. See if there is a landmark there or some way you can establish where the halfway point is during the takeoff roll. Note your indicated airspeed as you approach that location, and if you have 75 percent of the required Vx speed, then you will make it (CE-150 Vx = 70 MPH; 10% × 70 = 7 × 7 = 49 + 3.5 = 54 MPH). One way to figure it.

If the speed is less than this 75 percent (i.e., fifty-four miles per hour) velocity, then immediately abort the TO and get on the brakes and stay on the brakes until your speed is cold. If you abort at the halfway point, there will still be enough runway remaining to stop. So stay on the brakes until you are cold (you're going faster than you think).

So we are back on the takeoff roll and normal rotation speed (Vr) is approaching, but we will accelerate past that to the higher Vx speed. Don't let the plane take off until it's at Vx, and then rotate assertively and smoothly, pitch up to ten degrees, and hold that best angle of climb attitude/speed with the yaw ball in the middle, until above all the hard stuff. Any "crooked" flying—meaning the ball is not "centered"—just degrades climb performance and decreases the safety margin. She flies best and most efficiently when lined up exactly with the relative wind.

Leave the landing gear down until the obstacles are cleared. During the retraction and extension cycles, various doors open then close, and some main gear turn sideways (a giraffe giving birth look) to the slipstream, increasing parasitic drag, which slows the acceleration/climb rate. Leave the landing gear down until safely up and over.

If it looks close but you are committed, then aim right at the obstacle to go as fast as you can. Right before getting *too* close, smoothly pitch up just enough to clear (a miss is as good as a mile) and "zoom" over the hurdle.

Once clear, push the nose down to regain your speed. Fifteen degrees of flaps deployed propitiously may also boost you over the high jump. Once, I just banked (seventy degrees) and sliced the left wing through a gap between two trees. The passenger remarked, "There's a lot of wood outside the windows." That was what we did in Alaska, but don't try this at home. You are cutting it way too close, but those tricks could allow your day to continue.

Renting a Piper Cherokee at a farm in Perrysville, Indiana, made it necessary to use the cow pasture as the runway. The takeoff technique these rich corn farmers employed was novel, but effective. They taught me to blast down this short and very bumpy field with flaps up and elevator neutral. A little hard on the nose gear, but it wasn't my plane.

As the Vx speed approached, the pilot would simultaneously pull back sharply on the yoke while jerking the flap handle up two notches (twenty degrees). The plane seemed like it jumped straight up and we popped over the trees. Very rough ride, and the timing and amount of the concurrent control (yoke/flap handle) "pulls" must be finely measured, but it worked.

Flaps with long emergency brake car-type handles are better than the much slower electric or hydraulic-powered flaps. They can be raised or lowered almost instantaneously, providing faster options. They may also be operated slowly by merely moving the handle gradually, which is especially handy on landing. By the way, those landowners purchased Piper's entire line of planes (nine back then), each year, and all their aircraft were brand-new or less than a year old. That's how it used to be.

That is the discussion on short field takeoffs.

Soft Field Takeoff

If it is truly a soft field, whether it be snow, mud, sand, or whatever, your main job is to not get stuck on the way to or from the runway. Assuming we are not already stuck where we are parked, then so far, so good. At a truly austere field, there is nothing like a ground reconnaissance. Walk your taxi path and the runway if you can.

Note all low spots, depressions, wet areas, and other hazards that may snare you. Visualize the taxi route and takeoff path to steer clear of those areas where you could bog down and become trapped. When your tank weighs fifty-three tons (M-60A1), you stay away from the wet spots.

The main difference for this type of operation is that we are going to get everything ready before we start to even move. Once we begin to taxi, we will not stop moving and will get to and on the runway and take off. So all checks, including the pre-takeoff, run-up, etc., are performed on the hard stand where we are parked. When we move off this parking spot, we will be ready to go, "All the Way" (Airborne), with everything set for launch.

Lower the flaps to the optimum lift angle (match the aileron down angle, ten to eighteen degrees). It is absolutely imperative that a full-up elevator position is held all through this soft-field taxi process right up to and through commencement of the takeoff run. Once moving, use enough power to maintain your momentum. Add whatever amount of power is required to keep rolling, full power if necessary. If the plane is allowed to stop, then even the application of maximum throttle may be insufficient to overcome the now-static inertia, and you are stuck in the mire. By all means, sustain your forward momentum.

Be making your radio calls, because here you come. Get to the runway and go—no stopping.

While holding full-up elevator, depending on the type of trike plane, the nose will come up real fast or just fast, with full power application. As the nose gear raises, release some back pressure so the tail doesn't touch, causing even more drag and possibly damage. Remember, right rudder.

Once the nose tire leaves the muck, we have lost almost a third of the ground drag resistance, which is our main enemy right now. Unlike a short field TO, we don't care about lift-inducing drag as much as shedding the rolling resistance drag. We want to transfer the weight of the machine from the tires to the wings and lift the gear out of the soft media as soon as possible. A lot of right rudder will be required to keep it straight as P-factor and gyro precession kicks in quickly as the nose raises abruptly.

Hold this nose-high attitude, and as the wing begins to generate lift, the main gear will be slowly lifted higher out of the soft stuff and the acceleration rate will increase. If this is a soft *and* short field situation, then I hope you did your homework on the predicted performance and that you know there is enough runway available. Once the airplane lifts clear, then release some yoke back pressure carefully and stay in ground effect. Still have enough right rudder pressure applied to keep it straight, as you do not want to settle back into the goo with the aircraft tires not lined up.

Concentrate in order to fly level, keeping the tires only five to eight feet above the surface, and hold that low altitude until your Vx speed is attained. Keep the flaps where they are and don't retract the gear. Raising the flaps at this point will cause a loss of lift (losing wing area), and retracting the landing gear adds more drag.

At Vx, pitch up to ten degrees if obstacle clearance is a factor and hold that speed until at a safe altitude. If the landing gear is retractable, then don't hit the brakes but let the main wheels spin to fling off contaminants. Now "milk-up" the flaps until they are fully retracted.

As we go faster, more debris is blown off the gear. An idea I had is to yaw the plane one way and then the other by pushing the rudder in almost all the way to one side and then the other. The slipstream and prop blast will now blow on the extended gear from different angles, helping to air-clean it.

Do a retraction cycle now, the tires have spun down, and wait a few seconds after the gear is up, then lower the gear again. If climbing to an altitude that is below freezing, any snow or mud in the wheel well could freeze the gear in the up position (ice-welded). Even the emergency gear extension method would not be able to lower it. With the gear back down, speed up to just below Vge (gear extension [retraction] speed), then retract the gear and leave it up. It should now be clean enough to function later.

That's a soft field takeoff.

Tail Wheel Takeoff

In a tail-wheel airplane, prevent getting the tail too high and the propeller tips too close to the surface. Don't slice the stuff. I avoid soft field takeoffs in the Super D (Decathlon). It has small tires for less air drag, along with very streamlined and tight-fitting wheel "pants."

A bounce on the takeoff roll, with the tail up, could trigger a prop strike, and the wheel fairings could also load up with soft field debris and become damaged and possibly prevent the tires from rotating on the next landing. Use the tail-wheel soft field takeoff technique of only raising the tail wheel a couple of inches above the surface, and let it struggle off. Accelerate to Vx while still in ground effect. This propeller tip strike risk is less of a factor if the bush craft has large "tundra" tires.

Crosswind Takeoff

Before the invention of the hard-surfaced runway concept (Ford Field, Dearborn, Michigan, 1928) there were no crosswind launches and recoveries necessary. An airfield was just that, a big open field. All operations were conducted into the wind. There's nothing like a direct headwind for TO and landing. When the wind changed directions, so did the takeoff and landing paths across the field. Perfect.

For this to happen at a modern airport, the runway would have to be mounted on a big turntable. An aircraft carrier is the only airport that can always line up the runway into the wind. Since we have neither, then crosswinds are a constant challenge.

One method of minimizing a crosswind component and effect on takeoff is to line up on the downwind edge of the runway, at the very end. If the runway has any width (one hundred feet or more), you can point the plane at an object on the upwind/far side of the runway (i.e., wind is from the right, then be lined up on the far left-side runway end corner).

Make this "aim point" a couple of thousand feet down the runway. Now visualize a line between you and your reference point. By angling across the runway, we have reduced some of the crosswind angle, thereby reducing its effect. Instead of a sixty-degree crosswind angle, it is now a few degrees less. Every little bit helps. In thirty-knot-plus conditions, use every trick in the book (or Manual).

Of course, we have been holding our flight controls properly as we moved into takeoff position. No flaps are used, unless it is a soft field takeoff, as flaps also add side area, giving more surface for a crosswind to push on. Our goal here, in this big side wind, is to get flying before we are blown off the downwind side of the strip.

Commence the takeoff roll with the ailerons deflected fully into the crosswind. With the wind from the right, the yoke will be twisted fully to the right (elevator neutral). Add power and head toward your reference target. As airspeed increases and the controls become alive, slowly decrease the amount of aileron but keep enough in to counteract the push downwind.

Accelerate past the normal Vr speed to ensure the plane doesn't settle back onto the runway from a down-gust after liftoff. At this higher speed, pull back on the yoke enough to pop the plane off the runway. It should keep going and not settle back down. Relax the aileron and allow the plane to weather-cock into the crosswind and establish your wind correction angle (WCA) to go the correct way over the ground.

If there are big trees and things on the lee side of the runway, then having a wind correction angle keeps the wind from drifting the aircraft downwind into the trees. Dragging a wing tip into trees is a bad thing and is even a greater danger in the dark when you can't see that hazard. Always know which way the wind is blowing. You don't need a weatherman.

If you're good, as the plane approaches liftoff speed, and with a safety margin from the edge (don't get fancy), then as it flies, don't turn into the wind to correct the drift but let the crosswind drift/blow you back over to the middle of the runway and then correct with a coordinated turn into the wind. You can't fight the wind, but you can use it. Make the wind your friend.

If there will be *in*sufficient airspeed to fly before the runway side is reached, then merely use the rudder to turn back parallel to the edge and keep going. Don't run off the runway. Note that your reference point was not far enough down the runway and adjust it for the next time.

Ironically, when this turn to parallel the runway edge takes place, the plane may become heavier on the upwind side, which is beneficial. With less-than-full fuel tanks, the fuel sloshes to the outboard edges of the tanks and shifts weight onto the crosswind side. With a left turn to parallel the edge, the fuel goes to the right, shifting weight that way. With full gas tanks, nothing happens (no room to slosh).

In high crosswind conditions, runways with wind-blocking obstacles are swirly dangerous places fraught with "dirty," turbulent air that we can't even see to avoid. We are trying to take off in transparent river rapids. After liftoff, hold Vx to reduce the time spent behind the trees/obstacles in these downdrafts and climb to "cleaner," less-unsettled air.

The faster the wind moves you, the faster you can move the controls back. Whatever it takes, to the stops if necessary. Make the plane do what you want it to do by quickly adding sufficient flight control pressure and holding it. If it wants to fly like a truck, then fly it like a truck. Use both hands if required.

The best technique for a crosswind takeoff is to begin at the far downwind side edge of the runway, as mentioned before. As the centerline is approached, it will then be captured and followed. For example, with a right crosswind component, the right rudder pressure can be released to capture the centerline, the nose will yaw left from torque, and then the right rudder can be added again to keep it going down the centerline once it is acquired. If the wind is from the left, then extra right rudder will have to be applied to swing the nose right (fighting torque) to hold the centerline.

Keep holding enough aileron to counteract wind drift, and as the nose lifts to the proper rotation attitude, then lift the downwind tire up off the runway and keep it going straight with the rudder. You point your nose with your toes. The plane is now only on its downwind tire and lifts off in this slip. Relax the controls now to establish the wind correction angle, and off you go.

Only do this in clean air that is predictable. A crosswind landing has the opposite touchdown point sequence of the upwind tire first, then the downwind, and finally the nose tire, with the controls being held at full aileron into the wind and full up elevator after touchdown. It is the reverse tire touching sequence of a crosswind takeoff.

These are some various ways to accomplish a crosswind takeoff.

Night Takeoff

This is one of the most dangerous parts of flying. The main goal is to get above the ground obstacles as soon as possible. Once up and away, we are safe. Especially for a night or an IFR launch, ensure the various gyros have been given enough time to completely spool up to operating speed. A Citation jet launched into low weather and promptly came back down out of the clouds and crashed.

The pilot had started the engines and then immediately took off. The attitude instrument gyroscopes were given insufficient time to "erect" (work), making for an inadvertent "partial panel" climb and a loss of control. Too much too soon for the pilot to handle. It takes a few minutes for the gyros to be at operating speed.

The first step in a night takeoff is to travel down the correct runway without hitting anything. Have the cockpit instrument panel lights adjusted as dimly as possible. Use only red or blue light in the cockpit, never white light.

Always confirm that the DG / compass degrees are showing the same heading as your runway of choice. An airport had right-angled runways with a common departure point located where the ends of the two runways met (one long and one short runway).

If launching in a regional airliner (Lexington, Kentucky), then use the long runway and confirm your lined-up direction matches the runway's magnetic heading number. If using Runway 36, for example, then you should see a big *N* through the whiskey window (compass). Tragically, the airliner did not confirm the heading, used the short strip, and went off the end.

Depending on the environment, we could ask airport personnel to "sweep" (drive on) the runway, looking for wildlife. After dusk, a warm runway makes a nice nap spot for coyotes and the like.

Avoidance techniques were mentioned earlier, and they work at night too.

Do a modified normal takeoff roll by rotating at Vr, then climbing to ten feet (to clear the deer), and accelerate to Vx speed. At Vx, pitch up to hold that speed and *climb*! If it is a tree-lined airstrip, then it is extremely important that the craft stays exactly over the runway. Any crosswind drift or uncorrected left-turning tendencies could allow a wing to snag a tree limb. I worked an amphibious Caravan (Ce-208) night takeoff crash that catastrophically caught their left wing tip in the (downwind) trees that were next to their own (unlit) private airstrip. Stay over the runway and *climb*!

Beware of the "black hole" syndrome. With a new (no) moon on a cloudy night (Ranger weather), there will be no outside horizon to reference. Rely on your flight instruments to climb to a safe altitude. I worked a B-747 disaster that had launched over the Bay of Bombay one moonless evening. The loaded jet left-hooked into the unlit and invisible water shortly after takeoff. Encountering a black hole scenario, as with a "whiteout" (snow) or a "brown-out" (sand/dust on a helo landing), places you in the Twilight Zone, for real.

The US Army has developed brown-out goggles for helicopter pilots, which should alleviate that dangerous takeoff and, particularly, landing phenomenon. During the flare, the rotor wash swirls up the unimproved landing zone (LZ) surface media (dust, sand), which blocks all outside visual reference. These new goggles can "see through" the debris. This is a much-needed invention and is a safety game-changer.

Without visual references, the human ears will provide erroneous information to the brain, so use the gauges right after takeoff in these conditions. Those lying ears also input false data when the aircraft accelerates and the nose pitches up for the climb. This somatogravic illusion makes it seem like the nose is too high (it isn't). Pushing the yoke forward soon after liftoff is a bad idea. If you can't see the horizon, don't look for it. Go 100 percent on the instruments. Keep it stable until a safe height above the surface is secured.

One last comment on night operations. There is no requirement to have the strobes or anticollision lights on while on the ground. In the dark, the strobe flashes are just night-blinding everyone as you taxi by. At night, just use the navigation lights and taxi light and leave the strobes off until fifty feet in the air after takeoff, and turn them off again on short final. Strobe lights will reflect off the runway surface and back into the cockpit and your eyes. Above fifty feet AGL, this won't happen. Always turn off the strobes when entering the clouds, as they can cause spatial disorientation *and* could hypnotize you.

Turn off the taxi light if it's going to point at another operating aircraft. Don't blind that pilot as you turn during the taxi, and sweep your very bright shaft of light across their cockpit. The new LED lights are so bright and focused that this is true even in the daytime. Like a lot of the new car headlights, they hurt my eyes. Extinguish that taxi light before it hits them and relight it once past. Common courtesy, like common sense, is such a misnomer as it's so uncommon.

It takes twenty or thirty minutes for the eyes to fully night-adapt. Safeguard your night vision, and everyone else's too. Close or cover one eye (dominant) if you are going to be exposed to white light. Reopen after the bright-light event has passed. At least one eye is still night-adapted.

Utilize the offset viewing technique of looking out of your eyes slightly sideways (six to eight degrees). This method uses the night-vision area at the back of your eye. Look around the edges of the object you want to see. Shift the scan regularly so you don't deplete the "visual purple" on that spot of the eye. Daytime viewing is direct; nighttime viewing is offset.

The wing-tip navigation lights and the red beacon provide sufficient illumination for most lit airport taxi purposes. Turn the taxi/landing light on and off every few seconds just to double-check ahead.

The above are the considerations for a night takeoff.

Circling Takeoff

Land planes cannot do this. This is only for water-capable airplanes. In a confined water situation (small lake), the craft keeps turning in a circle until liftoff speed is achieved. Go with the torque in the direction of the circle (left or right, depending on whether it's a pusher or a tractor-engine/prop design).

Use adverse yaw effect to tighten the diameter of the orbit. Hold the yoke opposite to the direction of the turn. This will cause the inboard wing to have its aileron deflected downward, which adds more induced drag on that side, thereby assisting in retaining the turn.

By the way, a *seaplane* has a boat hull for a fuselage. A *floatplane* is a landplane sitting on top of a pair of floats. If the craft can "land" on land as well, then it is termed *amphibious*. If water-capable only, then it is called *straight*. Only these types of airplanes can perform a circling takeoff.

Extreme Cold-Weather Takeoff

Once the temperature is below twenty degrees Fahrenheit, then the winter section of the POH must be consulted to comply with the manufacturer's guidance. If air "baffles" are required, then install them. These metal plates reduce the airflow through the engine cowling and sometimes cover half of the oil radiator fins.

Without these baffles, the residual moisture in the engine oil can freeze in the now too-cool oil radiator. The ice crystals then block the oil flow, resulting in excessive pressure and a blown oil line. You'd have to slip it to see straight ahead, as the wind, now (oil) shield is covered in streaming black lubricant. Install the baffles or don't fly when it's too cold.

There are a few extreme low-temperature tricks that help in getting and keeping the engine warm. I've flown in negative-twenty-degree-Fahrenheit conditions. At least there are no bugs. The run-up may have to be "on the roll," as the braked tires won't hold on the snow.

You may leave the carb heat on longer to help the stove to warm up. Don't worry about the unfiltered air, as the atmosphere is usually pristine when it is that cold-dry out and the snow "squeaks" when trod upon. Face the airplane away from the wind and leave the cowl flaps closed for now. It takes eleven minutes for the Debonair IO-470's engine oil to reach seventy-five degrees Fahrenheit (when it's thirty degrees Fahrenheit).

The biggest problem in very low temperatures is damaging the power plant by overboosting it during the takeoff and climb segments. As we learned earlier, the full throttle position dumps a lot of extra fuel into the cylinders to help cool it at high power settings. This additional fuel cannot burn under normal temperature conditions, as all the air in the cylinder has been consumed and there is none left to ignite any remaining fuel.

At ten below and colder, the air is much denser. The density altitude may be greater than two thousand feet *below* sea level. This very "thick" air now has the capacity of burning *all* the fuel given to the engine at full blast. This results in an overboost of the power output the engine is now capable of producing. A power plant can be damaged if operated at 110–115 percent of rated horsepower.

The solution is to take off and climb with the carb heat on. This heat going into the carburetor throat thins the intake air so it cannot burn the complete fuel load that is delivered. This lessens the total power output back to the proper parameters and protects the power plant from being "supercharged."

The other good thing about flying when it's cold is that the aircraft climbs like a homesick angel. So climb at a steeper pitch attitude to help warm the stove and to get to higher/thinner air. Adjust the nacelle cowl flaps as necessary or just leave them closed if it's really frigid out. Very cold air can be too much of a good thing.

That's a way to take off in the extreme cold.

The 180-Degree Turn Back

The normal takeoff flight path is to fly the upwind leg climbing straight out from the departure end of the runway until at least five hundred feet AGL. A wings-level airplane climbs faster than a banked one. All the lift vector is vertical, none horizontal. Once above five hundred feet, there may now exist the possibility of reversing back to the runway in the event of an engine failure.

This course reversal actually contains 270 degrees of heading changes, not just 180 degrees. Determine this in your training test flights at a safe altitude to see how much altitude is lost as you do a 225-degree turn one way and then a 45-degree turn back the other way. This is what it would take to line back up with the runway after turning around.

Figure that the loss of altitude will be at least five hundred feet and the lateral displacement from the runway's extended centerline to be five hundred feet also. The plane has to do a 180 to reverse with an additional 45 degrees heading change to be heading back toward the departure (now approach) end of the runway (total of 225 degrees).

Another 45-degree heading change is required at the end to realign with the runway direction, for a total of 270 degrees, including rolling in twice and rolling out twice, which further decreases glide distance because of the extra aileron and rudder drag that occurs when the craft is rolling/banking.

When this is practiced to establish this altitude loss, after the power is pulled off, count three seconds before doing anything. The human brain grinds to a halt when the loud noise thing suddenly goes quiet.

When it has happened to me, I find myself looking at the engine controls, which are all forward and proper, and my first question is, "WTF?" Realization kicks in (about three seconds), and you then start doing the Pilot thing. Now you are earning your money, and you only get paid for the last five feet. Air restarts will be covered elsewhere, and here we're assuming that it can't be done.

The initial question is, Which way to bank for the turn? Left or right? If there is a crosswind, we will turn into the wind to reduce our lateral displacement, by decreasing the turn radius due to wind drift.

In a no-wind condition, turn to the right. The "tweaks" on the airframe help to turn the plane to the right since there is no longer any torque twist and such. The left wing's higher angle of incidence and the cocked dorsal fin would be fighting you if the turn was made to the left. Flow with it, so break right. Don't worry about "clearing" your turn (unless in formation); just get the turn started.

Next question is, How steep to bank? We want to hurry up and get this turn out of the way, so make it forty-five degrees to sixty degrees of bank. The steeper the bank, the more degrees of turn per second occur. Make this a coordinated roll in and out, keeping the ball centered. Once level, holding some left rudder may be required to keep the ball where it belongs. Fly it as straight as possible to minimize unnecessary drag, thereby optimizing glide range.

The next question is, How fast should we be in the turn? Best glide/Vg is the speed to shoot for, but no slower. A sixty-degree bank will not be a full 2G turn, as we are not in a level turn, but in a descending one. Pull back on the yoke and tighten the turn to hold Vg.

Roll, then pull. If the stall horn "chirps," then release a little back pressure and hold at that edge until the heading change is complete. We want to roll from steeply banked to a wings-level attitude as soon as possible to return our lift vector to vertical. In a steeply banked turn, we are well below the average 9:1 glide ratio.

Maintaining this best glide speed is critical. As always, use constant, steady, smooth pressure. Most small planes will hold best glide speed at full nose-up trim, minus a glob or so. Crank the trim in to help you hold this airspeed. Most don't pull back on the yoke enough and are diving/giving away precious altitude.

Best glide speed is the best lift-over-drag airspeed and results in the maximum distance covered for the minimum altitude loss. Wings-level best glide pitch attitude is a nose-level pitch attitude. Keep the wings parallel with the horizon no matter what kind of airplane you are in. Trim for a level pitch attitude, and the plane will be near its Vg speed even if you didn't know what that speed is. Also, that Vg speed is usually close to that same airplane's Vx, or best angle of climb velocity, for the same reason (lift/drag).

The final reason this slow Vg speed is maintained during the turn is that the radius of a turn is a function of speed. The slower the speed, the tighter the radius. I was standing next to a runway at Oshkosh when a Mig-21 Fishbed fighter came down it (one hundred feet AGL) doing Mach .8 or so (I think I spotted). His turn radius was eleven miles (at 4Gs), which took him into the next county. We want to improve upon that and minimize the lateral displacement in order to reduce the amount of secondary banking required to realign with the landing strip. We do this by turning at the slower Vg speed.

The final question is, At what speed do we fly once level? Since the best glide speed is already very close to the stall speed, especially in a steep turn, we can't fly much slower. Maybe a knot or two slower if you are at a light weight. Otherwise, a speed less than Vg results in the craft "mushing" or sinking more with the increased induced drag factor steepening the descent rate. A speed faster than best glide (diving) also increases the descent rate compared to holding Vg.

If there is a crosswind, turn into/toward the crosswind, never with it. If you turn to run with the wind, then you are gone and won't make it back. You cannot stretch the glide. By turning into the wind, we are minimizing the turn radius due to drift, which makes for less maneuvering to line back up on final approach. More on emergency procedures later.

Advanced Takeoff Pattern Technique

This idea is brilliant, and I believe Captain John Carroll thought of it. Instead of flying the upwind leg straight ahead, we're going to do something completely different. Once the obstacles are safely cleared, bank and turn the plane to the left about thirty degrees (e.g., for Runway 36, use 330 degrees as the new departure course). We obviously can't do this at a towered field with a busy pattern without permission. At a remote location, however, where the departing strip is the only safe place to land in the area, this method could be safely employed using the appropriate radio calls and with extra vigilance.

Our goal is to aim for a point in space where we would be at least five hundred feet AGL, while displaced five hundred feet to the left side of the runway. From this strategic position, we would only have to execute a right 180-degree turn to be lined up with the runway again. This is far less than the 270 degrees of heading changes that are required using the standard departure pattern method. By the way, we are not actually climbing up into the opposing left downwind traffic, as they should be laterally displaced at least one thousand feet and at one thousand feet AGL, but watch it.

If there is no crosswind, after takeoff, we always turn to the left to fly down that side of the airstrip, because we turn more efficiently to the right (tweaks) if we are gliding. Once five hundred feet to the left side of the runway, continue climbing and turn to parallel the runway heading (back to 360 degrees).

Maintain the climb and that lateral distance (five hundred feet) for the length of the runway and to five hundred feet beyond the end. At that point, turn right 45 degrees and fly across the extended upwind leg centerline. If the engine failed now, the turn-back amount would only have to be 45 degrees plus 90 degrees, or only a 135 degrees heading change to be re-established on final.

Hold this heading, climbing all the while, until flying out of glide range, then go on course. This technique greatly maximizes the options available and the chances of succeeding in an emergency. If there is a crosswind, then after safely clear of the trees, turn away from the wind and aim for the 500'/500' key position on the downwind side of the normal departure path. If the crosswind is from the left, alter course (e.g., Runway 36 to 030 degrees) and steer to the right side of the runway for departure.

This, way the turn-back turn to the runway would aim us into the crosswind, which lessens the turn radius. In a strong crosswind, don't get too far away from the runway, maybe only a three-hundred-foot displacement instead of five hundred feet.

This is an advanced departure method that increases your chances of survival should an engine stop during the most dangerous takeoff/climb phase of flight.

Climb Phase

We have finally made it to one thousand feet AGL or so. Now transition the best rate of climb attitude/speed to a cruise climb pitch configuration. Simply reach down to the trim wheel (without looking) and add two or three notches of nose-down elevator trim. The nose will lower, improving forward visibility. Trim it so the nose is an inch or two below the horizon. This will result in a two- to four-degree nose-up pitch attitude. Don't get too shallow in the climb, as the fixed-pitch propeller/engine RPM needle will approach its redline.

To warm the engine up more quickly during the cold wintertime, climb with a steeper pitch attitude for a longer stretch. When it is hot out, the climb should be very shallow to boost the cooling airflow to this hardworking, very hot engine (see step climb).

Depressing the nose to the cruise climb attitude will not dramatically decrease the rate of climb, and the aircraft is now traversing more ground per minute. There are further benefits besides just forward visibility and ground speed gains.

You can slightly release some right rudder pressure, because as the airspeed increases, this higher velocity makes the "tweaks" more effective (having more air-per-unit time). One of the tweaks that makes the difference with increased airspeed is the off-centered dorsal fin, and another is the left wing's larger incidence angle. Doubling the speed quadruples the energy available, so even a small airspeed gain pays "tweak effect" dividends.

To roughly calculate the miles-per-hour conversion to feet per second (FPS), do the following arithmetic. Take half of the speed in MPH and add it to the MPH speed (e.g., 60 MPH + 30 = 90 FPS). At a one-hundred-mile-per-hour cruise climb speed, the tweaks are now traveling through 150 feet of air per second and become more energetic in canceling the left-turning tendencies.

Lowering the nose a couple of degrees for the cruise climb attitude also reduces P-factor force (less relative wind versus blade angle dissimilarity). The propeller slipstream effect is also being left behind as we speed up, so less prop vortex current is impinging on the port side of the vertical stabilizer, thus reducing the left-yawing propensities. These factors combined allow even less right rudder displacement, thereby decreasing drag and improving the efficiency of the airframe.

As the aircraft climbs into thinner air, the engine will no longer need the same amount of fuel as it did when lower. Some fuel pressure instruments are marked with altitude/fuel flow indices; for example, the gauge indicates 19 GPH at three thousand feet down from 22 GPH at sea level. Upon arriving at six thousand feet, the mark shows the mixture can now be leaned to 17 GPH. When you feel a slight and slow bumping/thumping vibration during the climb, it usually means it is time to lean the mixture a little. As always, err on the rich side.

Once the cruise climb attitude is set with elevator trim so the aircraft holds that exact pitch angle with no assistance from the pilot except for the rudder, we can start doing a complete cockpit check. The plane must be perfectly trimmed (as it almost always should be) so we can devote our attention to the inside cockpit inspection.

Starting from the far left side, look and touch to ensure the primer is still locked, the mags are on "Both," the lights are on (if required), the circuit breakers are all in, the carb heat is completely off, the engine controls are set and locked, the oil pressure and temperature are in the green, the alternator is charging, the vacuum pump is working, and there is enough fuel in the gas tanks.

Have a flow and be meticulous. This cockpit check should be performed at every phase of the sortie (climb, cruise, descent, etc.). This is the only time that mis-set items can be discovered. If you don't look, then you won't know. Otherwise, for example, we fly the whole mission that day with the navigation lights on (or whatever). Check everything you own regularly.

The cost of life is to pay attention, so specifically note the precise location of all engine-associated instrument indicators. For example, see that the oil pressure needle is at the very top of the green and the oil temperature pointer is over the letter T of the "Oil Temp" label printed on the gauge itself.

Any movement of a needle can now be detected, even if only slight. This will give you more time to discover that there may be a problem developing, so you can begin a diversion toward the nearest airport. If just a glance was made at these indicators during the cockpit examination, then they may have to move a few needle widths before the pilot was alerted to a deteriorating trend.

There is always the possibility of an engine gauge failure or an incorrect reading. If the oil temperature is rising, then the oil pressure should be falling. If only one needle is moving and the others aren't supporting this information, there may be a faulty reading instrument. Tap next to it.

One of our main jobs as pilots is to be on the lookout for anomalies or irregularities. Apply the DIMS concept: Does it make sense? Investigate and figure it out using your knowledge of the systems. Your comprehension of the aircraft as a whole is your primary defense asset, so be on top of the engine and airframe in all aspects of operation, particularly in the climb segment.

Step Climb

The Super Cub was unable to achieve a continuous climb to altitude in the Yukon, ascending over the Rockies. As the climb was maintained, the oil temperature slowly rose, making the oil pressure decrease. The climb would be held until the two gauges "green band limits" were approached. The oil temperature was getting too hot, and the oil pressure was becoming too low. Keep the engine instruments in the "green."

The solution is to lower the nose and level off. Leave the mixture as rich as possible (excess fuel cools) and keep the power at full throttle, if high enough (never over redline). Many pilots believe that they are helping the engine by climbing at less than maximum throttle. As we learned, the opposite is true.

After being level for a few minutes, the oven would then start to cool off. When the engine gauge indications returned to normal, the climb would commence again. This was repeated a few times before arriving at our required mountain pass crossing altitude. This is why it is called a step climb. Climb, level, cool, climb, level, cool. Always keep track of the engine parameters.

Spiral Climb

A circling climb has to be performed when there is insufficient area to climb out straight ahead, such as a mountain bowl valley bush strip situation. The "Kabul" climb/descent employs this helix maneuver too, but not because of terrain. Aircraft have to stay over the secured airport to avoid surface-to-air missile fire.

Make the turns to the left and use as much of the available space as you safely can. Most importantly, a pilot must receive formal mountain flight training and should always ask the locals for advice. Anytime you are flying and looking up at solid objects makes this a very serious business.

A larger circling turn circumference requires less bank angle, resulting in a higher climb rate. A steeper bank tilt has less vertical lift vector available. Stay away from the valley sides, particularly the shaded side, as there may be downdrafts there. Take note of any updrafts or thermal areas as you orbit. Bias the climbing route to dwell in that updraft area the longest. If one side of the expanse is in bright sunlight, making for rising air currents, then flatten the circle to an elliptical oval. Fly back and forth through this zone, making left turns at each end. Avoid the downdraft regions.

If the wind is blowing ten knots in the valley, then it's blowing forty-plus knots in the pass. Plan operations for the calmer morning and evening times. Gusts in a mountain pass can blow in a car's windshield. Williwaws and Chinooks can easily have a greater foot-per-minute sink rate than the max climb rate of the aircraft, especially if it's not turbocharged. Say, your plane can climb at 500 FPM but you are in a 3,000 FPM *down*draft. That was what happened to Stephen Fossett.

This is why the circling climb is continued above the summit of the peaks. If the departure heading is into the wind, then ascend to at least two thousand feet above the crest before crossing it. You are on the downwind or lee side of the barrier. This is where negative air currents thrive. Once two thousand feet over and clear, then steer to cross the ridgeline at a forty-five-degree angle, not perpendicular.

Be headed so the right wing gets to the ridgeline before the left wing does and cross that way. This sets you up for a left-turning escape maneuver. If severe downdrafts or turbulence were encountered, and we had to turn back, it would have to be a 180-degree turn (left) if at a 90-degree (perpendicular) overpass angle. By crossing at 45 degrees, the turn away would only require a 90-degree (not 180-degree) heading change to get away from the turbulence trouble. Fastest way to get out of Dodge.

Climb, Continued

The final question on climbing, topography notwithstanding, is, How high do we go? Higher in a tailwind and lower in a headwind, usually. A tailwind for a land vehicle is almost half of the circle (170 degrees); if the wind is anywhere from behind, it is helping. Nonland modes of powered movement (e.g., aircraft, hovercraft, and boats) only get a sixty-degree arc for an actual tailwind. Only thirty degrees to each side of the tail. If the breeze angle is more than that, then it is becoming a crosswind, requiring a heading change into the wind (WCA) to keep from drifting off course. So for us, three hundred degrees of the circle is a crosswind/headwind (not fair).

The FAA Regulations (FARs) say that first of all, do not be at an altitude that would pose undue hazards to those and their things on the terrain should the thruster terminate function. Over congested and adverse terrain, be as high as you can be. Observe the maximum elevation figures (MEF altitudes) depicted on the charts and be at least that high for each quadrant occupied. By the way, most bird strikes occur below three thousand feet AGL.

If at lower levels because of headwinds, maintain the required distance from objects. How *low* can we go (safely/lawfully)? A radio tower or antenna really represents a four-thousand-foot-wide domed cylinder of closed airspace that must be legally avoided. The top of the dome is one thousand feet above the obstacle elevation and extends horizontally two thousand feet all around.

If there is a "picket fence" of transmission towers (a row of them), then there is a solid wall of airspace that, technically, must be flown over (by 1,000 feet). Scud-running across ridgelines and flight below 350 feet AGL in general has become even more dangerous than before, specifically because of the proliferation of the huge three-bladed wind turbines. I call them the shredders.

CFIT (controlled flight into terrain) is still the biggest killer scenario. Don't push a bad situation. Perform the most difficult maneuver known to pilots—the 180-degree turn and runaway. (I wished my main battle tank transmission had two speeds forward and *four* speeds reverse; I wanted to be able to get out of it faster than I got into it.) See gray, turn away. See black, turn back. He who turns and runs away lives to fly another day. Don't find yourself succumbing to scud-running. It's not that the ceiling is getting lower; it's that the terrain is getting higher.

The next consideration in altitude selection is the "winds aloft" forecast. Depending on the length of the trip, which limits the rational apogee, the winds aloft can vary in your favor as the climb altitude increases. In my latitudes, if westbound, the winds can swing from a left front headwind down low, all the way around to a slight right tail / cross-impetus at thirteen thousand feet higher.

As a practical matter, unless equipped with supplemental oxygen, we should always remain below twelve thousand feet or less (five thousand feet at night). The eyes need O_2 to see, particularly in the dark. When over a mile high at night, you are unknowingly night-blind without oxygen. If going higher, then bring and use the brain elixir (aviator's breathing oxygen). Attend a physiological altitude chamber training session to fully appreciate how much more stupid we become without oxygen. Therefore, the *upper* limit of the cruise altitude decision depends upon the winds and human abilities.

Realize your passenger or buddy on board (who is probably very anxious) may not be able to physically endure a ten-thousand-foot cruise height. Keep very close track of a novice (newbie) passenger so as to not overstress them. There are a lot of physiological factors occurring that are exacerbated by less breathing air at a higher altitude, especially when coupled with the fear factor.

The cruising altitude can also be selected for the comfort of the ride, notwithstanding efficiency. Basically, it is smooth above the zero-degree temperature / dew point spread level. That condensation level is normally at the base of the clouds, if they are puffy. A cumulous cloud is the cap of a thermal. The cloud is there because its base is where the air vapor (gas) condenses into visible cloud water droplets. The turbulence "bumps" stop there, at the base of those clouds. Above that is hopefully very smooth, but be on an IFR flight plan. For a smoother ride, get above the base of the clouds.

When IFR, request a "block" of altitude from ATC to make it even easier on yourself and to have even more fun while en route. Normally, ATC will grant a block of space from six thousand feet to seven thousand feet or whatever.

Once a block clearance is received, holding your altitude within one hundred feet is no longer necessary and you can have some extra excitement by zipping around the cloud edges like a sports car speeding around a winding road (Le Mans). Our "zipping" is a lot less dangerous than the race car's, too. Wings clipping clouds suffer no damage.

Assuming there are no wind or other considerations, what is the best cruising altitude for a normally aspirated piston-engine aircraft? Consult the POH performance section and see that the engine can maintain 75 percent maximum cruise power up to eight thousand feet (at full throttle), depending on the ambient environment. The higher we go, the thinner the atmosphere, which results in less parasitic drag. At higher speeds, skin drag is the main speed bandit (double the speed, quadruple the drag).

Looking at the altitude-versus-speed chart proves there is an efficiency "knee" in the performance graph line that shows how high you can maintain full cruise power (75 percent). Above this altitude, your speed will diminish as the power falls off, and you should only go higher if the winds are favorable. Otherwise six thousand to eight thousand feet is the max cruise height for the best cruise speed. True airspeed increases 2 percent for every one thousand feet of elevation gained, and speed kills time.

This fastest altitude varies a couple thousand feet, depending on how warm it is. Warmer air will lower the altitude that the engine can still maintain for the 75 percent max. Cruise power setting. The warmer, less-dense air will feel like eight thousand feet, while only flying at a six thousand feet MSL altitude. Therefore, cruise at between six thousand and eight thousand feet MSL, depending on the winds, the temperature, and the length of the cross-country leg.

All things being equal, climb to the highest logical altitude for the distance involved. Calculate and make sure that the higher cruise altitude will actually be attained before you have to start back down. Don't try to climb to 6,500 feet on a thirty-mile trip. Plan to spend some time at the higher cruise level to allow you to reduce the GPH fuel flow for a while. Assuming you didn't go too high, there will be some savings in time and gas compared to traveling at a lower altitude.

The SST Concorde was never in steady cruise flight on a trans-oceanic crossing. It would continue its cruise climb until the mid-point, and then start back down. This apogee point (sixty thousand feet / FL600) was timed to be reached at the midpoint of the trip. We don't have that much "smash" (speed/power), unfortunately.

A higher altitude also expands your emergency radius of action. With a nine-to-one basic glide ratio, we can glide only a mile and a half from one thousand feet up. We could cover almost fourteen miles starting from eight thousand feet. Big difference. If there are winds, this radius of options is not a circle, but an oval. The glide radius will be reduced or flattened on the windward side and stretched out further on the downwind portion of the oval. Some computer apps now display this "glide range" area on the "map" screen, and the coasting expanse is also corrected for the winds and terrain.

A "point of no return" is calculated to determine where it makes more sense to continue on instead of turning back. If crossing an arduous area (e.g., large body of water, mountain range), then the point of no return will only be located exactly midway on the leg, when there is no wind. Otherwise, the winds aloft must be utilized to locate the turnaround point. Since you can glide farther downwind, this safety decision spot will be biased further into the wind.

The above is how to choose a cruising altitude. The bottom line is, airspeed is life, and altitude is life insurance.

Level Off

This is how many pilots transition from the climb phase to the cruise portion of the voyage. As the selected altitude is approached, they simultaneously push forward on the yoke and pull back on the power. The nose goes down, and the airspeed slowly rises from climb speed to cruise velocity. All the while the pitch forces are constantly changing. Altitude excursions result until the craft finally achieves cruise velocity and is trimmed. That's one way to do it.

A better method is to lead the level-off yoke push by 10 percent of the FPM climb rate. If ascending at a 500-FPM rate, then begin depressing the nose fifty feet before the desired altitude. Once the nose is actually level, add two or three notches of nose down trim. Many lower the nose, but not all the way to level; it is just less than what it was. The climb continues, albeit at a lesser amount, and the designated level is exceeded by more than one hundred feet (beyond parameters). Make the wing top or bottom parallel with the horizon (depending if a low-wing or high-wing). This is the level cruise and best glide pitch attitude for any airplane.

The throttle is still wide-open to assist in accelerating to cruise speed. As the RPM approaches redline (fixed pitch), reduce to the proper cruise power setting. Leaving the power up decreases the time spent attaining cruise speed.

The fastest way to attain escape velocity is to climb fifty feet above the altitude, then add three notches of nose down trim while descending back to your altitude. This "baby dive" puts the plane at cruise speed immediately. Reduce power as mentioned before.

The exact amount of trim required can be ascertained with aircraft familiarity. A three-axis autopilot can teach you how to efficiently level off. Watch how it does it. Look at the elevator trim wheel when the altitude "capture" feature engages. Observe how "George," the autopilot (as in King George VI of WWII England), slowly rotates in nose down trim until the airplane is horizontally level. That's how much you need to move it manually in the future to level off like a king.

Note the exact position of the trim wheel after the craft is perfectly trimmed and in a steady flight cruise configuration. Place the trim there when you level off from now on, and the workload will be lighter.

Pilots typically trim the elevator/aircraft one of three ways.

The puller. The craft is trimmed slightly nose down so the operator has to "hold" the plane up in the air. As soon as they are distracted and release their back pressure, the nose goes down. Not good if real low.

The pusher. Now the plane is trimmed for nose-up flight. I guess the thought is, "I'm safer now, because if I'm distracted, the craft will climb." Both of these "techniques" require constant attention and effort. Wrong! Many are not even aware they are doing this and that they are constantly battling with the machine to keep it level.

When the aircraft is slightly off level, then look at the power setting before reaching for the elevator trim wheel. If the nose wants to drop and the power is set a tad low, then adding power to where it should be may solve the nose-down attitude problem (and vice versa). Analyze the situation and try to accomplish the most with the least number of adjustments. Don't treat the symptoms; just cure the disease.

The only proper way is to have the trim adjusted so the air vessel flies itself, hands-off. It takes a while to get the trim perfect, but do that to reduce pilot workload. With the craft flying itself, your brain and hands are now released to perform other duties, like navigate and communicate. Adding the right amount of trim at any point in flight always makes it easier for the pilot. Let the plane fly itself—it knows how.

Cruise

After leveling off, we want to take care of the engine first (as always). Note the OAT and the inches of mercury set in the Kollsman window of the altimeter. Turn the knob on the altimeter to 29.92" Hg. Remember this "pressure" altitude number. Return the altimeter setting to where it was previously. Use the temperature and pressure altitude to discover the 75 percent power setting, as depicted in the cruise performance section of the POH. That page is tagged, remember?

Normally 75 percent is the maximum cruise power level authorized. Below 75 percent, use any power setting desired, all the way down to 45 percent. Below 45 percent of power, and the plane just won't keep going (mushing). I cruise at just below 75 percent, as I have the manifold pressure set for the 75 percent level, but the prop RPM is at a somewhat lower rate. And 2,450 RPM is allowed for 75 percent, but mine is back around 2,375 for less noise and reduced vibration purposes. Vary the prop RPM a bit to discover the smoothest running setting. At cruise speed, a lower prop RPM is more efficient and causes less wear per minute to the engine too.

With a constant-speed propeller, first reduce the manifold pressure, then bring down the prop RPM. Having the fan RPM "ahead" of the manifold pressure (MP) number is very important if flying a very large piston engine (e.g., Rolls-Royce Merlin V-12). It is not as critical with our private aircraft engines but is still a good operating practice to observe. Initially, adjust the MP to one-half inch below where you want it. When the propeller RPM is reduced, the MP will rise back to where it should be. This way, you only have to set the MP once. Reducing propeller RPM increases the MP, and increasing the prop RPM reduces the MP.

The engine has now cooled off from the climb, and we can adjust the mixture to properly lean it. If there is no EGT gauge on board, then pull back the mixture until the engine begins to stumble. Any further back, and it will die. Note how far the mixture control is out and push it in half that distance. Always err on the rich side. Don't save $5 of gas per hour and melt a $30,000 power plant.

If only a single-probe EGT is available, then lean the mixture and watch the EGT needle move, indicating the temperature is getting hotter, as the excess cooling fuel is decreased. There is a slight delay in this indicator needle movement, so don't move the mixture control too fast; however, the engine does not like this leaning action, so don't dawdle.

When the EGT needle stops moving and begins to reverse direction, then "peak" EGT has been established. Note that high point on the EGT dial and quickly "enrichen" to the prior setting. Some EGT instruments have a second needle that can be adjusted by the pilot to mark that peak temperature position. Precisely set that pointer there. This location changes every day, depending on ambient conditions.

Slowly relean the mixture and stop pulling when the EGT is seventy-five degrees Fahrenheit rich of peak (each tick mark on the gauge equals twenty-five degrees). This is the "best power" (fastest) fuel flow. Leaning more to fifty degrees rich of peak is best range (farthest) for that power setting, and just twenty-five degrees rich of peak results in the maximum endurance (longest) mixture adjustment. Operating at peak EGT will melt the engine.

The percentage of engine cruise power is similar, with 75 percent being best power and speed, 65–55 percent is the most range, and 45 percent provides for the longest duration. I flew a Cessna 150 for Shadow Traffic over NYC and could stay up for five and a half hours (with reserve) at a leaned 45 percent. That is the best power setting to "loiter" the longest in the air.

We are also assuming this single EGT probe is actually located in the hottest-running cylinder. This is another reason the mixture should always be set slightly rich instead of too lean. If set too lean for what we think is the hottest cylinder, then possibly another, un-probed hotter one is being secretly damaged.

I operate at seventy-five degrees rich of peak religiously. Don't be cheap. Be lower than a 75 percent power setting if planning to run extra lean. I am not a "lean of peak" (LOP) engine operator. My engine has air- and fuel-cooling happening all the time. A lean-of-peak fuel flow mixture setting burns all the fuel in the cylinders, leaving only air to cool the stove. I make no further comment on that subject.

If the craft has a sophisticated engine monitoring system, still set it for seventy-five degrees rich of peak on the hottest cylinder. By the way, if each cylinder has a probe, notice how the "hottest" cylinder location changes from day to day.

This is why the single-probe EGT indicator may not be telling you the whole truth and nothing but the truth. Also realize that the suggested gallons or pounds per hour listed in the POH has been massaged by the marketing and sales department. They are usually too lean, so add a little more gas to the fire. The POH-projected speeds, too, are rarely actually attained.

Now close the engine cowl doors/flaps, if available. At cruise speed, with the cowl flaps left open, you will hear and feel a subtle rumble down there, reminding you they want to be closed/retracted. Assuming we are still on our altitude and heading, then go ahead and perform a cockpit check again to confirm all is well.

During any time while in flight, but especially during the cruise portion, know two things:

1. Which way is the wind blowing on the surface?
2. Where is the nearest airfield?

Observing water waves, flags, smoke, and the like will confirm the wind direction on the ground. Always knowing the wind direction on the "deck" is important if a forced landing becomes necessary. Try to land into the wind (and a little uphill, if at all possible).

When the camshaft gear shattered in my IO-470K engine in the Debonair (with the family on board), I immediately broke right and turned to the nearest and only aerodrome in the area. If there was any hesitation in that turn to safety, we would not have made it. The alternative was the solid hills and trees of Western Kentucky. Pushing the Nearest button on the GPS (wasn't invented yet) would have taken too long. Having to grab at a chart and find our location and the closest airfield would have also used time we did not have. Know where you are as you hurtle along through space.

A pilot ran out of gas (which happens once a week in the USA) and dead-sticked onto a country road and saw a gas station ahead and coasted into it. Thinking he was messing with the attendant, the pilot said, "Fill her up, ethyl." The old guy didn't even bat an eye. The pilot asked whether it was a little strange to have an airplane at his service station. The guy agreed and mentioned that the airplanes usually landed across the street, at the airport. Which way the surface wind is blowing and the location of the nearest field (or landing site)—these are the questions always on your mind as the pilot in command.

If using an autopilot, select the "heading" (Hdg) option, in lieu of the "navigation" (Nav) choice. When tracking a VOR radial on "Nav," the craft will weave back and forth, chasing the signal. On "Hdg" mode, the heading bug can be used to stay on course without all that wasteful S-turning down the airway.

If traveling between city pairs using the magic GPS magenta line, then offset a couple of miles to the right before going "'Direct." Mid-airs are occurring as autopiloted craft precisely hold their exact course right into each other while going opposite directions between popular destinations.

Above 3,000 feet AGL, always be cruising at the legal altitude for that magnetic course to reduce the chance of a head-on encounter. Below 3,000 feet AGL, many cruise 100 feet or so above the rounded-off altitude number. Instead of being right at 2,000 feet, they will be at 2,100 feet or 2,200 feet to help miss the ones at 2,000 feet. However, if all do this, then the altitude chosen makes no difference.

If the cruise altitude makes the OAT below freezing, then "exercise" the controllable-pitch propeller every thirty minutes or so. Slowly reduce the prop RPM and then increase it to 2,450 and return it to the previous cruise RPM. This action exchanges warm engine oil for the very cold oil in the prop dome. When the prop RPM quickly responds to adjustment, it's operational. A sluggish RPM reaction indicates cold oil up front that must be exercised more to become warm and ready.

Switching fuel tanks, if required by design (left or right option only), should also happen every thirty minutes. This keeps the craft in lateral balance and makes it easier to handle. Only change the tanks when in gliding range of a landing spot. Crossing by an airfield is a good time to switch. As with anything like this, if the tanks are swapped and the engine dies, then undo whatever you just did. The term *bingo* fuel means there is just enough gas (with reserve) to RTB (return to base). You go home now.

Never switch tanks or do *anything* with the engine if flying over dangerous terrain. When we fly across the Great Lakes, all engine settings and adjustments are made well before we go "feet wet." Once over the water, don't touch anything that pertains to the power plant. There are no windows in the cowling, so the stove doesn't know it's over inhospitable terrain. But it will go into "auto-rough" as you are hyperaware. Leave it alone and let it hum along in steady state. Engine failures many times manifest themselves during power adjustments.

My old boss in Detroit was a former USMC F-4 Phantom aviator and was dropping bombs near Da Nang when a "dud" from a previous fighter-bomber blew up right in front of him. His fighter was badly perforated all over, but both engines continued to keep running (87 percent). He did not touch the throttles and shot a jet penetration approach back to the air station. When the power had to be reduced for the landing, both engines immediately ate themselves and shut down. If it is working, then leave it alone, until on the other side (feet dry).

Once established at cruise, then you become a cockpit resource manager and a systems monitor. Keep busy. Basically, if you are not doing or thinking something all the time, then you are not doing it right. Next is a way to keep occupied during cruise and at any time while flying.

Scan

Our primary responsibility outside the cockpit is to see and avoid solid objects. Review the various scanning techniques taught and realize the Mark 1 human eyeball can't see detail when the eyes are moving. Even when not moving, they only see detail in about 1 percent of our field of view (pitiful).

At night, your eyes are probably focused on the inside of the windshield. Look down a wing to its tip to get your eyes to focus further out. Move your head to look around the doorposts too. I've had three planes suddenly appear from behind those blind spots. Move your brain housing group around and look about like your life depends on it, because it does. Have your head on a swivel.

Most collisions happen on a clear VFR day, and 60 percent of all midairs come from behind. Many planes have windows back there, so look through them too. S-turn the airplane to check your "six." Have the passengers look out too. It gives them something to do, and they feel like part of the crew. My wife knows to look where I'm *not* looking. If my head goes down, hers goes up. If I'm scanning to the left, she is looking to the right. She is also a great loadmaster, navigator (she often tells me where to go), and has a great turbulence-indicator tracking system.

Explain the clock system to your passengers (you really have to nowadays). Twelve o'clock is straight ahead and on the horizon. If the "traf" (air traffic) is below the horizon, then the call is, "Twelve o'clock, low." Say "Twelve o'clock, high" if it is dead ahead and located above the horizon.

Where the horizon crosses an object indicates your elevation relative to that point. If the horizon line crosses a tower a hundred feet below its top, then that is where the impact point would be.

Aircraft located on the horizon are at your same altitude and are the most threatening, especially if they are not moving laterally, just growing larger (on a collision course).

Explain that a faraway craft represents no hazard and is therefore "no factor." This prevents the excited passenger from scaring the poop out of you, by proclaiming the presence of an airliner that is five miles away and thousands of feet higher. Explain the "no factor" factor to them, and always praise them, Captain, even if you had already noticed the potential traffic conflict.

Take each ten-degree sector of the view and hold still for a couple of seconds. Look for any movement or a glint. An aircraft's shadow traveling across the surface works well in alerting you to the presence of company. If the shadows are merging, then danger could be closing. Look upsun to see the shadow-maker.

When my craft is pointed out to another by ATC, then I roll the machine back and forth a bit to help make myself more visible. It works. By moving around, the sun can reflect off the aircraft differently, and the motion alone can help to catch the other pilot's eye. When ATC calls "Traffic at two o'clock," then look there, but also check the ten o'clock area just in case the radar was read backward.

The new "fish-finder" traffic locaters are nice but no substitute for looking around. My experience with these TCAS-type devices is similar to how I feel about the weatherman's forecast. They are not wrong enough to ignore but are not accurate enough to trust. Be like you are at the nude beach (back in the day; now it's tantamount to whale-watching): come home from flying with a sore neck.

Once traffic is spotted and ATC tells you to "maintain visual" separation, don't take your eyes off the target. If you look away, the eye focal distance to the traffic will be hard to re-establish. Lose sight, lose the fight. If contact is lost, then advise ATC and try to regain visual.

Run with your lights on. Many airplanes have a taxi light and a separate landing light available. A taxi light beam shines straight ahead, while a landing light beam is angled down so it can be used on the nosed-up approach to land. Use the straight-ahead taxi light when other aircraft are involved, and use the downward-angled landing light to aid the tower or anyone on the ground in seeing you.

We want to constantly fly the most difficult maneuver as we cruise along. It is called "straight and level." To most efficiently fly the aircraft this way, we must look outside and employ the attitude flying system (seat of the pants).

Cruise, Continued

To accomplish attitude flying, when level, note the exact amount of space between the nose of the craft (antiglare shield or cowling) and the horizon line. If that distance starts to diminish, then push the yoke forward a little to put it back where it belongs. If it drops a tad, raise it back up to the level attitude. Put the craft back where it belongs. If the aircraft wants to continue to climb or descend, then it needs to be more precisely retrimmed.

The pilot must maintain a wings-level attitude to keep Pegasus traveling straight ahead. Look at the wing tips and make them equally spaced with the horizon. The heading won't change unless the plane turns, and it won't turn if you don't drop a wing. In unstable air, a rising wing indicates the presence of a thermal on that side. In a glider, you would turn into it and soar, but here, we are just going to put the wings back where they belong. As soon as a wing drops, pick it back up, and the heading will be maintained. The faster the bumps move you, the faster you can readjust the controls to correct.

Looking outside is the most accurate way to control the craft, as you are seeing what is happening. Concentrating on the flight instruments will not work as well because you are reacting to what has already happened. There is a sufficient delay in the gauges to keep the pilot behind the plane while chasing the needles. Looking outside is more efficient and much safer. Spend 90 percent of the time looking outside, not inside. You don't want to see an aircraft come out of the instrument panel.

Look a few miles out front once on heading and select a landmark or two to aim for. This will keep you on the straight and narrow without having to look at the directional gyro (DG) all the time. To keep the DG accurate, always compare it to the magnetic compass at least every ten minutes. All gyroscopes precess, and they get stupid if not constantly corrected. You might as well be tracking outbound using the fuel gauge needle. It is difficult to get an accurate reading off the mag compass in turbulent conditions. Train yourself that when in a calm air area and the craft settles down for a bit, then quickly check the magnetic compass and update the DG.

Every ten minutes in cruise flight, a good rule is to compare the DG to the compass and turn on the carb heat for ten seconds (hold on to it). This will keep the DG refreshed and prevent carb ice. Remember to push the carb heat back to off. If the engine runs rough when the carb heat is engaged, it is eating carb ice now and has trouble breathing. Leave the heat on until it smooths out. Never turn the heat back off right away if it runs ragged, as that could kill the engine. Move the carb heat control slowly if newbies are aboard so the RPM noise change doesn't spook them.

Changes in heading will be required as we navigate along our route. Make small bank angles for small heading changes. Don't crank in a thirty-degree bank for a seven-degree course modification. You'll overshoot the new direction and have to turn back.

This is a smooth way to change directions. Use half of the required azimuth change as a bank angle target, up to 45 degrees of bank. If the heading difference is 30 degrees (e.g., 300 degrees to 330 degrees), then use 15 degrees of bank. Only 3 degrees of bank are needed for that small 7 degree heading variation.

Always turn your head and clear the turn before banking the aircraft. This is very true with a high-wing, as you can't see with a wing dropped. *Always* clear the turn! Remember, 60 percent of midairs come from behind, so crane your neck and check that four o'clock or eight o'clock location first.

Look straight ahead once the turn has been "cleared" and roll into the bank using coordinated controls (as always). To end up precisely on your new heading, lead the rollout by one-half of the bank angle. If going from 300 degrees to 330 degrees with a 15-degree bank angle, start the roll to level 7 degrees before the desired heading (i.e., initiate the roll-to-level at 323 degrees). Alter the unbanking rate so the rollout on heading works out perfectly (cheat).

Cloud separation regulation distances make good sense. The five-hundred-foot below-the-cloud requirement is because, like a bird, you can always just dive away from the danger that is now dropping out of the bottom of the cloud. Also, jets generally descend at a lower rate compared to their steeper climb gradient. That's why you need to be at least one thousand feet above the tops. A fast mover could be heading upstairs at a twenty-degree climb angle, and you are not going to outclimb it, so the extra five hundred feet gives more time to maneuver to avoid.

The larger two-thousand-foot spacing to the side of the puffs is because the aircraft in cruise flight are going even faster than a climbing one. They could come out of a cloud side doing 250 KTS (almost one and a half football fields per second). If head-on, then closure will be very quick. Remember, there are only two kinds of pilots. This is why there are these differences in cloud-spacing distances and why it is important to always maintain a vigilant scan.

The above are the things we think about and do as we fly along on our trip (and wonder what the poor people are doing today). There is a certain point, however, that we need to think about VNAV (vertical navigation).

On one of my first long cross-country flights, I could not find the destination airport (I was right over it). When I saw the aerodrome below me, I then realized that I had to descend five thousand feet from my cruising level. Duh?

At some point, we have to start down, although we do not want to give up our altitude until we have to. Don't squander that potential energy (elevation) that our gasoline and engine paid for. We do have to eventually descend, though, as it is too big a step from up here to get out.

Descent

The two main considerations, notwithstanding ATC, are, "When to begin the loss of altitude?" and "At what rate/speed do we come downhill?" The answers are mutually inclusive. The steeper the descent, the later the commencement of the dive. A JU-87 Stuka dive-bomber waits until it's over the target before starting down. We'll employ a less-steep descent slope.

The time of year influences this decision, as we will descend less steeply in the colder temperatures and will carry some engine power all the way down. This will keep the stove warmer, as we want to avoid "supercooling" the cylinders. After all, it is air-cooled. Leave it leaned on the way down, too. Just "enrichen" the mixture enough to keep it running. Don't shove the red mixture control in to full rich when it is cold outside, as now this extra fuel is helping to cool an already-cold engine. Leave it leaned all the way down. Only full rich if performing a go-around or a missed approach. Shallow, powered, letdown profile for the wintertime.

You can do a "slam-dunk" dive to a lower elevation in the summer heat. The power plant loves it. Excessive cooling is no factor when it's hot out. With my two Cessna trainers, in the hot summertime, we do a simulated "engine-out" for the last landing. Good emergency practice and cools the engine off before the shutdown occurs.

The standard small airplane descent rate is 500 FPM. By the way, this 500 FPM gravity-assisted pace is much easier to maintain in the letdown phase than it was in the climb-out segment, due to lack of engine horsepower and high-density altitude conditions.

There is one more control to manipulate once the descent has started and the speed has built up. Hold a little bit of left rudder the entire time the airplane is in the descent mode. The left-turning tendencies have now lessened to *de minimis* (a trifle) with the reduction in power and increase in airspeed. The "tweaks" (left wing and dorsal fin) have become invigorated and are now working too well. These combined tweaks are now yawing/rolling the plane to the right. The ball is out to the left, so step on it.

Right rudder on the way up and left rudder on the way down. Not catch and release, but constant, steady rudder pressure all the way up and down. The ball shows the quality of your flying and the alignment of the craft to the airstream. Use left rudder in the letdown.

There are various simple mathematical formulas out there to provide answers to the "altitude loss versus distance covered" question. My goal is to convert my hard-won height into speed and therefore ground traversed, by using "God's G" (in this downward case). I shoot for only a 200 FPM cruise-descent type of profile.

At a 500 FPM descent rate, with a 120 MPH ground speed (two miles per minute), then figure we travel four miles for every one thousand feet of altitude lost. Do the math for the amount of elevation change involved. At my 200 FPM cruise decline rate (one thousand feet altitude loss equals five minutes) and at 180 MPH (three miles per minute) ground speed, my descent needs to begin much earlier.

Starting at eleven thousand feet and going down to one thousand feet would require fifty minutes and 150 miles. For example, the nose-down maneuver would have to begin over Pennsylvania to arrive at Eastern New Jersey on altitude.

If on an IFR flight plan, and it is VFR the rest of the way to the destination, then cancel IFR but keep the squawk code and ATC's traffic advisories. If conditions are proper, then request a "cruise clearance." Or just ask ATC if you can descend at a less than standard 500 FPM pace. ATC would always grant the shallow rate request when advised that children were aboard (they were). It never hurts to ask.

For a proper descent profile, plan to be at the lower desired altitude (e.g., traffic pattern altitude) before you get to the airfield. Be at that TPA level at least a couple of miles before entering the pattern.

Do not descend into the pattern. It's poor form and dangerous. You cannot see the traffic below you in the pattern (unless you're flying an F-22 or 35). Rocketing along at 180 MPH behind a 70-MPH trainer also makes it difficult to stay in sequence.

The descent segment is the part of the trip where you are making money. With gravity's help, the speed will increase while the power only has to be reduced enough to keep it within parameters. You are cooking now.

There is a limit, however, as to how hot the cooking should be. There is a huge difference in going fast in smooth air and driving the tank too quickly down a rough tank trail. My driver broke a suspension road wheel torsion bar (three-inch diameter) on my tank because the TC (me) had us going too fast. So even a main battle tank can be hurt by harsh road conditions coupled with too much speed.

If you are not the first boat on the glassy lake and the air is not perfectly smooth, then monitor and keep strict control of your airspeed. There is great danger in going too quick in turbulent air, particularly if lightly loaded in a fast/hot air machine.

If you fly a high-wing airplane that doesn't have struts, stay out of the yellow or caution range (smooth-air-only band) depicted on the airspeed indicator. Since we know there will normally be bumpy air below the cloud base level, then we need to be slowed down to maneuvering speed (Va) before we reach that altitude. Va is not marked on the ASI as it varies with weight, but know your speed for your weight.

This is significant, as we could be doing 180 indicated in a high-speed cruise descent and yet our Va is only 110. That's 70 knots beyond "it stalls before it breaks speed." The reason Va exists and becomes an even slower speed with less weight on board is so the airplane will stall and thereby "let go" of the air, before it bends or breaks something (e.g., a wing). Afterward, it will then merely unstall and keep on trucking along undamaged.

When the bases of the clouds are reached, or whenever the turbulence begins, we need to slow down *now*. As much as we hate to give away this "smash," we have to decrease airspeed to protect the airframe that we are occupying. When I broke the tank, we pulled off to the side of the road. We can't do that here if we snap something by going too fast.

Plan ahead and anticipate the turbulence. Be under control and already slowed to Va when the predicted instability level is reached. If it is still smooth out, then add some power and lower the nose a little and resume the cruise descent velocity. Be prepared for that instability point in the descent and be under firm airspeed control.

Without adding additional stress to the airframe, how do we most efficiently decelerate an airplane that is going too fast? If you just encountered the violence transition zone and can go back up into the smooth conditions, then do that. Tell ATC if necessary. Once in smooth air again, we can comfortably slow down and then resume the descent.

First, of course, smoothly reduce the power to low green on the tach, turn the carb heat on, and pull back the throttle more to a high-idle power setting to decelerate. The speed decay rate will take some time, however. Gently raise the nose to level. How do we increase this braking rate and not add more G pressure to an already-strained and stressed bucking bronco? Pulling back on the yoke to climb or turn just adds more positive Gs to the load and is not the best answer. So what do we do?

First of all, never add flaps. The number one reason is that the craft is well beyond its white (flap) arc (Vfe) speed, and the wing would be severely damaged if this was done. The second reason is that flaps make the airframe weaker, as flaps add more wing area. Look in the POH under G "load limits" and see how the craft is one or two Gs weaker with the flaps extended. This is true for both the positive and negative G load limit.

Flaps are not the solution. Deployable speed brakes are ideal, of course, but few craft have them available. So how else can we safely but expeditiously decrease our velocity?

If it is over moderate turbulence (severe) conditions and the airspeed must be lost now to protect the ship, then drop the landing gear if available, the same as you would do in an "upset" scenario. The extended landing gear causes so much drag that Va is quickly achieved. You may need new landing gear doors, however. Drastic measures for drastic situations. There is a less dire option.

Just slip it. Slowly and gently feed in some cross-controls (aileron/rudder) to make the craft fly a little sideways. Add some right aileron and left rudder together, or vice versa. This adds skin and interference drag but does not add more positive or negative G load onto the wing, like a climb or turn would. Easy does it, particularly if cooking right along. Flying a little sideways for a while is the safest way to decelerate to Va.

Approach and Traffic Pattern

At the bottom of the descent, we need to do a reverse level-off. Most don't really go level but merely reduce the descent rate and still blow right through their target altitude. The easiest, therefore best, way is to slowly add sufficient elevator nose-up trim to level the pitch attitude. As the plane slows, keep adding enough trim to maintain this level attitude. Lead the level-off by slowly raising the nose 15 percent of the descent rate before your altitude (extra 5 percent to counter gravity's pull). For example, if descending at 500 FPM, then start the nose up seventy-five feet above the desired altitude.

Make all power reductions gradual and incremental. Pull back the throttle a couple hundred RPM and then wait some time before making a further reduction. Don't just retard the throttle all in one fell swoop. Take your time going up on the power, and take your time reducing the power too. The engine will like you better for it. Move the power lever slowly so as not to scare the people on the ground. A big chop in the engine noise makes everyone look up at you and could cause a loud backfire explosion in the exhaust system ("Hi, honey, I'm home!").

As the energy/speed bleeds off, release the left rudder pressure, as it is no longer needed. Begin the before-landing checklist and do a quick cockpit check. We are assuming all the proper radio calls are being made. Enter the traffic pattern at the correct altitude and in the proper way. See the "AIM" (the FAA Aeronautical [used to be "Airman's"] Information Manual).

Normal pattern entry is on a forty-five-degree angle to the midpoint (not end) of the runway. Do not fly a wide pattern, as someone could get in between you and the runway. At one thousand feet AGL, the runway should be down at a forty-five-degree angle from

180

you. That displaces the plane only one thousand feet laterally from the runway edge. Be predictable and fly a proper pattern.

Stay within gliding distance of a runway. The difference between a commercial pilot and a private pilot is that if a commercial pilot can see the airfield, he can glide to it by maintaining enough energy to do this. Stay close to the airfield and keep sufficient altitude and/or speed in order to "make" the runway if the engine should happen to stop.

On a windy day, the traffic pattern size can be reduced. If facing a tailwind landing, the base leg can be slightly longer. It is very critical to be on your landing (Vref) speed at the bottom. Excess airspeed on final, plus a tailwind, equals a go-around and another try.

Most midair collisions happen within five miles of the airport. Be extravigilant there and especially so when turning from the base leg to the final leg of the pattern. Ninety percent of all midairs happen here. That makes sense, as the base-to-final turn is where the approach path "funnel-necks" down and concentrates all the air traffic on final for that runway.

While on the base leg, always look for the "farmer on final," as we used to say in Kansas, the guy on the five-mile straight-in-final type of pattern. This is not an infrequent occurrence at a nontowered airfield. Don't just stare at the touchdown spot on the runway, but turn your head and look for this type of hazardous operation before joining the final leg.

Normal Landing

For a fixed-gear carbureted aircraft, the sequence of actions necessary for the landing process normally begins when the aircraft is abeam (across from) the landing runway "numbers" while on the downwind leg. Turn the carb heat on before reducing power. If it is cold out, wait a few seconds after engaging the carb heat before pulling back on the throttle. Always have the carb heat on before reducing the RPM out of the tachometer's green arc. Then, smoothly reduce the power to the approach power setting, around 1,500 RPM. Leave the mixture leaned, particularly in the winter. The POH says to go to "full rich" only for a potential go-around. We know to go to full rich at that time, so leave it leaned a little all the way down through the landing.

If flying a Complex aircraft, when the downwind leg is entered, and when you are below Vge (landing gear extension speed), then say, out loud, "Downwind, down gear." Activate the landing gear extension control and hold on to it while the gear is transitioning to the "down and locked" position. Warn novice passengers about the noise it makes and explain it is a good sound.

Announce that "gear is down and locked," after confirming all indicators are correct. By listening to the cycle, you can tell if all sounds are normal. Listen to these machines operate. They talk to you. If it doesn't sound right, then get it looked at before flying again. The down-and-welded aircraft do not have to worry about sliding on their belly like a reptile. Confirm the landing gear is down on each leg of the landing approach. Flying a Complex plane is the same as flying a trainer, except for the gear-and-prop option.

Don't allow the nose to drop upon RPM decrease, as you want to slow the plane down to the white arc flap range on the ASI. Always confirm the airspeed needle is in the "white" before touching the flap lever. Once slowed enough, lower ten degrees of flaps. As we know, only raise or lower the flaps when in wings-level flight.

Now add two-and-a-half globs of nose-up elevator trim. Feel the trim as it's added. Don't just do it mechanically. Be in tune with the desired approach path. Slow down to 1.3 of the stall speed (e.g., stalls at $61 \times 1.3 = 80$). When we are slow, the airplane responds in "reversed command." The yoke or stick controls our airspeed (not elevation), and the power lever controls the glide path angle or altitude (not speed). A nonpilot's response to being low on final is to raise the nose. Very wrong! When at approach speed, increasing the pitch just slows down an already-sluggish craft. Increasing the wing's angle of attack induces additional drag.

While driving a car and facing an uphill road, only pushing on the gas pedal will make you climb the slope, no matter how hard you pull back on the steering wheel. Same with a slow airplane. Only by pushing the throttle forward to adjust for an undershoot situation will you be safe. The power lever in your right hand is the up-and-down altitude control. The yoke in your left hand holds the speed/pitch regulator.

Energy/momentum control is what aviating is all about. Each of our craft's flight controls accomplishes an exact function. Don't move the wrong control. Look, think, then move. It is like a student in the taxi mode using the yoke (steering wheel) to drive down the taxiway. It looks impressive, but it doesn't work, and it wastes time and thought for what actually needs to be done. You always have time to do the right thing the first time.

Imagine a "skull and crossbones" decal depicted on the airspeed indicator dial face where the bottom of the green and white arcs reside. The no-more-fly speed region. The stall, spin, crash, burn, die speed.

Even with fifty-thousand-plus landings, I still look at the ASI every few seconds during the approach-to-landing phase. As long as you can trim and maintain a constant pitch attitude, the aircraft will hold a steady speed. If too slow, then lower the nose an inch or so and wait.

It takes a while (seconds) for the aircraft's mass to descend a bit steeper and accelerate. Do not chase the airspeed needle. Let it settle down. Normally, trimming the nose to remain a few inches below the horizon works well. To summarize: To go faster, lower the nose. To level off or decrease descent rate, add power. This is the only way to do it and prevent a LOC.

If you're way too slow and low, then add power and point at the ground. The opposite of what a nonaviator (NAMF) would do. If you do what they would do and jerk back on the pitch control, then that's called a LOC (loss of control) or stall-spin accident. The new, biggest pilot problem. Pilot, not aircraft, problem. Airspeed, airspeed, airspeed. Add full power and dive toward the surface to achieve Vx and *then* raise the nose and climb away. Do not have killer habits.

The more flaps that are added, the more nose-down pitch attitude is required. With over twenty degrees, the flaps are increasing the drag, requiring a steeper descent angle to maintain the Vref. That's one of the benefits of flaps, as they provide a better view of the runway, because the nose has to be lowered to overcome the additional drag. With forty degrees of flaps and the power off, the nose is pitched down ten degrees or more. The more flaps, the more pitch-down deck angle is mandated to maintain Vref.

After turning from downwind to the base leg, which is normally done when at a forty-five-degree angle back toward the approach end of the runway, ask yourself, "Am I high or low?" If too high, then add flaps and reduce some power too. The sooner you recognize the current situation, the less of a correction is demanded. If a bit high on base, then a power reduction of just a couple hundred RPM would make it work out. If high, then also add the flaps earlier and add more if necessary. The later you delay an accurate assessment of the glide path, the more that has to be done to remedy the approach. Realizing on short final that the airplane is high and hot is too late. Even with the power at idle, flaps full and a slip, the landing still cannot be salvaged. Go around!

Keep track of where you are in the pattern (heading and elevation) and constantly evaluate the projected path. See it. If low, then add some power and don't lower your flaps more than twenty degrees. Imagine the runway centerline extending out on the final leg. Time your turn from base to final to be over that path on the rollout. You are now lined up with the runway. Vary the bank angle of the turn, more or less, to make it work out. Maintain the turn coordinator's ball in the center during this (any) turn. This is critical. Nothing bad will ever happen to you during this procedure if the airspeed is proper and the ball is centered. Do that, and she'll never let you down, as it were.

On the final leg of the pattern, set the flaps to thirty degrees and control the descent angle with power. Many just point the nose at the end of the runway like they are going to strafe it and get going way too fast. Diving does you no good. Being on the proper altitude at the runway end has to be coupled with being at the proper Vref "over the fence" airspeed as well (1.15-1.2 Vso).

Look at the final approach segment as a mathematical problem. The answer we seek is to be at the right height, with the right speed, as we fly over the runway numbers. The more variables in this equation, the harder it is to solve. If we can make our approach speed a constant, the solution becomes easier. If we can also keep the descent rate constant, we can now predict our arrival point and adjust the power to make it work out spot-on. A stabilized glide path is the key to a good approach, which is a prerequisite to being set up for a great landing.

Your landing aim point is not the very end of the runway. Shoot for the runway numbers and plan to level out at ten feet above those numbers. The goal is to land on the first third of the strip. The shorter the runway, the more precise we must be to succeed on the first attempt.

Most students "target-fixate" and just stare at the runway end, which is bad for two reasons. You don't really know if the rest of the runway is unobstructed, and you are depriving your brain of valuable "ranging" input. Look to see if an aircraft is taking off toward you from the opposite end (I had that happen [Break Right]). Also, is there wildlife on the landing area? You can't see if you don't look.

Employ the same technique as used for inspecting the runway before takeoff. When established on final, look down the right side of the runway, all the way to the very end. Then sweep your eyes down the left edge, coming back toward you. You are looking for the same hazards as before. About a quarter mile away, look at the far end, and then look at the near end of the landing strip. Do this a couple of times to allow your brain to process this ranging/perception information. Blindly staring at the supposed touchdown spot deprives the pilot of this valuable data.

Only lower the flaps to forty degrees when on very short final (unless high). If this much flap is lowered too far out, then power will have to be added to counter all that extra drag. Otherwise, you won't make it to the runway.

When you have descended to twenty feet (not fifty feet) over the runway, reach down and add a glob of nose-up elevator trim. This will reduce the descent rate automatically (let the nose go up a little). Many raise the nose too soon on the approach. Resist this temptation. Don't be afraid of the ground. Be *afraid* of getting too slow while still thirty feet in the air. "Wait for it" before going level. Also, twenty feet doesn't mean two inches, either. Don't be too low until already pitched up.

The actual landing sequence consists of five distinct phases. By the way, the landing is one of the most fun parts of flying. Enjoy the landing process. Be a bird. Don't rush the plane. Witnesses will judge you as a pilot by the quality of your landings. Show 'em what you've got!

A new passenger doesn't know if you can talk on the radio or navigate well, but they do know when it's a scary, bounced landing. That is what they will remember and tell all their friends about. Remember, pilots only get paid for the last five feet.

The first step in landing is to level off and then stay at five feet over the runway. Once the runway is made, we smoothly close the throttle to idle. Any extra RPM at this time will increase the float distance and make the alighting process take that much longer. Some pilots cheat and drag the airplane in (too low) on final, expending copious amounts of power to even reach the runway. Twice the amount of runway is consumed when the power is not brought back to idle right away. Close the throttle completely, for a normal landing, once the runway "is made."

The second step is to wait a few seconds after going level. The airplane will balloon up if any but the tiniest amount of yoke back pressure is added at this time. This is even more the case if flying too fast. Those that come screaming in and try to force the plane onto the ground are always disappointed with the result. It's not the machine's fault. It's the pilot, not the plane. Stay above ground effect (thirty feet) if a bit too fast (if way too fast, do a go-around). Do a "baby slip" up there OGE (out of ground effect) to slow down before descending into the lesser drag region of the ground effect elevation. You slow down more slowly in ground effect.

As the airspeed decreases, the airplane will begin to descend. Now take the third step, where a small "bite" of yoke/stick back pressure is added and held. You are holding the nose up with your hand/arm tension. Keep it there. Cranking in more trim (without looking down) makes this pitch-up even easier. Give it one more little bite of yoke back-pull and wait again. If you rush at this point, the plane may "balloon" up.

If it does, don't do anything. Just hold what you have (or just release a very little back pressure) and let her come back down and catch it again. Never dump the nose and dive back down. If you are "too little and too late" on the pitch-up recovery from this dive, the nose gear tire will have an impact on the surface. This will initiate what is termed pilot-induced oscillation (PIO). *Go around!* Don't even mess with it. It happens (excrement occurs), and there is *no* embarrassment in flying a go-around. You are the Captain.

If this PIO is allowed to cycle on its proposing path and the pilot gets "out of phase" with the phugoid bouncing, then this will result in nose-gear collapse on the third nose-down (beak) collision with the planet (statistically speaking). This is not a great landing. The nose gear could break and "fold up" under the cockpit floor. This may pin your legs under the instrument panel. Turn the master switch off (to kill the still-running fuel pump), or just go around after the first bounce and try again.

We are now in the proper landing attitude, with the nose gear safely up and out of harm's way. We land on our feet, not our beak. You could stop pulling back right now and just let it land, and it will be an okay arrival. Most "fly" it onto the runway, and I guess that's fine (no, it's not) on a long, hard-surfaced runway, but don't try it on a sandy beach in a forced-landing episode (bat impersonation time).

The fourth step is to do everything we can (within reason) to keep this airplane from touching the runway. Act like you are going to fly all the way down the strip at a four-inch height. Don't let it touch down—hold it off. Keep adding little bites of yoke back pressure to keep her off the ground. As the speed dissipates, more and more back pressure at a faster rate can be used. Pull back a little and then hold that pressure fixed and constant. Don't relax this back pressure, or the nose will drop and clobber in.

In the flare, we are like a bird. Be warned that even though there is just a small amount of yoke rear travel left, the elevator is still surprisingly alive. Be very smooth with the yoke, even at the very end. If that last one inch of yoke is hauled back to the stop, the airplane may zoom up to ten feet and then stall and fall. Oops. If that drop does happen, a burst of power at the bottom of the fall will cushion the impact. Use small bites of increasing back pressure and hold it off. Feel it and flare with flair. This is the fun part!

An analogy I came up with to describe the amount and timing of yoke movement required in the landing would be like this: Place an uncooked egg in its shell on the kitchen sink bottom. Put an empty one-gallon bucket on top of the egg and hold up the bucket just lightly enough to keep the egg from rolling away. Hold the bucket handle with your yoke or stick hand. Turn the water faucet on (75 percent), so the liquid goes into the bucket, slowly adding weight.

The trick is to precisely add the right amount of handle lift pressure to keep the water's weight from cracking the eggshell, but not so much as to raise (balloon) the bucket and release the egg. The more water that goes in the bucket, the more bucket yoke holding effort is required. When the bucket is one-third full, turn the water on full blast.

This replicates how little effort and how deliberately slow the yoke pullback movement must be at the onset of the flare. This is because we are going faster. It also demonstrates how much more control movement is required at the end, in order to have the same control effect, because the speed/airflow is dissipating every second (less FPS).

This bucket experiment, like the flare, represents the challenge of metering our arm-and-wrist movement to *exactly* control the outcome. It is very hard for a human being to move that slow and slight, especially at the beginning of the flare pitch-up sequence. This is why I use "little bites" of back pressure (one-half inch). The goal is to keep pulling back on the yoke at such a varying rate that our altitude stays the same (four inches), while our airspeed bleeds off, until she can't fly anymore and *has* to land. Never try to *make* it land; it's like jerking the trigger on a rifle—you'll miss. Squeeze it off (or *on*, here).

The perfect landing is when the main landing gear tires "chirp" just as the back stop point of the elevator is reached. Hold the yoke there, or wherever it is when the plane touches down. If the yoke was released, the nose would crash down onto the runway. If an airliner was derotated that hard, it would break its fuselage in half. Keep the back pressure on, and the nose will slowly lower and land last. If the airplane touched down before the elevator stop was completely reached, then freeze the yoke in that position and wait. Obviously, we are using the rudder pedals to keep us going straight down the centerline.

Once the nose begins to lower, then smoothly add the rest of the remaining back pressure to now "land" the nose gear tire, the "third chirp." Hold the yoke full back all through the rollout. If there is any crosswind, then feed in the rest of the ailerons going that way into the breeze. If there is no wind, twist the yoke to full aileron displacement with the down aileron on the side of the runway exit.

The fifth and final step of landing is the post-touchdown rollout. With the throttle closed and all the primary and secondary flight controls exhibited to the slipstream, we are maximizing our aerodynamic braking potential. Power may have to be added to make it to the taxiway turnoff. By doing the rollout in such a fashion, I rarely need any brakes at all, except for the run-up part of the mission. Brakes and tires last a lot longer that way.

A good landing is any landing you can walk away from. A great landing is one where you can use the aircraft again. We are all trying to achieve the "perfect" landing (hole in one). Strive for that every time. It will always be different, and that is one of the absolute beauties of aviating. In golf, you drive for show and putt for dough. The landing is the putt of golf. Enjoy the landing!

Windy Landings

The main difference here is that we are just trying to get back on the planet without bending something. Nothing fancy now. On final, be on your speed or just a tad higher. The more speed at the bottom, the more you will float, prolonging the exposure to the blustery conditions.

The reason that many are too fast on final is, they are trying to make their "closure" rate (ground speed) to the runway end look the same as on a calm day. If approaching so the plane is covering the ground at the same seventy-mile-per-hour ground speed rate in a twenty-mile-per-hour headwind, then their airspeed is eight-five to ninety miles per hour (way too fast). Be on your Vref, or 1.1 Vref, no more than that.

Assertively control the glide path with power. If in heavy sink, then add enough throttle (full, if necessary) to stay where you should be and then reduce the power right back off when no longer required. Remember, when power is applied, the nose pitches up. Don't let it. Hold it where it belongs. Don't let the nose drop, either, when the power is reduced.

Keep doing this until at twenty feet AGL, and then close the throttle. Go level like before, but when it starts down this time, just give it a bite or two of nose-up yoke to raise the nose gear a few degrees. Once pitched-up in landing attitude, then let the plane descend and touch down. Don't try to hold it off. Let the main tires touch, if in a *fixed*-gear plane only, then raise the flaps as soon as you hear the chirp of the tires. Losing that flap lift and the extra wing area will keep you on the ground and protect you from a sudden gust, which could lift the plane back up if the flaps had been left down.

Once the mains have made contact, start applying the brakes. Get on them and slow down. The flaps retracting help in transferring the weight of the machine from the wings to the tires. We want the weight there now because that's where the brakes are. Keep adding some elevator back pressure to add more weight to the main tires. Be careful adding too much up elevator as a sudden gust could lift the airplane off the ground again. Stay on the brakes until the speed is "cold."

If it is really rough out, I will look and retract the flaps if flying a noncomplex airplane, just as the flare is begun, and while still in the air. If it's this windy out, I assume you can fly well. Raising the flaps makes for a shorter flare/float duration, and you are on the ground even quicker. Control the pitch changes as the flaps retract and keep the nose up for the actual touchdown. Only use this flap-retract trick when absolutely necessary. Your goal is to get safely on the ground and below flying speed as soon as possible. When that happens, you are safe and sound.

Landing Zone Reconnaissance

Most of our landings take place at surveyed airports. Obstacles are Notam-ed (notices to air*men*) and lit. We know how much room we have and that the runway approach paths are inspected and unobstructed. Flying into an austere, remote location provides none of these safety margins. We become the surveyor and inspector. As I learned in the Rangers, there is nothing like a ground reconnaissance. Walk the field and look around. Maps and aerial photos are nice, but they are no substitute for actually being there. If you are going to fly into a friend's field, then drive there and check it out in person, if at all possible.

If not, then study the charts and check the computer maps. After arriving at the remote field, conduct a high reconnaissance circle of the field at one thousand feet AGL. Slow down to loiter speed and add half-flaps and trim (of course). While circumnavigating the site, identify the approach and go-around departure paths. Are they clear of obstacles, especially wires?

Wires can easily stay invisible to the naked eye for 330 degrees of a 360-degree orbit. For only a 30-degeree slice is the sun angle proper to allow us to see the wires that are there. Also look for power line pole shadows. Do a couple of loops around the pattern and satisfy yourself that all hazards have been noted. If a wire is actually encountered on approach or departure, we won't see it until it's too late to avoid. Wires are killers. Really look for them!

After the high one has been completed, do a low recon circle at five hundred feet AGL. Look for the same items and study the landing surface closely. Tall grass can hide rocks and logs from view. Keep your airspeed all the time and check it regularly. Don't do a "moose turn." While circling wildlife, the pilot gets too slow and stalls in, or hits a tree. Watch what you're doing when down here.

The last very low recon of the process is to "drag" the field. Fly next to the right side of the "runway," at one hundred feet up, and really study it hard. The importance of these reconnaissance techniques cannot be over-emphasized, and they give you the best chance for a successful outcome. Still, always be prepared for surprises.

Short Field Landing

Our objective here is to clear the obstacle at the end of the landing zone, get down on the runway, and stop, as efficiently and safely as possible. Always use full flaps and land uphill if presented with a sloped strip (TO downhill).

Always land uphill unless the winds are really howling the other way. Remember to "double-flare" when landing uphill. The first pitch-up is to establish the plane going "level" up the slope. The second flare is the actual landing flare. Get going uphill first, then flare and land. Don't stab the upslope with the beak.

There are two basic methods to "clear" the ever-present obstacle. If there are no obstructions blocking the approach path to the landing field, then just drag it in at Vref, using engine power to arrive at the runway. Chop the power over your spot and land. Not the safest, but that's a way to do it when there are no blocking barriers off the bush strip end.

Depending on the region, the trees at the end may actually be ninety feet tall and not the standard fifty-footer. This makes a vast difference in total distance required. If necessary, extrapolate this calculation from the POH to confirm that a landing is even possible. Remember, almost all general aviation airplanes require (much) more takeoff room than landing space. Brakes are more powerful in the deceleration mode (assuming traction) than a small engine is in the acceleration mode. Don't land somewhere if you can't get back out. Always do the math and also "worst-case" it. This *is* a tactical operation, after all!

Speed control is critical on short final. Have it trimmed to hold Vref. The first short field landing method is to maintain a constant descent angle that is just going to clear the trees. Keep ample distance from the tops of the trees in gusty conditions. This safe glide path is maintained over the obstacle and all the way to the "deck," where the power is chopped in order to land. This is the safest way to do a short field approach (stable/powered glide path).

The next technique will shave off some of the distance that is used to get into a very short-field airstrip. Once established on final, aim for an undershoot approach. This glide path aims at the treetops off the near end, not the runway. Be exactly on your Vref, but no slower. Add sufficient power, as the treetops come closer, to level off with thrust and just go over the treetops.

As the obstruction passes beneath and the craft is now clear to descend, chop the power and lower the nose to hold Vref on the steep decline. Landing is similar to a windy landing method. Aerodynamic braking is nice but is nothing compared to gripping, braking rubber tires on the runway. Raise the flaps and keep applying the brakes as soon as able.

Don't slide the tires initially by holding too much brake pressure before the full weight of the craft is on the mains (BTW, never land with the brakes on). Sliding damages the tire, makes blue smoke, and is less effective in slowing than a tire that is braking but still rolling and grabbing. Get on the brakes all the way to a slight slide screeching noise, and then release, just a little, and keep that pedal pressure on until slowed to taxi/turnoff speed (less than eight miles per hour [same as the "combat" speed for a MBT]).

Notice the tire slide marks at the end of a shorter airstrip. The black rubber lines only begin about thirty feet from the end. Why not further back up the runway? Speed is relative, and compared to the approach velocity sensation we just experienced, this new, slower rollout speed makes us perceive we are adequately slowed down. However, our speed is still thirty-five miles per hour—we just don't realize it. The ASI doesn't help either, as it won't read this lower speed.

A human's depth perception only works out to twenty feet. We are limited to that short range because our eyeballs are only a few inches apart. Beyond that distance, we use size comparison relationships. Because of this limitation, the pilot does not accurately comprehend the actual closure rate to the end until within fifty feet or so, then realizes he is traveling too fast and slams on the brakes and slides off the end. This can be prevented by getting on the hinder-binders and staying on them until you are cold.

There is one last, very advanced, and quite scary method to make a bush strip short field landing. Don't try this at home, unless you are a *real* bush pilot. It starts out with the same undershoot glide path toward the treetops as just described. Right above the treetops, add enough power to go over them. Once we are clear, the big difference begins.

The full technique involved requires an airplane that can rapidly raise and lower its flaps (Piper and such). I have done this in a Piper Super Cub (equipped with Tundra tires with cable-reinforced main landing gear). Once clear of the tops, then chop the power, raise the flaps, lower the nose, and do a full slip. The "glide" path angle heads toward vertical, and the runway surface is now approaching very rapidly. The descent rate of this barely controlled "fall" is quite astounding, as you can very well imagine.

At about forty feet AGL, rudder-swing the nose straight, add full flaps and full power to pitch up, and arrest the vertical sink/fall rate. Don't cut this recovery too thin and don't get too slow. Don't ride the elevator car to the basement floor.

Level off close to the surface and then chop the power, raise the flaps, and slightly pitch up and land. Decelerating is the same as before, but the flaps could be relowered for extra drag during the rollout segment. Display full ailerons, too (hang everything out). Timing is everything with this maneuver, so be very careful if it is ever actually utilized. A good pilot knows their own limits (and those of the aircraft).

On the previous, much safer, short field methods, you could still slip it once clear of the obstacle. Do not go below Vref on the way down, but don't dive it—give yourself sufficient margin to stop the vertical rate and align the plane with the runway. Don't get cocky. Anyway, the above are some ways to land at a tight airstrip.

Soft Field Landing

The objective with this type of arrival is to first gauge whether the surface is even safe to land on. If it isn't, we can still go around if we start to sink in too deep. Otherwise, we commit and touch down as gently as possible. We don't want to "plant it" in the mud, or whatever. The conditions of soft field surfaces change with the season and with the temperature. We don't ever want to get stuck.

A soft field landing is the best type to practice regularly. Most importantly, this is how we would land on an off-airport "forced" (not crashed) landing site. If a pilot can do a soft field landing well, then he can safely land on the beach and not flip over onto his bat, er, back. Additionally, the finesse involved in precisely controlling the pitch to ensure a delicate contact with the surface is just good yoke/ stick and rudder skill practice.

The salient difference with this landing is that we will not cut the power once over the landing zone. Or actually, we will close the throttle, but then reopen it to just add "noise." From the closed throttle position, add only one millimeter (one-sixteenth inch) of throttle control throw. Listen to the engine at idle, and then add some noise. This additional prop RPM "cleans up" the airflow around the tail surfaces of the plane, providing enhanced slow speed control. The propeller is not pushing the air but is allowing it to pass, as it were.

Crank in full nose-up trim (with feeling) but maintain the proper pitched-up attitude approaching the surface. There are two scenarios that make a difference as to how we play the next part. The first is if this is an established soft field airport that is regularly utilized and is usable, a *known* quantity/quality.

We can commit to a landing knowing this. At one foot above the soft surface, begin to hold off the landing by steadily increasing yoke back pressure. The goal is to be as slow as possible before contact is made with the friction-causing surface. Have the plane going the same way as the tires rotate. Don't let it touch in the mire if it is cocked/yawed.

Don't let it land, by holding it off, and when it does, cushion it on with the remaining yoke back pressure. Now hold the yoke all the way aft the whole time, until we are parked. Keep the flaps extended. Turn the carb heat off and go to full rich mixture. Slowing down is normally not an issue, depending on the frictional nature of the surface. The problem could be in maintaining your momentum all the way to a safe parking/stopping spot.

The other soft field scenario involves an *un*known landing zone. Conduct a thorough reconnaissance of the area, as mentioned earlier. Once on short final, add some engine noise as before. We must ascertain the condition of the surface to confirm it is suitable for landing. We do this by lightly sinking into the muck as we add power to keep from getting sucked into it. If it feels like it will be too deep or whatever, then go around now!

Ski-planes will sometimes make multiple semilanding passes to pack down the snow for landing and (more importantly) for takeoff. The key is to leave the go-around option open by easing into the soft stuff with power and staying under control. Keep the nose up as always. If the decision is to land, then do it as before. Ease the power off and let her settle in. Just as in the soft field taxi technique, use ample amounts of power to keep in motion and don't get mired. Stick to the high/dry spots. Read the field contours (the putting green).

Landing on a snow-covered runway with high snowbanks on the edges presents the distinct possibility of a "whiteout" condition. A complete loss of discernable visual reference vanishes in certain lighting conditions. A sightseeing airliner tour flight (DC-10) flew into an Antarctic hillside due to that reason (CFIT). They just didn't see the surface. Depth perception is impossible when everything is the same color.

In Michigan, I was thirty feet over a snowy runway, as just described above, and experienced a complete whiteout environment. Since all was set up perfectly, I just held what I had and let it touch down. If all looks good, then simply "freeze" the controls and land. If a go-around is initiated, then be aware of the potential adverse physiological effects as mentioned in the night takeoff section.

The same thing happened another time while landing in fog when I was flying road watch for Shadow Traffic. You can see through a thin layer of fog from above. However, once on final, you are looking at the side edge of the layer (slant range) and forward vision is now blocked. As before, if set up perf, let her land. This assumes you can't just go to another airport and are low on fuel (hoping the fog would "burn off").

A "glassy-water" landing presents a seaplane pilot with the same emergency conditions. In this case, set up a stabilized descent using power. Trim for a shallow rate of descent (100–200 FPM). At least the air is very smooth in these conditions. Maintain this slight descent until contact with the surface. Don't move anything when it splashes in. Leave the power and pitch controls where they are. If the plane bounces, then it will just land again. Don't chop the power until you see that the floats are in the water.

Landing without power on a glassy sea is basically impossible. You don't know when to start the flare. Too high, and you stall in. Too low/late, and you've already impacted the surface. This is probably what killed Amelia Earhart (there was a glassy-ocean surface that day).

You can't teach an old dog new tricks (unless he's a tricky dog). But if you could glide over the featureless surface on the downwind leg and throw stuff out the window that would float on the water (charts/maps, newspapers, etc.), then after you turn around on final, you can land next to the jettisoned jetsam. The top of the water/snow is now defined, and you can judge when to flare.

Now back on soft fields, try this to keep from flipping over onto your back in a tail-wheeler during the landing rollout. If a conventional-gear airplane starts to tuck nose down due to excessive braking at too low a speed, or because of an obstacle or hole that was encountered, then release the brakes and give it a big burst of power while holding the elevator full up/aft. Hopefully, the prop blast will blow the tail back down onto the ground. What have you got to lose? But this must be a quick and immediate response to a developing nose flip-over issue. Once the propeller blade tips touch the ground, it's a moot point.

If facing a short *and* soft field scenario (the worst), then use a combination of the various methods discussed and really be on your game. You'll need it. Especially departing.

An excellent way to practice soft field landings is to do a touch-and-go. Be in soft field landing configuration and touch the main tires as lightly as you can. Add some power and keep the nose (tire) flying a foot above the runway. Don't let the nose go down or touch. As you are doing a "wheelie" down the runway, reconfigure the plane for a soft field takeoff. Raise the flaps from full down to half up. Confirm the mixture is at full rich, the carb heat is off, and the trim is reset to the takeoff mark. Keep the nose up the whole time by using the yoke and the throttle. Keep it exactly on the center line too. Have fun, as this is good duty.

Now, smoothly bring in full power and perform a proper soft field takeoff. This is very good practice for a number of reasons—speed and pitch control feel, for one. For the last landing on a hot day, do a simulated engine-out short approach to a power-off soft field landing to a full stop. This maneuver helps cool the stove off and illustrates how the craft behaves in the glide and in a dead-stick touchdown scenario. Priceless practise (UK spelling). The above are some ways to do a soft field landing.

Tail-Wheel Landing

Use the same approach as before, and if the winds are easy, then do a "three-point" full-stall landing. All three gear tires touch at the same time. If it touches down prematurely then freeze the stick position, don't pull back anymore; otherwise, it will balloon back up. Stay on the ground and get cold now, as always.

If there are more winds, and they are of a cross-type, then do a "wheel" landing. Just fly the mains onto the surface and begin braking. More brake application can safely be used at the beginning of the rollout, as the elevator and top of the horizontal stabilizer will prevent a nose-over at the higher speed. Once the airspeed decays, release some of the braking pressure, as the airflow over the tail will now be insufficient to stop a pitch-over tuck demonstration.

Crosswind Landing

This landing is the opposite of a crosswind takeoff and climb-out. Use the same principles, just going the other way. Use the necessary wind correction headings to maintain proper pattern position. If there is a tailwind component when turning from base to final, then start that turn earlier than normal. Try not to overshoot the final leg. Use coordinated flight control inputs only to be where you should be on the final approach.

Landing at Alpena, Michigan, in an F-33 Bonanza with a forty-knot crosswind (seventy degrees) made my wind correction angle almost forty-five degrees off the runway heading. The breeze was from the right, and I was now seeing the runway through my left-side vent window. Establish a wind correction angle on final and stay on the proper final approach path. Don't fly it in a slip the entire way down the final course. That's too much work and will wear you out. Instead, there is a safer and easier way.

Hold this WCA "crab" heading all the way down to twenty feet AGL. On the way, practice yawing the nose straight with the runway, then re-establish the WCA to stay on the final course. If the plane cannot be aligned to the runway heading with full rudder applied, then we need a new plan. Or just clobber it in at the bottom by pushing in full downwind rudder and some upwind aileron, raise the flaps, and "touch" down now. Bam, done. A kill's a kill.

As the runway approaches, begin a windy landing-type flare and swing the nose straight with downwind rudder and lower the upwind wing. This prevents the crosswind/air from blowing the airplane off the side of the strip. Chop the power and let the upwind main tire touch down. Now you have a grip on the situation.

If any of the flight controls reach their stops, then it is time to land. The plane can't do anything more with the air, so get some rubber on the road to hold on. Raise the flaps in the flare to assist in alighting. This is the safest way to land in gusty, turbulent crosswind conditions.

If there is a smooth, steady crosswind at the runway environment, then land on the upwind tire only. Keep it going straight with rudder, but keep twisting in more upwind aileron to hold the downwind tire up in the air.

It's tricky to keep it tracking straight and true on one tire, but not that hard. This tire will "talk" to you if it's not rolling straight. Eventually, the other wing comes down, and that main tire lands as full aileron travel is attained. Continue to hold that full yoke aileron twist. Now land the nose tire with the elevator as described before. Hold the yoke controls at their stops during the complete rollout.

Use this one-tire crosswind landing technique if one of the tires is low on air or flat. Always look at the main tires before landing (if in a high-wing, obviously), as a flat tire will look "dimpled-in" by the wind. At least now you know. During landing, hold that flat tire off the ground as long as the ailerons will keep it up. I've done it in a Skyhawk (at night), and if there is enough of a headwind, the plane is almost stopped before the nonrolling tire touches. Taxiing is no longer an option, though.

The last crosswind landing method involves avoidance. On a long ferry flight from Wyoming to New Jersey in an Aviat Husky, with a huge tailwind that day, I realized the planned fuel stop could be bypassed. Just as well, because there was a ninety-degree, direct, twenty-five-knot crosswind to the one runway. Looking down the cross-country course line on the chart revealed that every one of the next ten airports had north-south runways, which would not work with this brisk west wind. Aerodrome number 11 had two runways. We have a winner. So crosswind avoidance is an alternative, when your destination can be flexible. I'm not loose, but I'm flexible.

These are a couple of ways to accomplish a crosswind landing.

Night Landing

To not run into anything but air is always our primary goal. The level of difficulty in accomplishing this is increased during nocturnal operations, as it's darkish out. On a truly dark and stormy night (cloudy, with no moon), you wish you were wearing NVGs (night vision goggles). Seventy percent of all Army Ranger operations are conducted at night (using *no* lights). Do all you can to protect your night vision.

Notwithstanding that, there are some distinct advantages to flying and operating by an airfield at night. There is usually much less air traffic, and it is far easier to see them, and them us. The wind is light or calm, normally. This makes for a nice, smooth ride. Many airfields have glide path guidance aids available (e.g., VASI, PAPI). If there is an ILS for your runway, then utilize that glide slope data to guarantee a safe arrival over the runway threshold. This is our night landing initial objective.

While approaching the field, look for the airport beacon. Small airfields can be difficult to discover particularly in well-lit, congested areas. Ensure the beacon is only flashing one white and one green light as it revolves. A double white and then a green flash indicates a military airbase.

Activate the REILS (runway end identifier lights), if available. Adjust the PCL (pilot-controlled lighting) to its brightest setting initially (seven clicks on the PTT), then dim them down when on final (three or five clicks). Otherwise, the REILS and the too-bright runway lights will flood the cockpit with white light at the worst time (landing flare).

Flying the ILS will prevent a landing at the wrong aerodrome, too, or on a taxiway (done that). Be cognizant of co-located airports with similar runway directions. Especially at night, it is easy to "latch on" to what you think is your runway. Freightliner pilots (B-747) have committed this embarrassing and potentially very dangerous mistake. A good preflight chart recon will alert you to this possibility. "Forewarned is forearmed."

Since most ground clutter (trees and such) is not lit, then we don't see it in order to be able to miss it. So we use glide path control guidance. We will still conduct a normal landing approach and will now aim for the painted touchdown stripes or the first third of the runway.

The biggest danger on final is to "scallop out" or undershoot. Don't do that. The best advice for a safe night landing approach is to execute an *immediate* go-around if the runway threshold ever disappears from sight. There is something (probably hard stuff) in between the aircraft and the runway, and you are getting ready to hit it. Go around now (full power and a Vx climb) and try again. Stay on or slightly above the normal descent path when on final at night.

In Kansas, if we couldn't get the airport personnel to sweep the runway, then we would drag the landing strip ourselves to frighten the fauna off their snug siesta spots. This is similar to the very low landing site recon pass that was discussed earlier. That's the best we can do to ensure the landing zone is open and clear.

Turn the strobes off at fifty feet AGL or higher. Turn the landing light on if it's not on already. Do a normal landing level-off and flare while closing the throttle and hold that pitch attitude (five degrees) until the mains touch. Don't overly flare at all. Let it land.

When taking off at night, note where the runway edge lights are in reference to your eyes. This is what they will look like when back on the ground. See those runway edge lights at your ten o'clock and two o'clock position in the flare and watch them rise as the plane settles in. Keep it over the landing area and land. Flaps up and brakes on to become cold, and there you are.

Airmail airports used big, wood-burning bonfires to illuminate each end of the runway prior to rural electrification. If one was too fast and high on final and slid off the end of the runway, it was said that he landed "hot." Be on your approach game for a dark landing episode, especially if it involves circling over remote terrain. Be able to fly a level turn without losing altitude. Hold the nose up while banked in a turn; don't let the nose drop in the turn.

Also, don't raise the nose *before* or *as* you roll. Resist this pitch-up at this time. Roll, then pull; bank, then yank. In that order. Only ten degrees or less of bank angle will require no yoke back pressure. However, the steeper the bank, the more the yank/pull (sixty degrees equals 2Gs). Keep your nose up in the turn.

A night circling approach in a remote hilly region is an emergency situation. I worked a restaurant chain owner's B-58 Baron CFIT crash that demonstrates this danger. The pilot inadvertently descended during a night circling approach turn in mountainous terrain and impacted while on the base leg to his home airfield. Also see the Hormel meat plant strike jet helicopter CFIT crash while merely performing/attempting a 180-degree reversal turn from low altitude. Don't hit the ground while turning around. "Try" equals attempt, but fail. *Do*, not *try*.

Old V-tailed Bonanzas had three spring-launched parachute flares (two-minute burn time) loaded into ejector tubes on the left side of the fuselage. The first parachute flare would be ejected while on the left downwind for an unlit night-landing spot. It would float down, illuminating the landing area. The second flare would be fired upon reaching the downwind to base turn location. The last flare would be launched once the airplane was established on final.

By now, the first flare had landed/extinguished itself (hopefully) and was not bothering the pilot's vision while looking down and ahead on final. The second and third flares were positioned beautifully (eight o'clock and six o'clock) to light up the landing zone while on final. Now, that's pretty neat stuff, but not a good idea during the dry season.

If using car headlights to light the runway, park them at the approach end, pointing the lights down the landing runway edges if there are two autos. Otherwise, light up the left half (not the middle) of the runway showing that edge to the pilot, with high beams on. The light source is now behind and to the left the aircraft, once over the runway, and won't night-blind the pilot or cause a shadow.

Searchlights did this for the Shuttle's (STS) night landings. Each of my seven MBTs had a 100-million candlepower xenon searchlight (infrared and white light) that could produce a 150-million candlepower output in "overdrive." With a combined illumination of over a billion candlepower (350,000 car headlights), you would be able to see that runway from space. Or there is this duller way.

The Piper Cub (PA-11) I learned to fly at night in had neither alternator nor battery (you hand-propped it to start it). There was a landing light, though, and it was powered by a ten-inch wooden propeller that was attached to the front of a generator that was situated between the main gear strut oleos. The relative wind would spin the prop and light the light. At idle power, and when slowed down to approach speed, the "light" was just a pale yellow glow. As the runway got closer, the engine would then be revved up to brighten the landing light (from prop blast), and then the power was reduced back to idle. You'd do this a few times on short final to see the lay of the land.

One of the worst of many possible worlds is a dead battery / no electrical power night landing. This is why the charging system is the second most important system on the aircraft when it is dark out. This is why there are three hand torches on board with extra batteries and bulbs. Holding your last burning match by an unlit airspeed indicator while on short final is what you are trying to avoid by having all these dead battery storage devices in the cockpit. Good thing you brought matches.

If your aircraft *ordinarily* has electrically powered landing gear, now it's going to be a manual-extension exercise. You will also be making a "flaps-up" landing, if they are amperage-activated. Therefore, hire a CFI and do a couple of practice night landings with no interior or exterior lights, and no flaps. While you're at it, turn off the runway lights, if it's a moonlit setting. At least you'll have done it now and know you can. With no flaps, the airplane has a much more nosed-*up* angle on final approach. Use the higher "flaps-up" Vref speed, if applicable (Thurman Munson's Citation crash).

By keeping very close track of the charging system throughout the flight, we can prevent all this effort and sweat. We know the low-voltage light works because it went out when the alternator was engaged after start. In a dark cockpit, you can't miss it. If it illuminates, then check the charging meter. If it is showing a discharging state, at night, then the price of admission just went up.

Turn the alternator side of the master switch off. Check all circuit breakers. If one is popped, then identify it. If it is your plane and it has never done that before, then re-engage it one time. If it is a rental/unknown aircraft, then do not reset it at all and go with it. Who knows how many times it has previously blown, and it may be now ready to *really* blow. Circuit breakers must be allowed to cool off (a minute or so); otherwise, they will not reset.

Begin shedding the electrical load by shutting down unnecessary equipment (e.g., ADF, interior lights). Wait for thirty seconds at least. Time it. It may just be an overheating problem. Let the alternator cool off. At night, we have almost everything electrical on, and the charging system is operating close to its limit of amperage output.

After half a minute, purposely re-engage the alternator switch (use the force, Luke). If on, good; if not, then new rules now apply. Turn the alternator back off. Look at the switch with a flashlight. Jiggle the alternator switch when you re-re-engage it once again and snap it right on. If you're lucky and good, it will start charging again. If not, then turn the alternator back off. And here's the new deal.

If in contact with ATC, then say, "ABC approach, this is Cessna 123, Pirep." (Pilot report.) This gets everyone to pay attention. Then tell them slowly and calmly that you are on battery power only. If stated too fast, there will be many "Say agains." Tell them your exact intentions—what airport and what entry pattern to what runway—so they know your plan in case all communication eventually dies. If there is any doubt, then say "Pan-Pan" three times (pronounced "Pahn," French for "a [mechanical] breakdown") over the frequency. Pan-Pan indicates an urgent situation, whereas "Mayday" stated three times (French for "come help me") means an emergency. Doing this guarantees ATC's attention and gives you priority handling if you need it.

Now shed the electrical load and turn off all nonessential items. I've had sixteen in-flight electrical charging failures over the decades (fortunately, none at night). There are a myriad of ways to fail a charging system ranging from a V-belt or wire ring connector breaking to various wires and nuts that disconnect or just a worn-out switch or alternator.

If everything is shut down and the master switch is turned off, then the battery will last for weeks. (After all, even after sitting all winter, it'll still start the plane.) If there is some distance to cover before reaching the airport, then see if you can just go "dark" for a while. This will save the battery so the gear and flaps can be lowered normally (electrically) at the end of the flight. Of course, this all depends on the ATC environment and traffic density. You will still be able to see the other air traffic, but you are "cloaked" and invisible to them.

This all assumes the charging malfunction was identified quickly. If this electrical deficiency is not realized until the radios begin to fade, then good night, Irene. Flashlight city. At least a low-voltage light can't be "sun-washed" out at night. Buy a volt meter that plugs into the cigarette lighter socket. Get the one that sounds a low-voltage alarm.

The more electrical items that you extinguish, and the quicker you do it, the longer the battery will last. A good battery should run one radio, a transponder (7600) and the red beacon for thirty minutes. Slow down (less drag) to lessen the strain on the battery when extending the gear and flaps. Lower the flaps to half first and trim to maintain a slow pattern speed. If the battery finally gives up the ghost, at least you have some flaps. The gear can still be lowered by hand. Now extend the landing gear, and hopefully there will be sufficient juice remaining to lower the flaps the rest of the way when required.

The above are night landing tips and techniques.

Go Around

If ever in doubt, then just go around and try it again. It is your *command decision* (the PIC is the final authority)—end of discussion. In a go-around, we are faced with transitioning the aircraft from a low-power, slow-speed descent to a maximum effort climb configuration.

We begin the go-around process with the throttle (that is already in our hand). Push it in all the way, nice and smooth, and "enrichen" the mixture and turn the carb heat off. Everything forward. Be careful pushing/shoving the throttle control forward too fast on a big piston engine, as it will flood/gag and deprive you of power right when you need max thrust.

I worked a Skyhawk go-around crash at Dodgeville, Wisconsin, where the 172 hit the very tops of the trees off the departure end of the runway. They almost made it. The upside-down cockpit showed that the throttle and mixture were full in, but the carb heat was still pulled out/*on* (a 10–15 percent power loss). If the carburetor heat had been turned off, they would have cleared the trees. In a go-around, everything pertaining to the engine is now pushed in (including the propeller control).

As the power comes up in the go-around, the plane will want to yaw left *and* pitch up to begin an inside loop, depending on how much nose-up elevator trim was dialed in. The newer airplanes have less trim authority, making it easier for the pilot to control a full power application pitch-up. My 1973 Skyhawk is a handful (or two) to tame with full power, max up-trim, and forty degrees of flaps. It would pitch up and loop over onto its back, if you let it. This is a go-around, not a bad air show.

We know that when power goes up, then the right rudder goes in. Keep the ball in the middle as always, especially now (low and slow). Let the nose rise to the horizon only, then stop it with forward elevator force. Now raise the flaps to twenty degrees or 50 percent. Do not raise them all the way (not yet), as we already know.

After this is done, remove some of the excess nose-up elevator trim, thus reducing the yoke/stick pushing effort required. As Vx speed is achieved, then pitch it up to ten degrees or less and clear the obstacles and fly the upwind leg to re-enter a normal traffic pattern. Leave the landing gear down. At one hundred feet AGL, milk up the remaining flaps and retrim it to hold this Vx/Vy climb attitude.

The sooner the pilot understands that a go-around is required, the easier and safer the maneuver becomes. If you are unpurposefully porpoising down the runway (PIO) or are already sliding/smoking the tires when you start this escape procedure, then it may be too late to salvage the situation. When performing this exodus plan, the sooner, the better.

When watching another airplane's approach, an experienced eye can see a go-around coming way back on the base-to-final turn (too high and too close in), particularly if there is any tailwind component on final. If the power is back all the way and the flaps are completely down and you are still high while holding a full slip, then what else can you logically do but go around?

Some common mistakes are not adding full throttle, not adding right rudder, and letting the nose climb too high. A killer mistake is to let go of the "answer," the throttle, and instead, reach over and raise the flaps. Really!? Only the gas pedal makes the car go uphill. Be able to do a go-around quickly and efficiently and practice this control flow regularly. Know how to play the "get outta jail free" card. When in doubt, go around.

Emergency Landing

This is where a pilot has to really be a Pilot. A go-around is no longer an option. It's called a *dead*-stick landing for a reason. This new action movie scene only gets one "take." Most of mine have happened at lower altitudes, where it was less than two minutes from the time the engine went quiet to touchdown. I've been lucky enough to have made it to a runway five times and a golf course once. However, one engine power loss did happen at FL060 while IMC (in the clouds) and over a foreign country. What makes the difference in my mind is decent living providing good karma (and a lotta luck). I'd rather be lucky *and* good.

From a throttle cable disconnecting, to a cam shaft gear failure, etc., I always happened to be at a point in space where there was a clear field landing option available. When I think back and realize that for the major portion (95 percent) of all those flights, we were over solid trees, and the power only happened to quit when we had a chance to go somewhere safe, then I realized that fate is the huntress. As far as I'm concerned, that's why it's important to always conduct yourself as a Sky Knight.

I once had an engine stop at night over Kansas, where there is an abundance of landing fields almost everywhere (good tank country). When I moved to Detroit, the company check pilot showed me the metro area in the dark and asked where I would go if the fan stopped. I pointed at a big dark, unoccupied area. The next day, we went up and I realized I had selected a high-power transmission line easement. Sparky. I don't fly at night in the NYC area unless I have to for a student lesson. Night's not nice when over densely populated neighborhoods.

If power is lost, then determine if there's time to troubleshoot the unsolicited shutdown. If there is, start from the left side of the cockpit and mess with anything pertaining to the engine. If you just did something, then undo it. Establish and trim for Vg, as we discussed earlier. Dead-stick landing is a misnomer, as our job here is to keep the joystick "alive" by maintaining glide speed all the way down. Don't get too slow and perform a self-burying dirt nap demonstration.

Check that the primer is locked in, or boost pump on, then try the L and R mag switch positions and leave it on the one that works best. Make sure the carb heat is on (whenever in doubt, carb heat *on*). Move the throttle and mixture controls to see if anything happens and select a different fuel tank (and leave it there; it may take thirty seconds, by certification code). Try pumping the engine fuel primer.

If it's still quiet up front, then "secure" the stove. We don't want the engine firing back up and then dying again during the forced-landing flare. Throttle back, pull the mixture out, turn the key and fuel to off. Pull the propeller control all the way aft to reduce the windmilling drag for the glide.

Also, reopen the throttle all the way (full forward) to reduce engine (compression) drag on the prop. Having the throttle open and the prop back results in an even better glide ratio. Or just stop the prop by slowing way down, if there is sufficient altitude and time available for this and you need the extra glide range. To induce the propeller to more quickly cease rotating, leave the prop control full aft (coarse pitch) and close the throttle. By the way, if you haven't stopped the prop and it's still spinning at the bottom of the glide, you can push the prop control in and close the throttle for a slight air-braking effect.

Leave the gear and flaps up. Squawk 7700 and make the "Mayday" call. Try to give a location and state your intentions. Most forced-landing scenarios play out as follows. The airplane arrived at the landing spot on altitude, but at too high an airspeed. Those pilots merely target-fixated on the touchdown point and dived down to it. After arriving there, they float down the entire length of the landing area and then crash into the trees at the very end. Even if they manage to get it on the grass field, there is little or no braking action and they still run out of room and slide into the trees. Ninety percent do this. Diving does you no good.

Instead, aim to glide to the "key position." This is where the downwind-to-base leg turn would occur in a normal traffic pattern. Depending on which side of the emergency field you are approaching from, make it a left or right base leg. Arrive at this key position with eight hundred feet of altitude and the proper glide speed. Now everything is back to normal. Just complete the pattern and land the aircraft like you always do. You practice this scenario all the time—no difference here.

Lower the gear and add half-flaps. Tighten all safety belts. Unlock and open the doors so they won't become jammed or stuck. Brief everybody on how to "de-ass" the aircraft after it stops and show them (by pointing) the rally point (RP) on the upwind side of the strip.

Trim to hold Vg, then Vref or a little higher speed, so there will be sufficient energy to raise the nose and stop the vertical rate for the level-off. You *cannot* stretch the glide. Don't get too slow and stall. Landing nose-up, you live; nose-down, you die. If you are not going to make the intended spot, then land as well as you can. Make it the best one you've ever done, even if it's into the treetops. If you added too much flaps too early, then take some off to see if that extends you a little. Wait to use full flaps until the "runway" is made. Forty degrees of flaps will make for a steep-approach angle with no engine power. Now, turn off the master switch.

If too high on base, then make that leg a little bigger by turning away some; S-turns can also be made on final to gain time to lose additional altitude. If low, then cut the corner and head right for the landing locale. You can always lose height, but you can't gain it. You are gravity-fed and air-cooled to the surface of the planet. Exploit your energy wisely.

The aircraft has "let you down" now, so if you have to sacrifice the airframe to maintain cabin integrity, so be it. Keeping the cabin in one piece is your ultimate objective. Go in between the trees and clean off the wings if necessary. Keep flying it until it finally grinds to a halt. Don't hit stuff with the nose; steer it around the obstacles. We can fix aluminum all day, and it's insured, anyway. So don't protect the plane—protect the people.

If there's going to be an impact, then make an effort to relax. A tight grip on the controls will break bones. That's one way crash investigators can tell who was flying. They have broken wrists and ankles. Loosen up like a drunk before a collision.

Once on the ground, use maximum braking and flight control displacement to stop. *Ta-da!* Get out now, particularly if there was an earlier fire or smoke symptom. Confirm that you are not on fire from *outside* the plane. That's why all are going to be gathered on the upwind side of the forced-landing area.

However, before the egress, as everyone is very excited, caution all to slowly and carefully dismount and just *walk* away from the craft. "Holy" Hollywood *always* has the air machine exploding at this point, but probably not in this script. If the passengers are not ordered to calm down and go slow, they will hurt themselves getting out and away. After a Helio Courier tail-wheeler chewed the tail off a parked trainer airplane, the student pilot in the trainer dismounted and ran away so fast he actually overran his legs, fell, and broke his thigh. So it's not over until your passengers, *Captain*, are outside and standing around safe and secure, taking selfies.

Normally, stay by the plane, activate your EPIRB, and inventory *everything* you have. An aircraft is hard enough to find from the air. A person walking is almost invisible to an air search plane (signal mirror). Make a big arrow pointing which way you went if the craft is abandoned. Find a stream and follow it downhill to civilization. Read a book about survival techniques and/or have one on board.

Studies show the pilots that have "made" it knew that it would work out. *Know* this. *Make* it work out. You will be too busy to even think about being scared. Keep working the problem and think a quick prayer. There are no atheists in the foxhole or cockpit. Good luck, Pilot!

Postlanding and Clearing the Runway

Since we have slowed to "cold" after landing, we can smoothly turn off the runway where we want. Notice all the black skid marks right before a runway/taxiway intersection. Those pilots were all moving faster that they thought and had to slam on the brakes to try to make the turn. Our airplanes can't maneuver like a sports car (on the ground, anyway).

If the turn is attempted at too high a velocity, the main gear tires could actually fold off their wheels. The taxi option is now over. If there is even more energy involved in this Le Mans change of direction, then the landing gear could collapse, particularly in a retractable-gear airplane. The gear is very strong, but it is not designed to take excessive side-loads and could be damaged. Be cool and get cold before the turn-off.

The "hold short" line is a "fence" facing the taxiway and a "wall" facing the runway side. "Hop the fence" and ensure the plane's tail is completely clear of the runway. Before the turn is begun, turn your head and make sure there's not a taxiing aircraft that could present a conflict at the intended turnoff intersection. Clear your turns even when on the ground. Give the tower a chance to tell you to call ground control. If the tower is busy, then just contact ground.

Taxi to Parking

On the way back to the tie-down spot or hangar, make sure the mixture is leaned one inch, as this is when the spark plugs will "load up" and will lead-foul. This will cause difficulties during the next run-up and can be eliminated by doing this slight mixture leaning during the taxi back to your "home plate." It is easy to let up at this point and reduce your concentration on what you are doing, but resist that temptation. Many strike their airplane's wing tip while taxiing down their own hangar row.

After a long flight, a Cessna 210 Centurion was shut down in front of its hangar and the pilot pushed the airplane back into its enclosure (that's what *hangar* means in French). Unfortunately, his Mercedes-Benz was still parked in the hangar. It cost more to fix the automobile than it did the airplane. It's not over until it's over. By *over* I mean not until you are safely home.

Be careful pulling in to your tie-down spot and watch your wing tips so you clear the fences, light poles, and other parked craft. Don't suck a tie-down rope up into the prop by using too much power. Be under control. It's better to just stop it when close, and push it from there.

Shut Down

Once we are stopped where we want to be, then it's time to turn off the fun fan. The last thing we should check before everything is turned off is the ELT. Tune a radio to 121.50 and turn the squelch to off. Now you know your "landing" didn't activate the emergency locator.

After doing that, we want to protect the electrical system here as we did during the start. Shut down all electrical items first. Avionics off, lights off, and master switch to off, too. Have a flow to do this.

Some leave the red flashing beacon switch on to remind them the master was left on once they are outside the craft. Since we flip the master off before we kill the engine, we don't have to do that. After all electronic items are off, then reduce the throttle to its lowest setting and rev down the engine.

After the revs are as low as they can go, pull the mixture to idle cutoff and listen closely to the engine. There should be a slight RPM increase just as it dies. The air/fuel mixture passed through the perfect stoichiometric ratio (14.7:1), causing the small rev-up at the very end. If that doesn't happen, then the mixture may be set too lean. Have it checked out by an A&P.

As we learned earlier, having the RPM at its lowest setting beneficially reduces the harmonic shaking of the airframe. There is also no need to rev it all up before we shut it down. Many do this (two thousand revolutions per minute or so) to burn any possible fouling off their spark plugs. We don't have to, as we leaned our mixture during the taxi, and we can therefore avoid superheating the stove right before we turn it off. Turbocharged engines and some jets need to "idle-dwell" for a few minutes to let things cool off first. Once again, time is relative, and that two- or four-minute cooling interval seems to last forever (like being in the dentist's chair).

An automobile engine is killed electrically. Some of its cylinders are still loaded (to fire), with unburned fuel. Since the car engine can't be moved by hand, it presents no inherent danger. However, an airplane power plant that was turned off that way (ignition key), as we know, is just a vicious trap. Remember, the three times the engine will be shut down using the ignition key are thus:

1. People (children) or an animal (dog) moving toward your whirling "wheel"
2. Imminent taxi collision
3. Severe engine vibration (prop tip separation)

Otherwise, always starve the engine by running it out of gas, using mixture control or fuel selector only. Now, if you hear a magneto impulse coupling make a loud "clack" noise, it will just scare, but not harm you. Store the weapon unloaded.

Post-Shutdown

Listen to the three gyroscopes as they "spool down" for those with a standard "steam gauge" instrument panel; these are the two air-driven ones (AI and DG) and the battery-powered one (TC). All three should sound smooth and take a while to finally come to a stop. The longer the noise, the better the bearings are. If there is a rough gyro, identify which one it is by touch and sound and think about getting it repaired or replaced.

Once the engine completely stops, then turn the ignition key to off and take the key out and put the control gust lock in place. Slide the seat back (think about the wind direction), open the door, take off your seat belt, and get out of the plane. The mission is not over yet, as the aircraft is still vulnerable until in its enclosure or safely tethered to terra firma. Key off and out, control lock-in, and tie down the plane.

Conduct a postflight walk-around, particularly if flying a helicopter. Touch any gearboxes that are reachable to calculate their heat and to identify any "hot boxes." If you can maintain fingertip contact, the temperature is below 140 degrees Fahrenheit. It's between 140–155 degrees Fahrenheit if it can be touched for a couple of seconds. If over 160 degrees Fahrenheit / 71 degrees Celsius, it will burn you. Tell maintenance about that gearbox, as it's going to fail soon.

Speaking of enclosures, *never* move an aircraft under a hangar door that is in motion. A Cessna 421 Golden Eagle was being pushed into the hangar as soon as the door was up high enough to clear the tail. The twin was about halfway into the bay when the hangar door "up-limit" microswitch failed. The up-door winch continued to operate and hyperstretched the support cables, causing them to snap. The very heavy guillotine fell and crushed the fuselage behind the cabin. Enough said.

Try to have a ground-guide helper if pushing the plane into a tight spot. This wing-walker can save the day. It is easy to concentrate on one part of the aircraft while another part impacts something. Trailing-edge damage to flight controls is expensive to repair. Watch the tips of the wings, tail, and rotor blades.

If the ambient noise level increases (e.g., a helo air-taxis by) while positioning the craft, then *stop* all movement and hold your position. If you can't hear the shouted warning or whistle from the wing-walker, then why have one? After the noise event has subsided, then resume movement. Always say yes to any that offer to help, even if you don't really need the assistance. If you say no, they will never offer again. Always offer to help someone else, as well. Pilots are part of the solution, not part of the problem.

Mooring

Electrics off, engine off, key off and out (and placed on the antiglare shield), control lock in, then tie down the plane. Say and do this every time. Once lashed down, the aircraft is then, and only then, secure. A flight school trainer had shut down and all were gathered around the plane to congratulate the "soloed" pilot. During the celebration, a large aircraft taxied by and blew the plane into a ditch. Tie down the plane, then party.

Do not use manila, cotton, or hemp rope to moor the airplane. This kind of rope will shrink when it dries after being wetted (a windy rainstorm). This drying/tightening rope could damage the airframe, especially if it was tied too tightly to begin with. The twisted polypropylene water-skiing-type rope is too hard to work with and untwists and unravels too readily.

Use nylon rope, as it has some give under a load (one-third) and will not shrink after becoming wet. I prefer the one-half-inch double-braided nylon rope. Nylon won't rot and is UV resistant. Get white-colored rope to enhance this UV protection. "Whip" (a knot) the ends or tape and melt the frayed end part so it won't slowly unravel. Tape the rope before you cut it and make the cut in the middle of the taped section. Then melt each end so it can't fray. Don't get melted nylon on your skin, as it will burn you. (That's why you don't wear synthetic clothing.)

To secure the "standing" end of a rope to the ground attach point, use two round turns and two half-hitches for that "anchor" knot. The "hurricane hitch" is the standard knot to use for the aircraft mooring rings. A double hurricane hitch will hold the devil. Be careful with the "working" end of the rope when pulling it through the tie-down ring so it doesn't flip you in the eye or crotch area. Owie.

As I learned during the mountain phase of Ranger training, anyone can tie a knot. The trick is, can you untie it after it has been under a load? I tie a half-hitch knot at the bottom of the second hurricane hitch to protect that knot from accidentally untying. Tie the rope so there is little free (working) end slack left over. A few feet of rope hanging down could whip around in a storm and lash the air machine (bad for the plane's morale). I also tie the "Remove Before Flight" streamer onto the Pitot tube cover for the same reason. If that banner is allowed to dangle, it will leave red stains where it whips that wing section in a windstorm.

We tie the plane down by securing the upwind wing first. Then the downwind wing and the tail is secured last. Once the wings are tied, then thread the tie-down rope through the tail tie-down mooring ring and pull the whole plane backward with the tail rope. Always exhale upon exertion, especially if doing this by yourself.

By parking the aircraft in this manner, the ropes form a triangle from the ground to the plane and the airplane cannot roll forward or backward. If the airplane is too far forward on its spot when it is "secured," then the tied ropes may look tight, but when the craft rolls aft in a storm, all three ropes will then be loose.

Once the aircraft is tied down, you can finally relax. Your main pilot jobs are now accomplished. Install the rudder gust lock. Leave the cowl plugs for the very last thing to do. Let the stove cool off for as long as possible before you plug up the air venting holes.

If it's parked outside, put the windshield visors down to block some of the sun. Put a white cloth or sun cover (nonreflective) over the antiglare shield and instrument panel to shade it from the sun. A reflective cover just fries the inside of the Plexiglas windshield. As mentioned, ensure all glass is clean if using an outside cover. Put the sun covers on the tires and make sure they reach all the way to the ground. If only one side of the plane is primarily exposed to the sun, then bias the sun covers for that light angle.

My nose tire inner tubes were rotting at the valve stem area. We believe we solved that rot problem by reversing the wheel/tire so the valve stem is now on the sunny side and can't stay damp like it did on the shady side. If your tie-down spot occasionally floods a bit, then put boat trailer bearing grease in your airplane's wheel bearings. If you hear loud squeaking or squealing from the wheels as you taxi, then stop or get ready to pay for new bearings—as they're saying, "Oil [grease] me."

Close all air vents if leaving the plane overnight. I saw a Skyhawk cabin that was filled up with snow (to the headrests) after a blizzard had passed (same Goodland, Kansas, windy flight). Dirt, grass, and bugs are also blocked from entering when all the vents are tightly closed. Make one last check of the cabin before closing the door. Does everyone have their phones and camera accessories? Got the headsets, keys, and everything else that shouldn't be left in the aircraft?

Hide the seat belt buckles under something that will block them from the sun. These seat belt metal attachment points get too hot to handle if left on the seat in the sunlight. Be careful leaving any delicate electronic gear in the cockpit, as the greenhouse effect will bake them. Never leave a clear water bottle in the aircraft where the sun can get to it. The sunlight shining through the water in the bottle can focus the light like a magnifying glass and actually start a fire in the cabin and possibly burn the plane down. Good luck figuring out the cause of that occurrence.

As you walk away from the aircraft, turn around and look at it closely to ensure all items are accomplished and everything is secure. Look at it like a scanning laser. Don't miss anything. This way, you will not have to worry about the machine during a storm as you confirmed all is copasetic.

Going Home

Now begins the most dangerous part of the sortie. Once we cross from airside to landside, we are on our own. You will now have to drive on the roads with the 99 percent. Good luck! Drive fast. Take chances. It's still not over until you're home. And there's no place like it.

Emergency Procedures

Write your aircraft's various POH/AFM emergency procedures on separate three-by-five-inch index cards, shuffle them, and keep going through them until they are memorized. Read, write, and rehearse while in the cockpit. It's not rocket surgery. If you understand the aircraft's systems, then it is all very logical.

Flying is very easy when the weather is good and everything is working. We earn our pay when something goes awry. Normally, there is time to analyze the situation in order to rectify the malfunction. I've been on plan G and plan H a couple of times before the situation was resolved. Don't give up. *Surrender* is not a Ranger word!

Once, in an A-36 Bonanza, the electric and manual landing gear extension systems failed. It got real hot in the cockpit, by the way, and the heater was *off.* Plan F was positive Gs to try to lower the gear, and plan G was lateral Gs, but to no avail. Inspiration is when I tried plan H of negative Gs, and it worked! Try everything. Why not?

I've seen planes with their main gear down but the nose gear is still cocked back at a forty-five-degree angle due to the slipstream airflow preventing it from swinging forward and down-locking at flying speed. To get it to swing forward and lock then land on the mains in a soft field configuration and hold the nose off the runway with back yoke pressure. While rolling like this and still holding the nose up, quickly jab the brakes on and off. That fast braking action may cause enough energy to swing the nose gear forward so it can lock in place. There is less airflow at this slower speed. I've been in formation with gear-problem airplanes a few times, and that's what I tell them to do with a situation like that. It works.

If landing on the belly because the gear won't extend, then do it on the runway. Don't land in the grass, as it's more unpredictable. If

STEPHEN M. LIND, JD, ATP

the runway is "foamed" with fire suppressant, then try not to "float" over it in the flare, like almost all do. You're in ground effect lower than ever before. Undershoot the foam and try to slide into it (Safe!). Make it one of the best landings you've done.

The *worst* emergency would be an in-flight fire, an aviator's nightmare. Secure the power plant, as we learned in the "emergency landing" section, and dive to increase the airspeed to try to blow the fire out, by hopefully making the air/fuel mixture too lean. Rudder yaw/slip the plane to keep the flames away from the airframe and, most importantly, the cabin. Be careful opening any windows or vents, as that may exacerbate the crisis.

When the cam shaft gear failed in my Debonair engine, the cockpit filled up with blue/gray smoke that was so thick you could not see the person in the right seat. In that situation, the vent window cleared the smoke out, as we were not actually on fire.

There is no such thing as friendly fire, so land *now*! Do not try to make it to an airfield unless you are over it. *Land now!* I worked a Beech 18 in-flight fire case where they tried to make an airport just a few miles away. The left engine fire blow-torched through the wing, causing spar structural failure while en route to the nearby airport. Unfortunately, the pilot was transmitting when it happened and held the PTT in all the way down (horrendous). Got it? Land *immediately* if you're on fire.

In any situation, if only a rough field is available, still lower the landing gear. It used to be taught that the gear should be kept retracted if landing on unimproved terrain. The problem was that the airplane's occupants would end up with broken backs due to a lack of shock absorption when the belly of the plane touched down too hard. So unless you can land lightly, like your life/spine depends on it, then lower the gear and rip it off on the rough field to help cushion it on and to slow down faster. The aircraft's job, at this point, is to sacrifice itself in order to protect the cabin (inhabitants).

Hopefully, you have memorized the emergency landing procedures. If there's time to get the checklist out, then do it. Make certain the wings are level with the surface as you approach. Do not catch a wing tip and cartwheel. Really not good. Make the crash landing last as long as you can. The faster the deceleration rate (stop), the more likely there will be injuries.

A boating friend once said he thought that flying over the water was less dangerous than being on the water. I agree. We are like a submarine (*supra*) and cannot be capsized or broached by a wave and thereby swamped and sunk. I mentioned that if *his* motor stopped, however, he gets to just merely float. We don't have that option. In boating, you can also pull off to the "side of the road." It's only two-dimensional, anyway (no offense). I had the absolute privilege of getting to pilot an airship for almost two hours, and even though blimps can definitely "float," they will not float indefinitely after engine power failure.

If something egregiously outrageous does happen in the air, we will end up on the water, just like the boater, only without a paddle, and the *on*-the-water part won't last long unless the airframe is full of ping-pong balls (e.g., C. Lindbergh's Lockheed 8 Sirius).

In an airplane (Land or Sea) water landing, leave the land gear up and clean. Study up on how to read the current, wind, waves, and swells to know which way to go when ditching. Know this if you are over wa-wa regularly, or even otherwise. (Not such a big deal in Kansas and Illinois.) Wedge open the cabin doors and have the flaps full down on the approach to a wet splash-down and flare and go level as low as you can over the surface.

Then raise the flaps and let it plop or skip it like a stone onto the surface. By having the flaps retracted, it will reduce the submarining effect by not having them dig into the water and pitch the nose down too hard. The more skips you can get out of this stone, the better the outcome.

If you are wearing PFDs, do *not* inflate them until you are out of the aircraft. We fly over the Great Lakes and carry a CO_2 canister-inflated four-person raft (thirty-three pounds). If something that can almost explosively inflate is ever in the cabin, then have a sharp knife available that you can use to stab it should there be an unexpected deployment. An inflating raft could overwhelm the cockpit, thereby preventing flight control operation. It's been swell, but the swelling must go down.

Operating an engaged three-axis autopilot can present a significant danger if there was ever an inadvertent nose-down trim runaway excursion event. It's outside loop time (about one-half, anyway). Grab the elevator trim wheel to stop it from moving. When the nose pitches down and you automatically pull back on the yoke, then George may not be able to be disengaged, as it's now been "locked up" by you pulling back on the yoke so hard. If you release any pressure, then the nose will tuck down even more severely. You cannot physically win this battle. Even with both feet up on the instrument panel and pulling with both arms, the trim tab is stronger than you are. Always know all the different ways to kill "George." If all else fails, drop the gear, disengage the A/P circuit breaker (practice that), and if all *else* fails, then master switch off.

Here's a final fallback option that I came up with. Cut the power and do half an aileron roll. The downward-diving outside loop will transform itself into a climb (inverted), and the yoke pressure can now be released, allowing the autopilot to be disconnected. Perform another half-roll to recover (see "upset recovery"). What else can you do, and what do you have to lose?

Thunderstorms

These are killers. Unfortunately, I have flown through two of them, and there are no rides like that at any amusement park. The rain is so loud it sounds like you are flying in a waterfall. Adjust the panel lights to full intensity, as the lightning strokes will flash-blind you. Look only at the instruments (it's like mountain climbing: don't look down or out—too scary).

Slow the aircraft as described before. The autopilot has probably already disengaged on the first air-jolt; if not, then A/P off, establish and trim for Va, adjusted for the actual gross weight. Maintain a level attitude. Don't worry about the altitude. There's probably no one else in this T-storm with you. Sparks and rocks (hail) are what you are worried about, in addition to the attention-getting and potentially destructive turbulence caused by wind shear.

Tighten up your already-snug seat belt. You will still hit the headliner on occasion, but as mentioned, the headset will protect you some if it is properly placed on the top of the head. *My* storms were both of the imbedded type, and it was before affordable small aircraft radar was available.

Once in the storm, maintain your heading and hope you get spit out on the other side. Heading changes, and maneuvering just adds stress to the airframe, could cause vertigo, and may prolong the duration you are in the storm (hope it's not a squall line or a cluster). While in a *huge* updraft, my VSI was "bending the needle" pegged. I dropped the gear (never the flaps), reduced the power to idle, and pitched down fifteen degrees and took the ride *up*, until the time we encountered the *downdraft*. Where there is an updraft, there is a downdraft. If not at Va, my aircraft (a company Debonair) would have bent or broken while violently transitioning from 3,000 FPM up to 4,000 FPM *down* (headliner time).

Now full power was applied, the gear was retracted, and the nose was pitched up to hold the Va speed. The VSI was now maxed out going down, even though we were in a full-power Va climb configuration. Six thousand feet of space may get you out of the downdraft before there is no sky left. The stall horn was routinely chirping, and occasionally, the bird's wings let go of the air and then unstalled and kept plowing on. Just sit there, hold on, and stay cool. Bruises on your hips from the lap belt because of the severe turbulence are like scars; they're tattoos with a story. This gear-up-and-then-back-down procedure was done a couple of times, and *poof*, we were out of the storm.

Yellow rain depicted on color radar is nasty, but definitely stay out of the red (or worse color) rain. Also, do not fly under a thunderstorm even if you can see all the way beneath it. Downbursts can push the aircraft onto the hard surface.

The ATC radar wavelength, at that time, was not designed to "see" the small raindrops but instead scanned for much larger aircraft returns. It was not reliable assistance, though no fault of their own. This has been much improved since then.

Realize that weather radar reflects off precipitation-size drops (rain or snow), which may not be dangerous in and of themselves. A heavy, *non*convective rainfall is a free wash job when you fly through it. The danger is where the convective updrafts slide next to the downdrafts. Wind shear slices like scissors.

As a cumulonimbus storm vertically matures, it transports millions of gallons of moisture into the ether. All this water weight is being buoyed by the uprising currents. When the moisture's gravity weight overcomes these up-currents, then the down part starts (a mature T-storm). A shear zone boundary is so violent that positive and negative ions are separated and migrate to divergent areas in the storm cell. This causes an electrical imbalance, which ultimately results in a lightning stroke, which equalizes some of the ionic disparity.

If there is no shear zone, no co-located updrafts and down-drafts, then there will be no lightning (there are five kinds), and the green and yellow radar returns represent no danger. The weather radar return may show moderate rain (dark green / yellow), but it is benign if there are no bright flashes around. By the way, I am not advocating tempest penetration, and always maintain the ten-plus-mile minimum T-storm separation distance when possible.

This is why it is good to have a lightning detector on board. The radar shows the rain, but the lightning storm or strike scope shows the actual danger. If there's no lightning, then it's just a wet and bumpy/loud ride. Prior to onboard radar, the ADF (automatic direction finder) was used to "point" to a lightning cell by tuning it to the low frequency band. It worked. A thunderstorm "broadcasts" on all frequencies. That's why AM radio stations crackle when a flash happens. The ADF needle would swing in response to a lightning bolt and show which way *not* to go.

Onboard lightning detectors use this same concept to depict in which quadrant and at what intensity (pseudorange) the electrical outburst activity is occurring. This, coupled with the radar infor-mation, provides the most complete picture of what you are facing out there. The strike detectors are "real" time, but the radar returns played over the computers have a significant-enough time delay so as to be unreliable when you really need it.

Unless you have aircraft radar and a lightning detector actually on board (real time), then all that "seat-pucker" screen data is just old news. The above information is provided for avoidance, not penetra-tion purposes.

So see gray, turn away. See black, turn back. Don't mess with a thunderstorm, but if caught in one, now you can survive it. They scare the hell out of me, and I don't scare easily.

Icing

Ice is not nice. It is easy to have a non-habit-forming experience with this phenomenon. Icing is a *cumulatively* nasty thing, as it adds weight, reduces lift and thrust, causes drag, blocks visibility, disables systems (the radio antennae are now over an inch in diameter and may depart as they whip in the wind), and may ice-lock the elevator control, thereby limiting or preventing flying authority. All bad.

To help to understand this hard water, examine the differences between Celsius and Fahrenheit temperatures. Say, 0 degrees and 100 degrees Celsius indicate when water will freeze and boil, and the choice of those numbers makes sense. What's up with the integer choices of 32 degrees and 212 degrees Fahrenheit? Actually, and approximately, 0 degrees Fahrenheit is when *saltwater* (ocean) begins to freeze and by that scale, 32 degrees Fahrenheit is when (unsalted) ice *begins* to melt. Ahh.

Technically speaking, though, unfrozen water can be supercooled to negative forty degrees Fahrenheit/Celsius (same temperature) and even colder (negative fifty-six degrees Fahrenheit for pure H_2O) and still remain in the liquid state. Don't fly through the top of a stratiform or cumulus cloud if it can be avoided, as undercooled (another term for supercooled) water droplets can immediately crystalize/freeze on the airframe (freezing rain).

A big four-engine transport (DC-6) was flying across the Atlantic when the captain flew through the top of a lone towering cumulus cloud. All four engines immediately shut down, and down they went. Twenty thousand feet lower and at only five hundred feet AWL (above water level), they got things working again and stayed out of the tops (of the clouds and waves) after that experience. That's why an ice storm is so devastating, as these very cold waterdrops instantaneously freeze and stick to any surface. Instant ice cube.

In general, if the bottom of the clouds is gray, not black, then the clouds are less than three thousand feet deep. When the clouds are thicker than three thousand feet, the sunlight is absorbed and can't penetrate all the way through, and so the base will appear black. If the edges of a cloud are "fluffy" and ill-defined, it is composed of water droplets. If the cloud edges are sharp and distinct, then its droplets are frozen ice crystals.

So this is not the icing on the cake. Even in "normal" icing conditions, these deleterious factors are inextricably interwoven, as the extra weight and drag requires a higher angle of attack, which exposes more wing to the ice, causing more weight and drag, and so on and so forth. I see a trend developing. Turn the autopilot "altitude hold" option off, or it will stall you.

Being in icing conditions, particularly freezing rain, is an emergency circumstance. Perform the hardest maneuver known to pilots, execute the turnaround *now*, and get out of there. Pitot heat should always be on if in any visible moisture, no matter what the temperature (OAT) is. This heat keeps the pitot-static system "dry" in rain, as intense precipitation could otherwise overwhelm the tube opening. Have the defroster heat on all the way too, and you may have a little ice-free vision hole in the windshield to see through (tank driver).

If a possibility of ice is present, then have all anti-ice equipment engaged already. Warm up the wind (soon to be ice) shield in advance. To confirm that ice is slowly building up, look at the bottom of the windshield and the leading edge of the wings and horizontal stabilizer for evidence. If IFR, then immediately request a higher altitude from ATC. Climb while you can. If they can't approve it, continue the climb and advise them you are doing so anyway and explain why.

Go to full RPM on the prop. The faster the blades are spinning, the less ice can adhere due to centripetal force. Go to full power and start a gentle flat climb upward. The more the nose is pitched up, then the more underwing surface is exposed to the sticking ice. You can even deploy a couple of degrees of flaps to maintain this flatter climb attitude. Our goal is to ascend into warmer air or break out on top, where the ice will melt or slowly sublimate away.

If climbing on an IFR flight and you encounter an overcast, which may contain ice, level off just below the base of the cloud layer and accelerate. Leave all the power full up and wait until you're going as fast as you can, and then zoom into the clouds and quickly get the first few hundred feet of muck out of the way. If not picking up ice, you can resume the cruise climb configuration. Climb less steeply if there is accretion. Monitor the OAT regularly. If it is too cold or too warm, then ice won't form. (*Normally*, zero degree Celsius to negative ten degree Celsius / fifteen degrees Fahrenheit. It's still possible down to negative twenty degrees Celsius to negative forty degrees Celsius.)

Unfortunately, I've had a couple of inches of ice on a non-FIKI (flight in to known icing) airplane a couple of times. The stall horn had iced up and was inoperative (no warning now). I had to keep activating/pulling on the engine alternate air door with the mechanical T-handle, as even that anti-ice air intake was trying to freeze shut. I had to climb to seventeen thousand feet to get on top and finally get out of it. Thank God, as the Debonair wouldn't go any higher.

Ninety percent of the time, the airplane *can* carry the ice load. Fly as fast as you can and head to an airport with a long runway. The carb heat will probably have to be left on to bypass the ice-plugged air filter, allowing the engine to continue running, albeit with less power, right when we really need more. Only make shallow banks and be very smooth on the flight controls and exercise them regularly to prevent ice-locking. You are a test pilot, as no one has ever flown a wing shaped like yours is now.

If there is a vibration up front, the propeller may have asymmetrically shed some of its frozen load, causing the shaking imbalance. Vary the RPM smartly and see if the rest of the ice will come off the other blade(s).

While on top of a solid deck at eleven thousand feet approaching Atlanta in a Debonair, the ATC SIGMET (not AIRMET) warned of severe icing in the area. Great! Twice, ATC tried to get me to descend and fly around in the ice, but I rejected both of those clearances. We *are* the final authority after all.

I requested a descent that would get me through the mile-and-a-half-thick ice-laden clouds (three-thousand-foot ceiling that day). I advised I would vector if required so the descent could be continued until breaking out of the bottom of the overcast. Once cleared, I went down to the tops of the clouds and leveled off and slowed. I turned on all anti-ice items (defrost and Pitot heat) and dropped the landing gear and lowered half-flaps for maximum drag. I mildly stalled the plane just above the cloud deck and lowered the nose and dived in. What a rush! The speed quickly increased and was maintained at the maximum "approach flap" setting velocity, and down we went. The first thousand feet went by almost immediately. I broke out at the bottom and cleaned up the plane and completed the approach.

If you can go fast (two-hundred-plus knots) in the descent, then the compressibility of the air will increase the leading edge temperature a few degrees, which could be enough to de-ice/anti-ice the wings and tail. My planes won't go that fast (bummer). The approach part of an ice flight is where most lose control and crash (a quarter mile off the end of the runway, normally).

Slowly reduce power on final but leave some on. Perform a glassy water (no pun intended) landing. Do not use flaps unless you must, and then only what is absolutely necessary. Lowering the flaps will block and disrupt the airflow over the iced-up tail and may cause the tail to stall. The tail stall recovery method is to *pull* back on the yoke, not *push*, as in a normal (wing) stall.

The leading edge fillet radius of the horizontal stabilizer is much smaller than the wing-leading edge radius. This makes the tail more susceptible than the wing to icing issues (like stalling). Do not get too slow, test pilot. Use power and fly the ice cube onto the runway. Once confirmed down, then reduce the throttle to idle and get cold. You made it. I took a chunk of the ice home and put it in a large scotch and water.

Stay out of the ice or get out of it as soon as possible.

Loss of Control and Upset Recovery (Wake Vortices)

The best defense to these scenarios is to receive some basic aerobatic ground and flight training from a qualified CFI; it's money well spent. The aircraft doesn't care which way it's pointed, but you should.

As a general note, fixed-gear and retractable-gear airplanes accelerate from slow flight to redline (Vne) speed at about the same rate (power-off dive). A fixed-gear airplane can't really go any faster (parasitic drag), but one with retractable gear will keep on going to three hundred miles per hour and its destruction. Similar to a thunderstorm recovery technique, drop the landing gear and convert your bird into a trainer. Speed can kill more than time.

It's especially important, if "upset," to always sit straight and tall in the saddle, cowboy (no spurs), and don't lean away from the roll direction. If we roll inverted, are you going to stick your head through the floor? Be part of the plane so that your flying sight picture remains stable.

Don't think of the elevator as an up-or-down control but rather understand that pulling back on the yoke/stick moves the nose toward you and pushing moves the nose away. The rudder can act like an elevator if the plane is rolled ninety degrees onto its side (knife edge).

Some basic aerodynamics are that the airplane won't stall if it has flying speed and is within its critical angle of attack for that flight condition. It won't spin unless it is stalled *and* a wing is allowed to drop. If you are fast and smooth enough with the rudder, the airplane can be held wings level as it falls in a stall. Do that in an aerobatic airplane with a CFI. At any point, the back pressure on the stick can be relaxed and she simply starts flying again.

The order in which the flight controls lose their effectiveness as the airplane slows is thus: first goes the aileron, then the elevator, and the rudder is last. When flying speed is regained, they come back "online" the reverse way. First is the rudder, then the elevator, and finally the ailerons start working. So the rudder is more important than the ailerons are. Basic radio-controlled airplanes don't even have ailerons, and they fly just fine, if a little sloppy (really air-boating).

Especially when slow, pick up a dropped wing mostly with opposite rudder, not just the ailerons. This is important, as drooping an aileron on a very slow wing can cause it to stall first. Rudder usage avoids that problem. Tell your feet to wake up and step on the rudder pedals to fly straight.

An airplane can stall at any altitude, any attitude, and at any airspeed. You can stall it going straight down (if it doesn't break first). I've done over sixty thousand stalls or near-stalls. Thankfully, they were mostly landings. My kind of stall (three-inch AGL).

Tail-slide/whip stalls are prohibited in most powered airplanes as the violent swoop to the vertical nose-down position at the end of the tail-slide will literally *throw* the engine off the firewall (CG problem again).

I unintentionally did one in an aerobatic glider (thankfully), and the negative G *force* was unmistakably sufficient enough to break something heavy (like the stove) off a normal plane. Do not be going straight up, or even close to vertical, when you run out of smash (airspeed/energy).

As the aircraft ceases going up, *stops* (in midair), and then starts to slide/fall backward (a couple hundred feet), hold all the primary flight controls (yoke/stick and rudder) in their neutral positions as *hard* as you can and pray (say, "Oh, poop!"). Don't crack the whip (or plane) by never having the nose pitched up too high when it stalls.

Stalls and spins have to be performed for student and CFI applicant flight training, but I don't like it. I figured out why (besides being a scaredy-cat): pilots like being in control, and when you are stalled and (particularly) spinning, gravity and aerodynamics are in command.

In a spin, you are just self-loading cargo riding the downward helix. The three phases of a spin are incipient, developed, and recovery (hopefully). It may take a couple of rotations to really "wrap up" and develop into a very fast spin rate (blur). For example, a Super Decathlon does this.

When the spin recovery is initiated and the flight controls are where they should be, there is always a split second of *nothing happening*, and *then* it stops spinning (one-fourth turn or so in a trainer). However, you are so hyperaware that in that split second, you think, "It's not stopping." I hate that.

As a practical matter, even if you bailed out of the plane (jump to the *out*side of the spin), then how can you get away from the plane to pull the chute? During Airborne training, I became entangled with another paratrooper's chute, and you should know that it's hard to get away from something that's falling with you. So unless absolutely necessary, keep your airspeed up and fly smoothly on the controls, and nothing will ever happen LOC-wise. That's the best and safest way.

Basic spin recovery is accomplished by closing the throttle, holding the stick full aft, ailerons neutral, full opposite rudder (to the spin direction), and as the rudder gets to its stop, then briskly move the yoke forward to the neutral elevator position. Don't push the yoke too far forward, as you'll tuck under onto your back. Hold this flight control(s) position until the rotation ceases, then neutralize the rudder, or it will start spinning the other way. Start easing back on the stick to recover from the dive, using trim to help if needed. Do not add power until restored to a level flight attitude. Know and do what the POH says.

If the back pressure on the stick is released too soon, the plane will unstall and transform into a steep spiral, or if power is added too early, then the airspeed redline (Vne) could be exceeded. If ever going that fast, be very smooth (*smoooth* with three *O*s) on the controls or just use nose-up trim to slowly raise the nose.

Stall/spin training is learning what to avoid, *not* learning how to get into and hold a spin (two turns max recommended). Where I'm from, you do not do spins for recreation. Don't mess with a High-Performance/Complex hot machine, as it will bite you and go flat in the spin (usually unrecoverable). We don't want to ride this thing all the way in and buy the farm.

If spin recovery plan A isn't working and the nose is rising while in the spin, then the spin is becoming flat (less than sixty-degree nose-down by NASA definition). Try *everything* now, ailerons, power, move the seats forward, flaps, open the doors, and deploy the antispin chute. See what I mean? Pass. Make the spin aircraft preflight a very thorough one, concentrating on full flight control movement and no binding or catching/capturing, especially at the rudder and elevator control limit stop points.

Before flight instruments, the way the airmail pilots would get down through the clouds was to spin through the undercast and hope to break out in time to recover. Hard-core! If spinning in the clouds or at night and you don't know which way you are rotating (bad day at Black Rock), then check the turn coordinator and push the rudder on the raised-wing side of the miniature airplane symbol.

Unless the turn coordinator is mounted in the middle of the cockpit panel, the ball doesn't work correctly while in a spin. If this instrument is on the left side of the panel (six-pack), then the ball will always be out to the left side, no matter which way you are spinning. The miniature airplane shows the direction of the spin with its lowered wing and depicts the recovery rudder on the up-wing side. Push rudder *in* on the *up*-wing side of the TC; disregard the ball.

The original spin-recovery technique was to delay the forward movement of the yoke until the rotation had stopped and the rudder was straightened. When the manufacturers swept back the vertical stabilizer of the various airplane models for a sleeker, more modern jet look, they made them harder to recover in a spin. That's why they have such long dorsal fins.

A straight-tail plane will stop spinning and unstall with just a slight forward yoke movement because the vertical tail surfaces are still in free air and retain effectiveness. A swept tail now hides behind the horizontal tail surfaces when the nose is down seventy degrees and is rotating. This blanks out the free airflow to the vertical stabilizer/rudder due to the spin's rotational velocity.

This now-required, additional forward-yoke movement shifts the rudder area past the horizontal stabilizer and into free air (unblanks it). This is why the nose is almost straight down in a spin recovery in a swept-tail airplane. The reason the minimum altitude regulation is 1,500 feet AGL is to give you space for two more spins (600-foot loss/revolution) and a little room for recovery. Airspeed is life, and altitude is life insurance.

There are two additional methods that can be employed in an "upset"/LOC situation, such as one caused by wake vortices or violent turbulence. The first is PPRR and is translated as thus: P, power idle; P, push the yoke; R, rudder toward the horizon; and R, roll (aileron) toward the horizon. Returning the craft to straight and level is your goal. Power, push, rudder, roll—that's the mantra.

The second technique recommended by a champion aerobatic pilot is to "freeze" all the flight controls in their neutral positions and hold on until it stops gyrating, then PPRR. This is all you can do if there is no discernable up or down and you really don't know what the aircraft's doing right now. Any control input by the pilot could very well accentuate this already-serious, whirling predicament. By tightly holding everything in the middle, with the power at idle, of course, she should straighten up and fly right.

If ever inverted for whatever reason, always recover by rolling, not pitching, back to upright. Do a half-aileron roll. Do not pull back on the yoke and try to do a split-S maneuver (half-loop), as your airspeed and the resultant G forces could break the plane. Roll out, not pitch down, to recover from upside down.

If you cannot recover or if something big broke, then de-ass the aerobatic vehicle ("nylon letdown"). There are cheap parachutes available, but the classified ad normally reads, "Used once, never opened. Small stain." Don't purchase a Maxwell House parachute ("Good to the last drop"). The US Army ensures high quality control of their parachute riggers (packers) by having them "jump" one of their own-packed, randomly selected chutes. Brilliant. Nothing like a motivated employee.

Having decided to depart the aircraft in-flight, keep your wits about you and move slowly and deliberately. The way to go fast is to go *slow*. An AD-1 Skyraider pilot friend related to me that his squadron commander made the pilots fully suit up and completely strap into the cockpit and then get back out. This drill happened before *every* mission.

He told me that when he was shot down at only five hundred feet AGL, it was that practice that saved him. Rehearse like you've never done it and perform like you always have. In any training session, strive to do it the correct way. Practice may not make it perfect, but it does make it permanent.

When getting *out*, jump/dive toward a wing tip in order to clear the tail and delay opening the chute for a few seconds to gain parachute deployment clearance from the aircraft structure. Can you imagine what this would be like?

However, the basic deal is, if you take the aircraft out, then you should also bring it back. I'm going to skip the various parachute landing fall (PLF) methods for dealing with landing in trees, water, or wires. Do your aerobatic training over parachute-landing-friendly terrain (e.g., open fields, sod farms) and know how to do a PLF on the drop zone (DZ). Don't pussyfoot when pulling the parachute deployment D-ring. After pulling it using both hands, hold on to the handle, as they're not cheap (kidding). Rehearse that parachute "open" move on the ground while wearing the chute (don't "pop" it for real, though).

There are other ways to become "upset," too, and as we learned in the "taxi" section, there is always a danger when Small and Large aircraft mix; this is even more dangerous when we are unhooked from the ground and up in the air, flying. The ideal way to deal with a wake vortex hazard is to, of course, avoid the wake. Review AIM on this subject and be able to visualize this invisible but present hazard.

Wake vortices descend (600–800 FPM) and always travel downwind. Observing the two-minute wake turbulence subsidence time is prudent. Wake vortices are caused by lift generation. This wake phenomenon begins when a helicopter's main rotors curve upward or when an airplane's nose gear lifts off. A large airplane is still creating thrust turbulence on the takeoff roll even before the plane rotates.

Finding yourself in a "horizontal tornado" has you now starring in a double roll in this new action movie scene. Cut! If that happens, then maybe go with the roll instead of fighting it. Keep the nose up as you roll around, by using top rudder and elevator. Once clear, then PPRR.

If taking off or landing and the runway is wide enough and when the crosswind is strong enough, we can stay on the upwind side of the wake path and out of trouble both in leaving and landing. Go further into the wind after airborne and stay there until clear. The departure and approach paths are flown on the upwind side of the jet's path.

We can stay above their glide path on final as large airplanes are only at a flat, three-degree descent angle on a stabilized approach. A wake vortex descends because it is denser (heavier) than the surrounding air and is initially shoved downward by the wing itself, similar to a boat's wake, only invisible.

If in a light aircraft that is landing on a perpendicular runway to the jet's takeoff runway and the wind is blowing down your runway, then his wake will eventually flow to you. Be prepared—it's coming. My student and I landed a tail-wheeler in a similar circumstance. The jet's nose went up (rotation is when the wake begins) just before the runway intersection. The student was slow on retracting the sixty degrees of flaps, notwithstanding my reminder, and the jet's wake picked us up vertically into the air about fifteen feet. Oh, boy! I gave him a split second to apply full power and then did it myself, and it was a very mushy go-around initially. Be able to *see* the air and be prepared.

I hit the top of a large helicopter's wake during a night landing once, and it felt like a solid object. These wake vortices continue until an airplane derotates. The mains touching down means nothing, as wake is still being generated. Watch for the smaller puff of blue smoke indicating the nose tire is down. Even when the nose is down, there still is jet blast present.

So stay in clean air, above and upwind. Face piles of trials with smiles and don't get upset.

Hijack

Be careful who you have in the cockpit with you. Trust your "spider sense." If it happens on the ground, then crash his side of the airplane a little bit during the takeoff roll. Being in flight provides some maneuver options (also squawk 7500).

If the perpetrator is not wearing a seat belt, you can shove the yoke forward and hit him with the aircraft's ceiling and knock them out (or snap their neck). If he is wearing a seat belt and you can reach it, then distract, unbuckle, and shove the stick/yoke forward. There's only one rule here: No rules.

If he is sitting next to you, then a sharp elbow jab to the side of the head at the temple will disable (render unconscious) or, if done with sufficient *force*, kill. Move your arm with the speed of a "startle reflex" (see *Hikuta*). These hijackers are just *kamikaze*-type killers (no offense to Japan). This isn't TV. Take them out hard, just to be sure. *Their* mission failure is *your only* option, hero pilot.

Cold Weather and Snow Operations

I'm from Wisconsin, and I oughta know (old beer commercial slogan). When it's below twenty degrees Fahrenheit, the main trick is to free the craft and get it started and warmed up, which can be a major project. Unfortunately, I endured Arctic conditions training as an Army Ranger (nylon pup tents at negative twenty degrees Fahrenheit) and learned how "cold-brittle" man-made things can become. The M-14A1(E2) rifle *wood* receiver stock was always impervious, though (but not in hot/humid), and that was about it. Not much is invulnerable to extremes.

Here's a trick: put a drop or two of car gasoline in your survival weapon gun oil, and it won't freeze and lock the bolt/slide action in *situ* (otherwise, it's just a single-shot bullet launcher). It's an old Russian Army trick that works all the way down to negative forty degrees Celsius/Fahrenheit. Jet fuel doesn't like severely cold temperatures, either. To thin the now-thick jet fuel in the extreme cold, a mix of kerosene (jet A) and avgas (up to 25 percent) had to be employed. Don't do that with a diesel engine (never add gas to diesel fuel). Fortunately, avgas has no jelling issues with the cold.

The thin metal and plastics of an aircraft become very sensitive to any abuse in the harsh cold (I'm the same way). Be very gentle with everything, or it will crack or break. A frozen door lock can snap the key off in the lock. Now what?

Remove the wheel pants during the winter to prevent ruining them. After flying a blood resupply mission during a snowstorm at night for the Red Cross, I found the wheel/tire fairings to be damaged and cracked from all the deep snow that we plowed through.

When it comes to snow, no matter how fluffy, it will *not* come off the aircraft during the takeoff roll. If a launch is attempted, then you are now a test pilot again, as no one has flown a wing of this specific camber shape. Much more importantly, the aircraft will not fly. Unless you abort the takeoff in time; you're going to be sliding off the end of the runway with some snow still on the wing.

Because of the airflow pattern around the top of the wing, the snow will merely air-sculpt itself into an un-airworthy shape, destroying your lift. All the snow must be completely removed; ideally, the craft would be placed in a heated hangar for a couple of hours. Don't use hot water, as it just refreezes somewhere else. Hoar frost can be polished smooth with a towel (rubbing it in circular motions) or can be removed chemically using de-icing fluid spray.

Ensure that the wings, and particularly both the horizontal stabilizer and elevator, or ruddervators, are smooth and clean. The wings must be contaminant-free from at least the top of the main spar, around the leading edge, to the bottom of the spar underneath. At the *very* least, the front half of the wing must be perfect. There was a report in which a lightweight experimental aircraft put a decorative pinstripe paint line down the center of the wing leading edge, and it disrupted the airflow sufficiently to prevent the aircraft from flying. It does not take much.

After a heavy snowfall, the planes parked outside will be unbalanced so that they are sitting on their tail tie-down points. The nosewheel is way up in the air (hyperrotated). This is why we secure the machine with tie-down ropes that stretch a little. Use this tail sit-down stance to your advantage. (Hi-ho, Silver (snow), away!) The difference between winter and summer is at least you don't have to shovel heat.

Start by removing the snow up front on the top of the nose cowl and shed the weight there; we want the plane to remain sitting on its tail tie-down ring. Very carefully, remove as much snow as you can from the windshield, really trying not to touch and scratch it.

Next, use a push broom to shove the snow off the wings first, before doing the horizontal tail. The wings are tilted up now, and most of the snow can be easily pulled back and off the trailing edges to fall down into your boot tops. Careful with the antennas and the paint job so no damage is inflicted to the air machine's outer surfaces.

I have my outdoor-parked airplanes waxed during the late fall to aid the snow in slickly sliding off, sometimes all by itself, creating a beneficial "avalanche," allowing for self-shedding snow removal if the conditions are perfect. Nice option!

It helps a lot if the airplane is moored with its tail pointed toward the afternoon and evening sun during the winter season. This orientation promotes this self-sloughing action. In a perfect world, we would schlep ourselves out to the aircraft right after the storm and move the snow right away. When shoveling, switch arms so that your body can be symmetrically sore the next day.

If it is really cold out, and therefore dry enough, a leaf blower could do the trick and merely puff the powder away. The longer you procrastinate about cleanup, though, the tougher it will get, especially after a couple of freeze/thaw cycles.

Once the wings are free of snow (as much as possible), then go down the dorsal fuselage and clear it of snow, watching out for the ELT whip antennae. Back at the tail, which is still adhered to the ground, ensure you don't step on it, as it is buried in the snow and hidden from view.

Walk well around it and dig down carefully to confirm the elevator trailing edge isn't frozen to the ground. If it is, carefully chip it free. The colder it is, the more numb and dumb our brain becomes, so stay "cool" and watch your step. Once the tail is unstuck, and as the snow is removed from the tail plane, it will "jump" up, and the nose tire will self-land. Be ready for that jerk movement.

We still have to dig it out of the tie-down spot. If the ramp in front of the airplane has been plowed, then only narrow snow trenches have to be dug in front of the three tires. Clear three straight snow-free lanes for the tires—just a snow-shovel-width wide is fine.

Once free, move the plane around so the sun strikes it at different thawing angles, making it easier to clean those now-warming surfaces. If no preheat is available, then angle the plane so the sun shines on the engine block if the cowl can be easily opened to allow for that. After a big storm, it may still be cold out, but the freshly scrubbed air makes for very intense sunshine. Exploit that *free* solar thermal energy. It's the only thing warm around here, anyway.

If you have a non-south-oriented hangar door, then get on the snow-removal mission ASAP. If the solid moisture becomes a little liquid and flows under the hangar door and refreezes, then the now "undoor" is severely ice-welded to earth. If the forecast is for continued cold, then Pegasus is safely (and annoyingly) sealed in her aluminum stable for the duration of time that's it's colder than forty degrees Fahrenheit. At least the threat of aircraft theft or repo has been eliminated for now. An ice-bonded hangar door cannot be remedied without a supreme effort.

To not lose the use of your hangared craft for the entire winter, shovel the flakes away, right away following a snow squall. Leave a bottom-touching hangar door surface slightly open and off the ground. Don't close the door all the way if anticipating a snowstorm/ice storm. Place a couple of short wood blocks (two by two inches in size) symmetrically at the bottom edge to hold the hangar door weight at this slightly elevated level. This way, even if you don't remove the snow in time, its moisture cannot freeze the door closed for the rest of the winter.

When digging out the hangar, ensure there is/are drainage channel(s) dug that will direct any melted runoff away from the hangar. When sufficient water freezes on the hangar floor because it couldn't drain, the plane is now ice-chocked in its shaded parking place. Never use salt to melt the ice. Salt melts aluminum. Negative NaCl at an airport.

Slide your feet over a slick surface. A heel can slip out if you walk normally. Lean forward if walking downslope. Leaning back will allow your feet/heels to slide out so you fall on your butt. Lean backward, not forward, when going uphill, so your toes don't slip out and you fall forward. Turn your feet forty-five degrees, toes out, to "herringbone-walk" for better traction.

When pushing or pulling an aircraft on a patchy, slippery surface, be very careful of your footing/grip for each propelling step. If you are pushing hard on the wing-leading edge and slip, you can dent the wing with your forehead—always a nice touch. If pulling the land machine backward, then pick up your heels, not slide them, so they can't catch on something on the ground that you can't see and maybe trip you backward.

While pulling the Debonair out using the tow bar, I stepped on an ice patch, "lost purchase," and fell on my butt as the still-rolling nose tire was heading to crush my crotch. Bad James Bond movie scene, and highly embarrassing and painful, *inter alia*. I stiff-armed the tow bar and let the plane's momentum slide my bottom over the ice and stayed clear of the tire.

Another time, I slipped but twisted and caught myself with my right arm and dislocated my shoulder. That'll bring a tear to your eye. I had two very pretty passengers waiting, and they weren't watching, so I tugged/jerked the ball back into the shoulder socket and flew the "mish." Ow!

After the winter flight is over, with the plane now stopped in front of its spot or hangar, we have to move it. But even with a powered tow bar, it won't move onto its tie-down spot or into the hangar. Too slippery, so no grip. So now what? You've got a car to get home, right? Very carefully drive it to a couple of feet in front of the spinner at a perpendicular angle. Ensure the automobile transmission is in park, with the e-brake heartily engaged, and dismount without hitting the door on the plane.

Get in between the two machines, put your butt against the car, and push the plane back as far as you can without falling down. Move the auto again and repeat until the airplane is properly positioned for parking.

If your winters are like a bad "Dr. Chicago" movie, then anchor a tow-cable winch onto the rear hangar floor. Hook the tow cable, with a split Y junction, to the main landing gear using nylon tow straps. Watch your wing tips as always and merely winch the wench in.

Winter Cold Start

If the engine has not been preheated and the temperature is below freezing, then you are going to damage your power plant. Dissimilar metal thermal-creep growth rate is the reason. An aircraft engine is made of many different types of metals and materials. All these things expand and contract at different rates when heated and cooled. These various metals are all properly sized and fitting once the stove is at its operating temperature.

The problem is temperature-related, as the colder it gets, the more the metals are contracted and internally tight. The normal engine interior clearance tolerances will open up and return to normal as it warms up after the start. That warmup takes quite a few minutes, and this is when the cold-start scenario power plant damage is materializing, particularly right after she fires up.

There are several ways to accomplish the necessary preheat. *The Aviation Consumer* would be the reference source as to what to buy and how to use it. I have an electrical engine-block heater on the hangared planes, which I plug in the day before the scheduled flight. We don't fly the two kept outside if it is below freezing. It's just too hard on the old girls, and I'm too cheap to pay for an FBO preheat.

To properly use a propane-fired system, only set the thermostat as recommended (140 degrees Fahrenheit or less). If the temp is set too high (71 degrees Celsius / 160-plus degrees Fahrenheit), the superhot air blast could damage the cowling paint and melt plastic and other parts under the hood. I've seen them catch the heater hose and almost the entire nacelle on fire in an attempt to hurry the heating process. Now *that's* a preheat.

Replace the stock preheater hose with a four-inch aircraft-grade air duct hose. Hold your bare hand in front of the heater hose to check the heat level. If it is too hot for your skin, then reduce the burner flame/temperature, as it's too hot for the aircraft's skin too. Be able to hold your hand comfortably in the heated airstream to ensure it is not too hot.

It really takes about thirty minutes to do a proper preheat, and the discharge hoses should be shifted to different locations, including the underneath, to do it correctly. Most do it for just a few minutes instead of the half-hour and are merely going through the motions and just wasting their time.

Many pilots don't fly during the winter and are under the mistaken belief that by starting their engine and running it on the ground only (not flying), they are helping it. The opposite is true. When ground-bound, the engine can't be run hard enough, for long enough, to do it any good. And by doing that, additional damage is occurring also. When actually flying, the engine oil can properly get hot enough (plus-212 degrees Fahrenheit) to vent the oil's water vapor (steam) overboard and yet still not overheat the engine itself, as it is receiving its velocity air-cooling supply.

Piston engines convert air and gasoline into water, which is why a car's tailpipe drips. The Zeppelin airships captured the exhaust from their engines to supply pure (distilled) water for drinking/cooking and for droppable ballast (just five hundred gallons weigh over two tons). You can see the water ballast drops made by the LZ *Hindenburg* during the first-ever filmed crash sequence. Most of that water came from the engines.

The POH describes "long- and short-term storage procedures." Just do them. The prop can be hand-pulled through, five or six times every five or six days to try to impede the rust-formation rate. But don't start it unless you are going to fly it.

As mentioned in the "normal start" section, the colder it is, the more prime is needed for any piston engine. Here's a Northwood's way to do a cold start on a small piston-engine airplane. It takes two pilots, ideally, to do this, or at least someone that can pull the propeller through its cycle (but not to start it, of course).

Leave the tail tied down. The pilot in the cockpit leaves the mixture at idle cutoff and sets the throttle to a high-idle setting (one-half inch). The carburetor heat is turned on, and the primer is unlocked and "cocked" (pulled out). The ignition key is out and on top of the antiglare shield for all to see. Set the parking brake and have your feet on the brakes as well. It shouldn't start yet, but you can't be too careful when someone is moving the engine blades.

Have your well-instructed assistant pull the prop through a few times (normal operation direction). Order him to always stay out of the prop arc and to watch his footing, since he can hear the magneto impulse coupling firing every other prop blade pull.

He should remove all rings and watches and clean the spot where he will stand. Have him stop every couple of prop pull-throughs / primer strokes and have him look under the engine cowling. Advise your aide to advise you if there is liquid dripping out down there. This means you can stop priming now, as it won't hold any more fuel.

Shoot the primer in as he moves the prop and keeps pulling the prop through. You shoot a shot of prime for the number of cylinders in the engine (four or six) while the prop is being pulled through. Just so you know, there is a "long" stroke and a "short" stroke type of primer. Use the number of primer-pushes that are recommended in the POH for a cold start. Once it's all fuel-primed, have the prop-puller step well clear, hold the fire extinguisher, and observe the start.

You can leave the tail tied, as he is going to remain outside, manning the fire extinguisher during the actual start sequence. Once the stove is fired up, they untie the tail and carefully and coolly (prop-wind chill) get into the plane.

Prime it, get him clear, put the key in, make the mixture rich, and crank it. Leave the primer out and push it in as the engine is turning over. It should start. Leave the carb heat on, as it will help warm up the stove and reduce the chance of a carb air-box fire.

If necessary, keep it running initially with the help of primer stroking, then secure the primer. It is critical to keep the cold thing going, as if it dies now, the spark plugs may frost over and ice-bridge their electrode gaps. You're done for now (no more spark). No amount of cranking will activate it.

The plugs will have to be pulled and cleaned off. So once it's running, *keep* it running. Damn the RPM limit for now, and hopefully it's not your engine anyway. Business is business. Remember that we can tell if a small engine is warmed up if it smoothly accelerates with the throttle. The stove is not ready yet if it stumbles when power is added.

If the battery is low and the prop barely heaves, then try to let go of the key as the propeller stops and begins to swing back, and then hit the starter again using the prop's rebound energy to boost the blade rotation. That little extra prop swing could start it, if she was all properly gassed up for the cold, then bang, it starts! Otherwise, it's jump-start time, which can be even more perilous. Use POH!

If the engine backfires and a power plant compartment fire starts in the lower cowling area (from pooled fuel), then continue cranking and try to suck the flames back into the engine once it starts. A horizontal figure 8 is the arm and hand signal for (you're) "on fire." If it won't start and is still smoking, then turn everything off and extinguish the fire now. Don't miss with the mist.

Some cold-weather bush operators do the following to counter the effect of unforgiving winter temperatures. First of all, the aircraft (or a tank, for that matter) is parked on pine boughs or some other type of nonfreezing material (e.g., cardboard, wood planks). If the tires/skis/tracks rest directly on the snow or muck overnight, the machine will be ice-glued and become "one" with the surface and difficult or impossible to move (ice can be stronger than steel).

Right after the last flight of the day, the pilot drains the engine oil and places the oil bucket next to the woodstove inside the "hooch"/cabin. The aircraft is tied down, and nylon wing, nose, fuselage, and tail covers are affixed. The prop even has blade bootees that are slipped on and secured.

In the morning, besides unmooring, the drill is to remove the protective snow/frost covers and perform the preflight and get everything ready. The last item is to pour the oil back into the engine and start it. That's one way, anyway, but it works and the engine starts at twenty below. A start is a start, but the hooch always smells like a refinery.

Taxi through the snow as described in the "soft field" section. Always maintain your momentum, but don't forget, you may slide on the stop attempt. Parking "by touch" is not the cheapest way. I once observed a ski plane slowly skid a wing into a hangar wall. You could see the pilot pushing the nonexistent brakes as hard as he could. The taxi, takeoff, and landing principles are the same in the snow and ice; it's just another soft field operation.

The cabin heat is provided by a heat-exchanger that surrounds part of the exhaust pipe. If there's a crack in that particular section of pipe, an exhaust gas leak could enter the cabin at any time, especially when the heater control is pulled on. Carbon monoxide (CO), an insidious, colorless, odorless, poisonous gas, will incapacitate the cabin occupants. Have a CO detector mounted in the cockpit.

Look at the CO detector regularly. If it has changed to a darker color, then check your fingernails. If they are turning blue, you are being polluted and are happy about it (euphoria is one of the first symptoms of CO poisoning). Turn the heater control off, engage the firewall cutoff control, if available, and open the vents and windows to get fresh air into the cockpit. If the pilot passes out from this exposure, then at least the toxicology report would reveal the cause of the crash. CO poisoning is an additional winter flying hazard.

Winter landings also present novel situations. I've landed on a *glare*-ice runway. Flying a Skyhawk from Manhattan (Kansas) to Wisconsin after an ice storm, I was confronted with the information that every airport within range was still "iced in." I chose Fort Dodge, Iowa, for the fuel stop, as its runway was best lined up with the wind and was slightly uphill, too. Stopping would not be the problem. Turns out, turning around was going to be the trick.

The runway wasn't very wide, and as advertised, it was a sheet of ice, slick as a curling rink. Trying a normal turn failed, as the change of direction ceased after about forty-five to fifty degrees of left-turn rotation, because the wind now hit the vertical tail and weather-cocked my ice-plane back into the wind. Hmm. I could see my left tire sliding in the turn attempt.

A seaplane turn combined with a serpentining path did the trick (correlation). I got the plane S-turning, back and forth, using the "brakes," rudder, and opposite ailerons, while being very careful to stay on the landing surface. It was timed so that as the tail started to swing to the right, I nailed left rudder, left brake, and full right yoke.

The combination of swaying inertia (similar to a shoulderless lizard's) and adverse yaw effect turned the ice-craft 120 degrees, but now I had to stop it at 180 degrees as it wanted to do a complete 360 (back to Go). The left aileron down (yoke right) input was held until the yaw rotation ceased at around 200 degrees and were then neutralized as we came back to the 180-degree/reversal direction. Left deployed, the opposite-facing ailerons would act like asymmetric sails too and increase our sliding speed. The left aileron being down helped the initial swing to turn around and also helped to slow the yaw rate as it came around into the wind from the back. Double duty.

The flaps had been left down for air-drag reasons, but I raised them during the course reversal. They would act like sails once I 180'd and would push me downhill/downwind on this slick strip even faster than I was now traveling. The brakes/tires were already "locked" the whole taxi/slide back down the runway.

The last thing I could do to slow down was switch the mags from Left to Right, back and forth, every few seconds, to reduce engine residual thrust to the absolute minimum RPM (not unlike approaching a dock during water plane operations). I kept the engine running, as it was the only thing around here that had any "traction" (air). I still had thrust and rudder/torque control.

I managed to turn off the runway and get on the hockey-rink-like ramp and stopped. If I had slid past the turnoff, I was going to nail the left rudder, give it a burst of power, and flip the plane back around into the wind. It's easy to do, as it wants to weather-cock by design, and stopping the rotation at the 180-degree reversal point is almost automatic for the airplane. I would then use power to taxi back in uphill and pull onto the ramp (plan B). Always try to have at least one fallback position in mind.

My "door-gunner" dog (Zelda had 1,500 hours) could not stand up on the ice. Her legs would slip outward, and she would slowly spread out until her belly touched the ice. The poor thing was dumbfounded. The taxi out and takeoff were easy (air traction).

The nice thing about an ice- or snow-packed, smooth, slick landing surface is that the airplane can be touched down in a crab during a crosswind. You don't have to swing the nose straight to line up the tires; they can just slide sideways now. Be careful, as you don't want to encounter any dry spots or bumps while you are slip/sliding away sideways.

An additional major snow hazard at airports are drifts, banks, and snowplow tailings. A low-wing airplane can "touch" piled-up snow, whether natural or man-made, and do major damage, as this "snow" soon transforms into frozen white concrete. We had to replace a Piper Cherokee's left wing that "clipped" (four feet in from the tip!) a snowbank during taxi. And that pilot hit the wing on his side!

During and shortly after a plowable snowfall event, be very alert approaching runway intersections, as snowplows may have, hopefully temporarily, left a bank of plowed snow across your runway. This stuff is *not* soft. A soft field becomes a Jersey barrier made of snow. This danger can be invisible during certain light angles, and it is also well-camouflaged.

At a small airfield, after landing the same type of plane (PA-28), I noted the narrow taxiway to the ramp was plowed. It was difficult to see the exact height of the side snowbanks, and I had been calling the UNICOM, asking if it was open or not. "Negative contact, out."

It looked okay, so away we went, and about halfway through, the higher drifts now lifted the airplane tires off the taxiway as we slid along on the snowdrift tops. We were skijoring on the outboard wing bottoms (no pitot damage risk), so the engine thrust was used to maintain our inertia (right rudder), and after twenty feet or so, we "landed" just as the UNICOM advised that the taxiway was indeed closed. "Roger." So it is possible to have more landings than takeoffs (not counting bounces).

Lastly, there's landing in unplowed snow a foot or two in depth. When I had to do it at a very tight airstrip in the Detroit suburbs, the runway's outline, and therefore its exact location, could not be determined. It was my home plate, so I had an idea where the strip was. The wind was blowing down the runway at twenty knots, so the Debonair would be nice and slow for this snow field landing. Gear down, flaps down, and as soon as touchdown, I added power to keep moving in the two feet of (thankfully) powdery snow.

I went off the runway a little, and as the right tire started to track down into the drainage ditch, the bottom of the right wing touched the snow, signaling an excursion. The wing slid along as before, and now I was landing "by touch." I corrected, added power, and kept going all the way back to the hangar. Soft/snow field taxi technique. Once "landed and cold," the taxi lane outlines could be seen. I had almost two inches of ice on the plane, too. There was a two-inch-long curly "pigtail" sculpture of ice still protruding from the spinner point (weird). Whew! Tough mission. I never tried that crap again.

When there are snowbanks plowed up around the tie-down spot, be aware that your horizontal tail tip cuts a big arc in a tight turn and can slice its outboard end into a mound of snow/ice. Thankfully, they usually aren't there most of the year, but that's why you don't think about it. Don't scythe the horizontal stabilizer into things on a tight turn.

If your tie-down spot is going to be unoccupied, then remove and stow the mooring ropes so the snowplow can't cut them up. When coiling rope or an extension cord or garden hose, *don't* coil it. Instead, figure 8 the line.

Coiling twists the stuff, and it is hard to unravel. By making a figure 8 pattern, this doesn't happen, and the rope, wire, or hose can be tossed and it will land straightened out and ready to go. As a quick aside, if throwing a rope over a cliff or wall, make four to five coils (not forty-five) in your throwing hand. Don't toss that like a purse; instead, throw it overhand like a football pass, and then lob the rest of the coil over the edge.

The above cold weather techniques work but are dangerous, so watch your step and always appreciate a heat source. Winter sucks!

Overview

This is the final test of a pilot's correlation ability and is a true story. A Shadow Traffic Cessna 150 is flying over the Hudson River one night when, suddenly, the nose pitches down a couple of degrees all by itself. When the pilot pulls back on the yoke, there is no change in pitch angle and the craft continues descending at a slow rate. The elevator trim does not change the situation either (time to check the heater control knob).

This aviator now has three minutes or so before he's swimming in the river. Besides making his radio calls, what should he do? Analyze the scenario. Adding full power merely increases the airspeed but does not alleviate the declining flight path (plan C). Let's think about this (while we have time).

Where is this problem most likely located? Since the elevator and elevator trim don't work, then look there. You can see out the back of a 150 (marketed as OmniVision), and you do have a flashlight, don't you? The flashing red beacon/strobes will also provide brief glimpses of this area. Look at the right-side (starboard) elevator, as that is where the trim tab is located.

Sure enough, there is a superhero (Bat type) kite wrapped around the horizontal stabilizer and elevator, "locking" the elevator and trim tab, thereby preventing their movement. I guess someone by the G. W. Bridge decided to fly a kite at one thousand feet over the Hudson. Trees catch kites, and I guess kites can catch airplanes. Two minutes left. What to do? Think!

How can we shed this impediment? Simple: just push a rudder, and maybe roll, too (both of those controls still work). But which one, and which way? You get one shot at this. Think it through. Roll to the right and nail the right rudder. The air slipstream, coupled with gravity, should work to make the kite slip off. At least enough to regain pitch control.

Even if the kite does not completely slough off and gets hung up on the outboard elevator control horn, the trim tab itself will at least now be unfettered. The airplane can now be controlled in pitch with the trim tab alone. It will work opposite of normal since the elevator is "frozen." Usually, a trim tab moves its control surface, and that flight control surface moves the plane.

In this situation, the trim tab is the new "baby" elevator and is what will pitch the nose. Dial in some nose-down trim to raise the pitch angle. Once you are back in command, you can experiment by using the flaps to establish what the nose does when they are deployed and ascertain if the ulm authority is sufficient to maintain stability. Think about how you are going to land. Land long so the kite can't catch on anything during short final. Use the same type of approach if landing with a hung advertising banner. If the kite stays on, you have a nice souvenir.

When this actually happened, unfortunately, our young flyer (not for long) never did any of this correlation analysis and had to swim to shore. Your knowledge and brain are your main weapons to defend yourself in all situations. Solve the problem if it's solvable, and always hang in there, Pilot.

Now embark on your aerial adventures. *Bon voyage!*

Credits and Acknowledgment

Obviously, I have shamelessly stolen knowledge from all that I have had the privilege to meet and learn from. We are all merely the sum of our memories, so it is impossible to list all those from whom I have gleaned knowledge and wisdom. One cannot be all-inclusive, and I don't want to be guilty of inadvertently excluding anyone. So thank you all for the many lessons learned.

Johnny Hatz (Hatz Biplane) was my initial instructor and must be a Master Angel by now. My commercial airplane and helicopter CFIs had each flown in three wars (WWII, Korea, and Vietnam) and were amazing in their flying and teaching abilities. Thanks to all my other CFIs, too.

I always tell my students to read Wolfgang's *Stick and Rudder* book (few do). Additional volumes I recommend are *Taildragger Tactics* by Sparky Imeson; *Stalls, Spins, and Safety* by Sammy Mason; *Roll Around a Point* by Duane Cole; and anything written by William K. Kershner. Read the classics, like *Weather Flying* by Robert N. Buck and *Instrument Flying* by Richard L. Taylor and *Flying a Floatplane* by C. Marin Faure. There are many, many more out there, and Rod Machado has done a superlative job in explaining aviation in his various books.

I have my worthy students pick up (after I dropped it) a copy of *Illusions* by Richard Bach, as that tome makes everything very easy and fun.

I want to dedicate this book to my beautiful and very smart wife, who has graced my cockpit for decades and worked as hard on this project as I have. Thank you, Nurse Kristina, for everything. (Happy wife, happy life.)

Everything in this Manual is true, or at least close enough for piloting purposes. Good luck and Godspeed!

About the Author

Captain Stephen M. Lind, JD, ATP

Stephen started flying in 1969 at the age of seventeen. His FAA ratings include air transport / commercial pilot for multiengine and glider aircraft, instrument instructor for air and seaplanes, and helicopter flight instructor. He has made six emergency landings without damage.

With over sixteen thousand hours of flight time, he has operated as a banner-towing and Skycaster pilot and as a bush pilot in Alaska and the Yukon. He flew for WCBS's Shadow Traffic as the chief pilot / reporter for seven years and has nine thousand hours flying over the NYC area. He also holds a FCC technician-class radio license.

A bachelor of science degree in international politics was earned at the University of Wisconsin (1973), where he was in the Army Reserve Officer Training Corps and was deemed a distinguished military graduate and received the AMVETS National award. Steve was commissioned as a second lieutenant in the US Army and served during the Vietnam era as an Airborne Ranger platoon leader and a main battle tank unit commander in the First Infantry Division.

While living in Kansas, he was the operations officer (general manager) for a private security guard company, responsible for 120 armed security guards and one hundred job sites. Steve attended the Washburn University School of Law and graduated on the dean's list, received his juris doctor degree (1979), and is registered as a state and federal attorney.

Two years were spent with the New Jersey Insurance Guaranty Association as the environmental claims team leader. Prior to that (1979–1991), he worked for a large aviation insurance company as a claims attorney in Detroit, a regional claims manager in Chicago, and as the vice president in charge of all ten regional claims offices nationwide. He has worked over two thousand aircraft accidents and claims.

Steve runs Sky Insight Consultants, which is presently safety-managing a Morristown Airport private jet terminal. Sky Insight is also hired by attorneys to assist in aircraft accident investigations and to testify as a pilot expert witness on aviation insurance and environmental claims issues. He also flies aerial photo and aerial resupply missions, along with giving aerobatic/spin training flight lessons and rides.

He is currently a captain in the USAF/Auxiliary as a search-and-rescue pilot and was nominated for the country's highest civilian air medal and, in 1979, was presented the Bronze Medal of Valor by the governor of Kansas after piloting a blood resupply mission in a blizzard (at night). Steve also has been the chief flight instructor for the Eagle Flight Squadron since 1999 and has over 6,900 hours of student flight instruction (eight of his flight students have been accepted to the US Military Academies; four to the USAF, two to Annapolis and one each to West Point and the USCG). Largely because of his association with the Eagle Flight Squadron, in 2009, he received the New Jersey State Aviation Award and the Governor's Aviator of the Year Medal. He has a son (former USMC) and daughter (pilot/veterinarian) and is married to Kristina Stickel, RN, LNC.

CPSIA information can be obtained
at www.ICGtesting.com
Printed in the USA
FFHW022309010519
52203677-57563FF